ARIZONA TRAILS

WEST REGION

A P C
PUBLISHING

Printed in the United States of America

Cover photos
Clockwise from bottom left: (bottom and top left) Nellie Mine Road, Signal Road

Rear cover photos
From left: White Hills Trail, Moss Mine Trail

ARIZONA TRAILS
WEST REGION

PETER MASSEY
JEANNE WILSON
ANGELA TITUS

APC
PUBLISHING

Contents

Sidebars

Before You Go

Why a 4WD Does It Better

The design and engineering of 4WD vehicles provide them with many advantages over normal cars when you head off the paved road:

■ improved distribution of power to all four wheels;

■ a transmission transfer case, which provides low-range gear selection for greater pulling power and for crawling over difficult terrain;

■ high ground clearance;

■ less overhang of the vehicle's body past the wheels, which provides better front- and rear-clearance when crossing gullies and ridges;

■ large-lug, wide-tread tires;

■ rugged construction (including underbody skid plates on many models).

If you plan to do off-highway touring, all of these considerations are important whether you are evaluating the capabilities of your current 4WD or are looking to buy one; each is considered in detail in this chapter.

To explore the most difficult trails described in this book, you will need a 4WD vehicle that is well rated in each of the above features. If you own a 2WD sport utility vehicle, a lighter car-type SUV, or a pickup truck, your ability to explore the more difficult trails will depend on conditions and your level of experience.

A word of caution: Whatever type of 4WD vehicle you drive, understand that it is not invincible or indestructible. Nor can it go everywhere. A 4WD has a much higher center of gravity and weighs more than a car, and so has its own consequent limitations.

Experience is the only way to learn what your vehicle can and cannot do. Therefore, if you are inexperienced, we strongly recommend that you start with trails that have lower difficulty ratings. As you develop an understanding of your vehicle and of your own taste

for adventure, you can safely tackle the more challenging trails.

One way to beef up your knowledge quickly, while avoiding the costly and sometimes dangerous lessons learned from on-the-road mistakes, is to undertake a 4WD course taught by a professional. Look in the Yellow Pages for courses in your area.

Using This Book

Route Planning

The maps on pages 24 and 25 provide a convenient overview of the trails in Western Region of Arizona. Each 4WD trail is shown, as are major highways and towns, to help you plan various routes by connecting a series of 4WD trails and paved roads.

As you plan your overall route, you will probably want to utilize as many 4WD trails as possible. However, check the difficulty rating and time required for each trail before finalizing your plans. You don't want to be stuck 50 miles from the highway—at sunset and without camping gear, since your trip was supposed to be over hours ago—when you discover that your vehicle can't handle a certain difficult passage.

Difficulty Ratings

We use a point system to rate the difficulty of each trail. Any such system is subjective, and your experience of the trails will vary depending on your skill and the road conditions at the time. Indeed, any amount of rain may make the trails much more difficult, if not completely impassable.

We have rated the 4WD trails on a scale of 1 to 10—1 being passable for a normal passenger vehicle in good conditions and 10 requiring a heavily modified vehicle and an experienced driver who expects to encounter vehicle damage. Because this book is designed for owners of unmodified 4WD vehicles—who we assume do not want to damage their vehicles—most of the trails are rated 5 or lower. A few trails are included that rate as high as 7, while those rated 8 to 10 are beyond the scope of this book.

This is not to say that the moderate-rated trails are easy. We strongly recommend that inexperienced drivers not tackle trails rated at 4 or higher until they have undertaken a number of the lower-rated ones, so that they can gauge their skill level and prepare for the difficulty of the higher-rated trails.

In assessing the trails, we have always assumed good road conditions (dry road surface, good visibility, and so on). The factors influencing our ratings are as follows:

■ obstacles such as rocks, mud, ruts, sand, slickrock, and stream crossings;

■ the stability of the road surface;

■ the width of the road and the vehicle clearance between trees or rocks;

■ the steepness of the road;

■ the margin for driver error (for example, a very high, open shelf road would be rated more difficult even if it was not very steep and had a stable surface).

The following is a guide to the ratings.

Rating 1: The trail is graded dirt but suitable for a normal passenger vehicle. It usually has gentle grades, is fairly wide, and has very shallow water crossings (if any).

Rating 2: High-clearance vehicles are preferred but not necessary. These trails are dirt roads, but they may have rocks, grades, water crossings, or ruts that make clearance a concern in a normal passenger vehicle. The trails are fairly wide, making passing possible at almost any point along the trail. Mud is not a concern under normal weather conditions.

Rating 3: High-clearance 4WDs are preferred, but any high-clearance vehicle is acceptable. Expect a rough road surface; mud and sand are possible but will be easily passable. You may encounter rocks up to 6 inches in diameter, a loose road surface, and shelf roads, though these will be wide enough for passing or will have adequate pull-offs.

Rating 4: High-clearance is required, 4WDs is preferred, though some stock SUVs are acceptable. Expect a rough road surface with rocks larger than 6 inches, but there will be a reasonable driving line available. Patches of mud are possible but can be readily negotiated; sand may be deep and require lower tire pressures. There may be stream crossings up to 12 inches deep, substantial sections of single-lane shelf road, moderate grades, and sections of moderately loose road surface.

Rating 5: High-clearance 4WDs are required. These trails have either a rough, rutted surface, rocks up to 9 inches, mud and deep sand that may be impassable for inexperienced drivers, or stream crossings up to 18 inches deep. Certain sections may be steep enough to cause traction problems, and you may encounter very narrow shelf roads with steep drop-offs and tight clearance between rocks or trees.

Rating 6: These trails are for experienced four-wheel drivers only. They are potentially dangerous, with large rocks, ruts, or terraces that may need to be negotiated. They may also have stream crossings at least 18 inches deep, involve rapid currents, unstable stream bottoms, or difficult access; steep slopes, loose surfaces, and narrow clearances; or very narrow sections of shelf road with steep drop-offs and possibly challenging road surfaces.

Rating 7: Skilled, experienced four-wheel drivers only. These trails include very challenging sections with extremely steep grades, loose surfaces, large rocks, deep ruts, and/or tight clearances. Mud or sand may necessitate winching.

Rating 8 and above: Stock vehicles are likely to be damaged, and drivers may find the trail impassable. Highly skilled, experienced four-wheel drivers only.

Scenic Ratings

If rating the degree of difficulty is subjective, rating scenic beauty is guaranteed to lead to arguments. The West Region of Arizona contains a spectacular variety of desert scenery. Despite the subjectivity of attempting a comparative rating of diverse scenery, we have tried to provide a guide to the relative scenic quality of the various trails. The ratings are based on a scale of 1 to 10, with 10 being the most attractive.

Remoteness Ratings

Many trails in this region are in remote mountain or desert country; sometimes the trails are seldom traveled, and the likelihood is low that another vehicle will appear within a reasonable time to assist you if you get stuck or break down. We have included a ranking for remoteness of +0 through +2. Extreme summer temperatures can make a breakdown in the more remote areas a life-threatening experience. Prepare carefully before tackling the higher-rated, more remote trails (see Special Preparations for Remote Travel, page 11). For trails with a high remoteness rating, consider traveling with a second vehicle.

Estimated Driving Times

In calculating driving times, we have not allowed for stops. Your actual driving time may be considerably longer depending on the number and duration of the stops you make. Add more time if you prefer to drive more slowly than good conditions allow.

Current Road Information

All the 4WD trails described in this book may become impassable in poor weather conditions. Storms can alter roads, remove tracks, and create impassable washes. Most of the trails described, even easy 2WD trails, can quickly become impassable even to 4WD vehicles after only a small amount of rain. For each trail, we have provided a phone number for obtaining current information about conditions.

Abbreviations

The route directions for the 4WD trails use a series of abbreviations as follows:

SO	CONTINUE STRAIGHT ON
TL	TURN LEFT
TR	TURN RIGHT
BL	BEAR LEFT
BR	BEAR RIGHT
UT	U-TURN

Using Route Directions

For every trail, we describe and pinpoint (by odometer reading) nearly every significant feature along the route—such as intersections, streams, washes, gates, cattle guards, and so on—and provide directions from these landmarks. Odometer readings will vary from vehicle to vehicle, so you should allow for slight variations. Be aware that trails can quickly change in the desert. A new trail may be cut around a washout, a faint trail can be graded by the county, or a well-used trail may fall into disuse. All these factors will affect the accuracy of the given directions.

If you diverge from the route, zero your trip meter upon your return and continue along the route, making the necessary adjustment to the point-to-point odometer readings. In the directions, we regularly reset the odometer readings—at significant landmarks or popular lookouts and spur trails—so that you won't have to recalculate for too long.

Most of the trails can be started from either end, and the route directions include both directions of travel; reverse directions are printed in red below the main directions. When traveling in reverse, read from the bottom of the table and work up.

Route directions include cross-references whenever two 4WD trails included in this book connect; these cross-references allow for an easy change of route or destination.

Each trail includes periodic latitude and longitude readings to facilitate using a global positioning system (GPS) receiver. These readings may also assist you in finding your location on the maps. The GPS coordinates are given in the format dd°mm.mm'. To save time when loading coordinates into your GPS receiver, you may wish to include only one decimal place, since in Arizona, the first decimal place equals about 165 yards and the second only about 16 yards.

Map References

We recommend that you supplement the information in this book with more-detailed maps. For each trail, we list the sheet maps and road atlases that provide the best detail for the area. Typically, the following references are given:

- Bureau of Land Management Maps
- U.S. Forest Service Maps
- *Arizona Atlas & Gazetteer,* 9th ed.

(Yarmouth, Maine: DeLorme, 2015)—Scale 1:260,000

■ *Arizona Road & Recreation Atlas,* 9th ed. (Santa Barbara, CA: Benchmark Maps, 2015)—Scale 1:285,000

■ -Terrain Navigator Topo Maps—Scale 1:100,000 and 1:24,000

■ *Trails Illustrated* Topo Maps; National Geographic Maps—Various scales, but all contain good detail

■ Recreational Map of Arizona (Canon City, Colorado: GRT Mapping, 2013)—Scale: 1 inch=12.5 miles

We recommend the *Trails Illustrated* series of maps as the best for navigating these trails. They are reliable, easy to read, and printed on nearly indestructible plastic paper. However, this series covers only a portion of the 4WD trails described in this book.

The DeLorme Atlas has the advantage of providing you with maps of the state at a reasonable price. Although its 4WD trail information doesn't go beyond what we provide, it is useful if you wish to explore the hundreds of side roads.

The *Arizona Road & Recreation Atlas* provides two types of maps for each part of the state. The landscape maps show changes in terrain and elevation while the public lands maps show what organizations control what lands. Aside from the maps, the atlas also provides a good recreation guide with a number of local contacts for different recreation opportunities.

U.S. Forest Service maps lack the topographic detail of the other sheet maps and, in our experience, are occasionally out of date. They have the advantage of covering a broad area and are useful in identifying land use and travel restrictions. These maps are most useful for the longer trails.

The Terrain Navigator series of maps published on DVD or via download by Maptech are also very useful. These maps contain an amazing level of detail because they include the entire set of U.S. Geological Survey topographical maps of Arizona at both the 1:24,000 scale and the 1:100,000 scale. These maps offer many advantages over normal maps:

■ GPS coordinates for any location can be found and loaded into your GPS receiver. Conversely, if you have your GPS coordinates, your location on the map can be pinpointed instantly.

■ Towns, rivers, passes, mountains, and many other sites are indexed by name so that they can be located quickly.

■ 4WD trails can be marked and profiled for elevation changes and distances from point to point.

■ Customized maps can be printed out.

■ The DVDs can be used with a laptop computer and a GPS receiver in your vehicle to monitor your location on the map and navigate directly from the display.

All these maps should be available through good map stores.

Backcountry Driving Rules and Permits

Four-wheel driving involves special driving techniques and road rules. This section is an introduction for 4WD beginners.

4WD Road Rules

To help ensure that these trails remain open and available for all four-wheel drivers to enjoy, it is important to minimize your impact on the environment and not be a safety risk to yourself or anyone else. Remember that the 4WD clubs in Arizona fight a constant battle with the government and various lobby groups to retain the access that currently exists.

The fundamental rule when traversing the 4WD trails described in this book is to use common sense. In addition, special road rules for 4WD trails apply:

■ Vehicles traveling uphill have the right of way.

■ If you are moving more slowly than the vehicle behind you, pull over to let the other vehicle pass.

■ Park out of the way in a safe place. Blocking a track may restrict access for emergency vehicles as well as for other recreationalists. Set the parking brake—don't rely on leaving the transmission in park. Manual transmissions should be left in the lowest gear.

Tread Lightly!

Remember the rules of the Tread Lightly! program:

■ Be informed. Obtain maps, regulations, and other information from the forest service or from other public land agencies. Learn the rules and follow them.

■ Resist the urge to pioneer a new road or trail or to cut across a switchback. Stay on constructed tracks and avoid running over young trees, shrubs, and grasses, damaging or killing them.

■ Stay off soft, wet roads and 4WD trails readily torn up by vehicles. Repairing the damage is expensive, and quite often authorities find it easier to close the road rather than repair it.

■ Avoid meadows, steep hillsides, stream banks, and lake shores that are easily scarred by churning wheels.

■ Stay away from wild animals that are rearing young or suffering from a food shortage. Do not camp close to the water sources of domestic or wild animals.

■ Obey gate closures and regulatory signs.

■ Preserve America's heritage by not disturbing old mining camps, ghost towns, or other historical features. Leave historic sites, Native American rock art, ruins, and artifacts in place and untouched.

■ Carry out all your trash, and even that of others.

■ Stay out of designated wilderness areas. They are closed to all vehicles. It is your responsibility to know where the boundaries are.

■ Get permission to cross private land. Leave livestock alone. Respect landowners' rights.

Report violations of these rules to help keep these 4WD trails open and to ensure that others will have the opportunity to visit these backcountry sites. Many groups are actively seeking to close these public lands to vehicles, thereby denying access to those who are unable, or perhaps merely unwilling, to hike long distances. This magnificent countryside is owned by, and should be available to, all Americans.

Special Preparations for Remote Travel

Due to the remoteness of some areas in Arizona and the very high summer temperatures, you should take some special precautions to ensure that you don't end up in a life-threatening situation:

■ When planning a trip into the desert, always inform someone as to where you are going, your route, and when you expect to return. Stick to your plan.

■ Carry and drink at least one gallon of water per person per day of your trip. (Plastic gallon jugs are handy and portable.)

■ Be sure your vehicle is in good condition with a sound battery, good hoses, spare tire, spare fan belts, necessary tools, and reserve gasoline and oil. Other spare parts and extra radiator water are also valuable. If traveling in pairs, share the common spares and carry a greater variety.

■ Keep an eye on the sky. Flash floods can occur in a wash any time you see thunderheads—even when it's not raining a drop where you are.

■ If you are caught in a dust storm while driving, get off the road and turn off your lights. Turn on the emergency flashers and back into the wind to reduce windshield pitting by sand particles.

■ Test trails on foot before driving through washes and sandy areas. One minute of walking may save hours of hard work getting your vehicle unstuck.

■ If your vehicle breaks down, stay near it. Your emergency supplies are there. Your car has many other items useful in an emergency. Raise your hood and trunk lid to denote "help needed." Remember, a vehicle can be seen for miles, but a person on foot is very difficult to spot from a distance.

■ When you're not moving, use available shade or erect shade from tarps, blankets, or seat covers—anything to reduce the direct rays of the sun.

■ Do not sit or lie directly on the ground. It may be 30 degrees hotter than the air.

■ Leave a disabled vehicle only if you are positive of the route and the distance to help. Leave a note for rescuers that gives the time you left and the direction you are taking.

■ If you must walk, rest for at least 10 minutes out of each hour. If you are not normally physically active, rest up to 30 minutes out of each hour. Find shade, sit down, and prop up your feet. Adjust your shoes and socks, but do not remove your shoes—you may not be able to get them back on swollen feet.

■ If you have water, drink it. Do not ration it.

■ If water is limited, keep your mouth closed. Do not talk, eat, smoke, drink alcohol, or take salt.

■ Keep your clothing on despite the heat. It helps to keep your body temperature down and reduces your body's dehydration rate. Cover your head. If you don't have a hat, improvise a head covering.

■ If you are stalled or lost, set signal fires. Set smoky fires in the daytime and bright ones at night. Three fires in a triangle denote "help needed."

■ A roadway is a sign of civilization. If you find a road, stay on it.

■ When hiking in the desert, equip each person, especially children, with a police-type whistle. It makes a distinctive noise with little effort. Three blasts denote "help needed."

■ To avoid poisonous creatures, put your hands or feet only where your eyes can see. One insect to be aware of in western Arizona is the Africanized honeybee. Though indistinguishable from its European counterpart, these bees are far more aggressive and can be a threat. They have been known to give chase of up to a mile and even wait for people who have escaped into the water to come up for air. The best thing to do if attacked is to cover your face and head with clothing and run to the nearest enclosed shelter. Keep an eye on your pet if you notice a number of bees in the area, as many have been killed by Africanized honeybees.

■ Avoid unnecessary contact with wildlife. Some mice in Arizona carry the deadly hantavirus, a pulmonary syndrome fatal in 36 percent of human cases. Fortunately the disease is very rare—by January 2017, only 78 cases had been reported in Arizona and 728 nationwide—but caution is still advised. Other rodents may transmit bubonic plague, the same epidemic that killed one-third of Europe's population in the 1300s. Be especially wary near sick animals and keep pets, especially cats, away from wildlife and their fleas. Another creature to watch for is the western black-legged tick, the carrier of Lyme disease. Wearing clothing that covers legs and arms, tucking pants into boots, and using insect repellent are good ways to avoid fleas and ticks.

Obtaining Permits

Backcountry permits, which usually cost a fee, are required for certain activities on public lands in Arizona, whether the area is a national park, state park, national monument, Indian reservation, or BLM land.

Restrictions may require a permit for all overnight stays, which can include backpacking and 4WD or bicycle camping. Permits may also be required for day use by vehicles, horses, hikers, or bikes in some areas.

When possible, we include information about fees and permit requirements and where permits may be obtained, but these regulations change constantly. If in doubt, check with the most likely governing agency.

Assessing Your Vehicle's Off-Road Ability

Many issues come into play when evaluating your vehicle, although some of the 4WDs on the market (excluding "crossover" SUVs) are suitable for even the roughest trails described in this book. Engine power will be adequate in even the least-powerful modern vehicle. However, some vehicles are less suited to off-highway driving than others, and some of the newest, carlike sport utility vehicles simply are not designed for off-highway touring. This information should enable you to identify the good, the bad, and the ugly.

Differing 4WD Systems

All 4WD systems have one thing in common: The engine provides power to all four wheels rather than to only two, as is typical in most standard cars. However, there are a number of differences in the way power is applied to the wheels.

The other feature that distinguishes nearly all 4WDs from normal passenger vehicles is that the gearboxes have high and low ratios that effectively double the number of gears. The high range is comparable to the range on a passenger car. The low range provides lower speed and more power, which is useful when towing heavy loads, driving up steep hills, or crawling over rocks. When driving downhill, the 4WD's low range increases engine braking.

Various makes and models of SUVs offer different drive systems, but these differences center on two issues: the way power is applied to the other wheels if one or more wheels slip, and the ability to select between 2WD and 4WD.

Normal driving requires that all four wheels be able to turn at different speeds; this allows the vehicle to turn without scrubbing its tires. In a 2WD vehicle, the front wheels (or rear wheels in a front-wheel-drive vehicle) are not powered by the engine and thus are free to turn individually at any speed. The rear wheels, powered by the engine, are only able to turn at different speeds because of the differential, which applies power to the faster-turning wheel.

This standard method of applying traction has certain weaknesses. First, when power is applied to only one set of wheels, the other set cannot help the vehicle gain traction. Second, when one powered wheel loses traction, it spins, but the other powered wheel doesn't turn. This happens because the differential applies all the engine power to the faster-turning wheel and no power to the other wheels, which still have traction. All 4WD systems are designed to overcome these two weaknesses. However, different 4WDs address this common objective in different ways.

Full-Time 4WD. For a vehicle to remain in 4WD all the time without scrubbing the tires, all the wheels must be able to rotate at different speeds. A full-time 4WD system allows this to happen by using three differentials. One is located between the rear wheels, as in a normal passenger car, to allow the rear wheels to rotate at different speeds. The second is located between the front wheels in exactly the same way. The third differential is located between the front and rear wheels to allow different rotational speeds between the front and rear sets of wheels. In nearly all vehicles with full-time 4WD, the center differential operates only in high range. In low range, it is completely locked. This is not a disadvantage because when using low range the additional traction is normally desired and the deterioration of steering response will be less noticeable due to the vehicle traveling at a slower speed.

Part-Time 4WD. A part-time 4WD system does not have the center differential located between the front and rear wheels. Consequently, the front and rear drive shafts are both driven at the same speed and with the same power at all times when in 4WD.

This system provides improved traction because when one or both of the front or rear wheels slips, the engine continues to provide power to the other set. However, because such a system doesn't allow a difference in speed between the front and rear sets of wheels, the tires scrub when turning, placing additional strain on the whole drive system. Therefore, such a system can be used only in slippery conditions; otherwise, the ability to steer the vehicle will deteriorate and the tires will quickly wear out.

These days, a substantial number of SUVs offer both full-time and part-time 4WD in high range.

Manual Systems to Switch Between 2WD and 4WD. There are three manual systems for switching between 2WD and 4WD. The most basic requires stopping and getting out of the vehicle to lock the front hubs manually before selecting 4WD. The second requires you to stop, but you change to 4WD by merely throwing a lever inside the vehicle (the hubs lock automatically). The third allows shifting between 2WD and 4WD high range while the vehicle is moving. Any 4WD that does not offer the option of driving in 2WD must have a full-time 4WD system.

Automated Switching Between 2WD and 4WD. Advances in technology are leading to greater automation in the selection of two- or four-wheel drive. When operating in high range, these high-tech systems use sensors to monitor the rotation of each wheel. When any slippage is detected, the vehicle switches the proportion of power from the wheel(s) that is slipping to the wheels that retain grip. The proportion of power supplied to each wheel is therefore infinitely variable as opposed to the original systems where the vehicle was either in two-wheel drive or four-wheel drive.

In recent years, this process has been spurred on by many of the manufacturers of luxury vehicles entering the SUV market—Mercedes, BMW, Cadillac, Lincoln, and Lexus have joined Range Rover in this segment.

Manufacturers of these higher priced vehicles have led the way in introducing sophisticated computer-controlled 4WD systems. Although each of the manufacturers has its own approach to this issue, all the systems automatically vary the allocation of power between the wheels within milliseconds of the sensors' detecting wheel slippage.

Limiting Wheel Slippage

All 4WDs employ various systems to limit wheel slippage and transfer power to the wheels that still have traction. These systems may completely lock the differentials or they may allow limited slippage before transferring power back to the wheels that retain traction.

Lockers completely eliminate the operation of one or more differentials. A locker on the center differential switches between full-time and part-time 4WD. Lockers on the front or rear differentials ensure that power remains equally applied to each set of wheels regardless of whether both have traction. Lockers may be controlled manually, by a switch or a lever in the vehicle, or they may be automatic.

The Toyota Land Cruiser offers the option of having manual lockers on all three differentials, while other brands such as the Mitsubishi Montero offer manual lockers on the center and rear differential. Manual lockers are the most controllable and effective devices for ensuring that power is provided to the wheels with traction. However, because they allow absolutely no slippage, they must be used only on slippery surfaces.

An alternative method for getting power to the wheels that have traction is to allow limited wheel slippage. Systems that work this way may be called limited-slip differentials, posi-traction systems, or in the center differential, viscous couplings. The advantage of these systems is that the limited difference they allow in rotational speed between wheels enables such systems to be used when driving on a dry surface. All full-time 4WD systems allow limited slippage in the center differential.

For off-highway use, a manually locking differential is the best of the above systems, but it is the most expensive. Limited-slip differentials are the cheapest but also the least satisfactory, as they require one wheel to be slipping at 2 to 3 mph before power is transferred to the other wheel. For the center differential, the best system combines a locking differential and, to enable full-time use, a viscous coupling.

Tires

The tires that came with your 4WD vehicle may be satisfactory, but many 4WDs are fitted with passenger-car tires. These are unlikely to be the best choice because they are less rugged and more likely to puncture on rocky trails. They are particularly prone to sidewall damage as well. Passenger vehicle tires also have a less aggressive tread pattern than specialized 4WD tires, and provide less traction in mud.

For information on purchasing tires better suited to off-highway conditions, see Special 4WD Equipment, page 20.

Clearance

Road clearances vary considerably among different 4WD vehicles—from less than 7 inches to more than 10 inches. Special vehicles may have far greater clearance. For instance, the Hummer has a 16-inch ground clearance. High ground clearance is particularly advantageous on the rockier or more rutted 4WD trails in this book.

When evaluating the ground clearance of your vehicle, you need to take into account the clearance of the bodywork between the wheels on each side of the vehicle. This is particularly relevant for crawling over larger rocks. Vehicles with sidesteps have significantly lower clearance than those without.

Another factor affecting clearance is the approach and departure angles of your vehicle—that is, the maximum angle the ground can slope without the front of the vehicle hitting the ridge on approach or the rear of the vehicle hitting on departure. Mounting a winch or tow hitch to your vehicle is likely to reduce your angle of approach or departure.

If you do a lot of driving on rocky trails, you will inevitably hit the bottom of the vehicle. When this happens, you will be far less likely to damage vulnerable areas such as the oil pan and gas tank if your vehicle is fitted with skid plates. Most manufacturers offer skid plates as an option. They are worth every penny.

Maneuverability

When you tackle tight switchbacks, you will quickly appreciate that maneuverability is an important criterion when assessing 4WD vehicles. Where a full-size vehicle may be forced to go back and forth a number of times to get around a sharp turn, a small 4WD might go straight around. This is not only easier, it's safer.

If you have a full-size vehicle, all is not lost. We have traveled many of the trails in this book in a Suburban. That is not to say that some of these trails wouldn't have been easier to negotiate in a smaller vehicle! We have noted in the route descriptions if a trail is not suitable for larger vehicles.

In Summary

Using the criteria above, you can evaluate how well your 4WD will handle off-road touring, and if you haven't yet purchased your vehicle, you can use these criteria to help select one. Choosing the best 4WD system is, at least partly, subjective. It is also a matter of your budget. However, for the type of off-highway driving covered in this book, we make the following recommendations:

■ Select a 4WD system that offers low range and, at a minimum, has some form of limited slip differential on the rear axle.

■ Use light truck, all-terrain tires as the standard tires on your vehicle. For sand and slickrock, these will be the ideal choice. If conditions are likely to be muddy, or if traction will be improved by a tread pattern that will give more bite, consider an additional set of mud tires.

■ For maximum clearance, select a vehicle with 16-inch wheels or at least choose the tallest tires that your vehicle can accommodate. Note that if you install tires with a diameter greater than standard, the odometer will under calculate the distance you have traveled. Your engine braking and gear ratios will also be affected.

■ If you are going to try the rockier 4WD trails, don't install a sidestep or low-hanging front bar. If you have the option, have underbody skid plates mounted.

■ Remember that many of the obstacles you encounter on backcountry trails are more difficult to navigate in a full-size vehicle than in a compact 4WD.

Four-Wheel Driving Techniques

Safe four-wheel driving requires that you observe certain golden rules:

■ Size up the situation in advance.

■ Be careful and take your time.

■ Maintain smooth, steady power and momentum.

■ Engage 4WD and low-range gears before you get into a tight situation.

■ Steer toward high spots, trying to put the wheel over large rocks.

■ Straddle ruts.

■ Use gears and not just the brakes to hold the vehicle when driving downhill. On very steep slopes, chock the wheels if you park your vehicle.

■ Watch for logging and mining trucks and smaller recreational vehicles, such as all-terrain vehicles (ATVs).

■ Wear your seat belt and secure all luggage, especially heavy items such as tool boxes or coolers. Heavy items should be secured by ratchet tie-down straps rather than elastic-type straps, which are not strong enough to hold heavy items if the vehicle rolls.

Arizona's 4WD trails have a number of common obstacles, and the following provides an introduction to the techniques required to surmount them.

Rocks. Tire selection is important in negotiating rocks. Select a multiple-ply, tough sidewall, light-truck tire with a large-lug tread.

As you approach a rocky stretch, get into 4WD low range to give yourself maximum slow-speed control. Speed is rarely necessary, since traction on a rocky surface is usually good. Plan ahead and select the line you wish to take. If a rock appears to be larger than the clearance of your vehicle, don't try to straddle it. Check to see that it is not higher than the frame of your vehicle once you get a wheel over it. Put a wheel up on the rock and slowly climb it, then gently drop over the other side using the brake to ensure a smooth landing. Bouncing the car over rocks increases the likelihood of damage, because the body's clearance is reduced by the suspension compressing. Running boards also significantly reduce your clearance in this respect. It is often helpful to use a "spotter" outside the vehicle to assist you with the best wheel placement.

Steep Uphill Grades. Consider walking the trail to ensure that the steep hill before you is passable, especially if it is clear that backtracking is going to be a problem.

Select 4WD low range to ensure that you have adequate power to pull up the hill. If the wheels begin to lose traction, turn the steering wheel gently from side to side to give the wheels a chance to regain traction.

If you lose momentum, but the car is not in danger of sliding, use the foot brake, switch off the ignition, leave the vehicle in gear (if manual transmission) or park (if automatic), engage the parking brake, and get out to examine the situation. See if you can remove any obstacles, and figure out the line you need to take. Reversing a couple of yards and starting again may allow you to get better traction and momentum.

If halfway up, you decide a stretch of road is impassably steep, back down the trail. Trying to turn the vehicle around on a steep hill is extremely dangerous; you will very likely cause it to roll over.

Steep Downhill Grades. Again, consider walking the trail to ensure that a steep downhill is passable, especially if it is clear that backtracking uphill is going to be a problem.

Select 4WD low range and use first gear to maximize braking assistance from the engine. If the surface is loose and you are losing traction, change up to second or third gear. Do not use the brakes if you can avoid it, but don't let the vehicle's speed get out of control. Feather (lightly pump) the brakes if you slip while braking. For vehicles fitted with an antilock breaking system, apply even pressure if you start to slip; the ABS helps keep vehicles on line.

Travel very slowly over rock ledges or ruts. Attempt to tackle these diagonally, letting one wheel down at a time.

If the back of the vehicle begins to slide around, gently apply the throttle and correct the steering. If the rear of the vehicle starts to slide sideways, do not apply the brakes.

Sand. As with most off-highway situations, your tires are the key to your ability to cross sand. It is difficult to tell how well a particular tire will handle in sand just by looking at it, so be guided by the manufacturer and your dealer.

The key to driving in soft sand is floatation, which is achieved by a combination of low tire pressure and momentum. Before crossing a stretch of sand, reduce your tire pressure to between 15 and 20 pounds. If necessary, you can safely go to as low as 12 pounds. As you cross, maintain momentum so that your vehicle rides on the top of the soft sand without digging in or stalling. This may require plenty of engine power. Avoid using the brakes if possible; removing your foot from the accelerator alone is normally enough to slow or stop. Using the brakes digs the vehicle deep in the sand.

Pump the tires back up as soon as you are out of the sand to avoid damaging the tires and the rims. Pumping the tires back up requires a high-quality air compressor. Even then, it is a slow process.

In the backcountry of Arizona, sandy conditions are commonplace. You will therefore find a good compressor most useful.

Slickrock. When you encounter slickrock, first assess the correct direction of the trail. It is easy to lose sight of the trail on slickrock, because there are seldom any developed edges. Often the way is marked with small cairns, which are simply rocks stacked high enough to make a landmark.

All-terrain tires with tighter tread are more suited to slickrock than the more open, luggier type tires. As with rocks, a multiple-ply sidewall is important. In dry conditions, slickrock offers pavement-type grip. In rain or snow, you will soon learn how it got its name. Even the best tires may not get an adequate grip. Walk steep sections first; if you are slipping on foot, chances are your vehicle will slip, too.

Slickrock is characterized by ledges and long sections of "pavement." Follow the guidelines for travel over rocks. Refrain from speeding over flat-looking sections, because you may hit an unexpected crevice or water pocket, and vehicles bend easier than slickrock! Turns and ledges can be tight, and vehicles with smaller overhangs and better maneuverability are at a distinct advantage—hence the popularity of the compacts in the slickrock mecca of Moab, Utah.

On the steepest sections, engage low range and pick a straight line up or down the slope. Do not attempt to traverse a steep slope sideways.

Mud. Muddy trails are easily damaged, so they should be avoided if possible. But if you must traverse a section of mud, your success will depend heavily on whether you have open-lugged mud tires or chains. Thick mud fills the tighter tread on normal tires, leaving the tire with no more grip than if it were bald. If the muddy stretch is only a few yards long, the momentum of your vehicle may allow you to get through regardless.

If the muddy track is very steep, uphill or downhill, or off camber, do not attempt it. Your vehicle is likely to skid in such conditions, and you may roll or slip off the edge of the road. Also, check to see that the mud has a reasonably firm base. Tackling deep mud is definitely not recommended unless you have a vehicle-mounted winch—and even then—be cautious, because the winch may not get you out. Finally, check to see that no ruts are too deep for the ground clearance of your vehicle.

When you decide you can get through and have selected the best route, use the following techniques to cross through the mud:

■ Avoid making detours off existing tracks to minimize environmental damage.

■ Select 4WD low range and a suitable gear; momentum is the key to success, so use a high enough gear to build up sufficient speed.

■ Avoid accelerating heavily, so as to minimize wheel spinning and to provide maximum traction.

■ Follow existing wheel ruts, unless they are too deep for the clearance of your vehicle.

■ To correct slides, turn the steering wheel in the direction that the rear wheels are skidding, but don't be too aggressive or you'll overcorrect and lose control again.

■ If the vehicle comes to a stop, don't continue to accelerate, as you will only spin your wheels and dig yourself into a rut. Try backing out and having another go.

■ Be prepared to turn back before reaching the point of no return.

Stream Crossings. By crossing a stream that is too deep, drivers risk far more than water flowing in and ruining the interior of their vehicles. Water sucked into the engine's air intake will seriously damage the engine. Likewise, water that seeps into the air vent on the transmission or differential will mix with the lubricant and may lead to serious problems in due course.

Even worse, if the water is deep or fast flowing, it could easily carry your vehicle downstream, endangering the lives of everyone in the vehicle.

Some 4WD manuals tell you what fording depth the vehicle can negotiate safely. If your vehicle's owner's manual does not include this information, your local dealer may be able to assist. If you don't know, then avoid crossing through water that is more than a foot or so deep.

The first rule for crossing a stream is to know what you are getting into. You need to ascertain how deep the water is, whether there are any large rocks or holes, if the bottom is solid enough to avoid bogging down the vehicle, and whether the entry and exit points are negotiable. This may take some time and involve getting wet, but you take a great risk by crossing a stream without first properly assessing the situation.

The secret to water crossings is to keep moving, but not too fast. If you go too fast, you may drown the electrics, causing the vehicle to stall midstream. In shallow water (where the surface of the water is below the bumper), your primary concern is to safely negotiate the bottom of the stream, to avoid any rock damage, and to maintain momentum if there is a danger of getting stuck or of slipping on the exit.

In deeper water (between 18 and 30 inches), the objective is to create a small bow wave in front of the moving vehicle. This requires a speed that is approximately walking pace. The bow wave reduces the depth of the water around the engine compartment. If the water's surface reaches your tailpipe, select a gear that will maintain moderate engine revs to avoid water backing up into the exhaust; and do not change gears midstream.

Crossing water deeper than 25 to 30 inches requires more extensive preparation of the vehicle and should be attempted only by experienced drivers.

Snow. The trails in this book that receive heavy snowfall are closed in winter. Therefore, the snow conditions that you are most likely to encounter are an occasional snowdrift that has not yet melted or fresh snow from an unexpected storm. Getting through such conditions depends on the depth of the snow, its consistency, the stability of the underlying surface, and your vehicle.

If the snow is no deeper than about 9 inches and there is solid ground beneath it, crossing the snow should not be a problem. In deeper snow that seems solid enough to support your vehicle, be extremely cautious: If you break through a drift, you are likely to be stuck, and if conditions are bad, you may have a long wait.

The tires you use for off-highway driving, with a wide tread pattern, are probably suitable for these snow conditions. Nonetheless, it is wise to carry chains (preferably for all four wheels), and if you have a vehicle-mounted winch, even better.

Vehicle Recovery Methods

If you do enough four-wheel driving, you are sure to get stuck sooner or later. The following techniques will help you get back on the go. The most suitable method will depend on the equipment available and the situation you are in—whether you are stuck in sand, mud, or snow, or are high-centered or unable to negotiate a hill.

Towing. Use a nylon yank strap of the type discussed in the Special 4WD Equipment section below. This type of strap will stretch 15 to 25 percent, and the elasticity will assist in extracting the vehicle.

Attach the strap only to a frame-mounted tow point. Ensure that the driver of the stuck vehicle is ready, take up all but about 6 feet of slack, then move the towing vehicle away at a moderate speed (in most circumstances this means using 4WD low range in second gear) so that the elasticity of the strap is employed in the way it is meant to be. Don't take off like a bat out of hell or you risk breaking the strap or damaging a vehicle.

Never join two yank straps together with a shackle. If one strap breaks, the shackle will become a lethal missile aimed at one of the vehicles (and anyone inside). For the same reason, never attach a yank strap to the tow ball on either vehicle.

Jacking. Jacking the vehicle allows you to pack rocks, dirt, or logs under the wheel or to use your shovel to remove an obstacle. However, the standard vehicle jack is unlikely to be of as much assistance as a high-lift jack. We highly recommend purchasing a good high-lift jack as a basic accessory if you decide that you are going to do a lot of serious, off-highway four-wheel driving. Remember a high-lift jack is of limited use if your vehicle does not have an appropriate jacking point. Some brush bars have two built-in forward jacking points.

Tire Chains. Tire chains can be of assistance in both mud and snow. Cable-type chains provide much less grip than link-type chains. There are also dedicated mud chains with larger, heavier links than on normal snow chains. It is best to have chains fitted to all four wheels.

Once you are bogged down is not the best time to try to fit the chains; if at all possible, try to predict their need and have them on the tires before trouble arises. An easy way to affix chains is to place two small cubes of wood under the center of the stretched-out chain. When you drive your tires up on the blocks of wood, it is easier to stretch the chains over the tires because the pressure is off of them.

Winching. Most recreational four-wheel drivers do not have a winch. But if you get serious about four-wheel driving, this is probably the first major accessory you should consider buying.

Under normal circumstances, a winch would be warranted only for the more difficult 4WD trails in this book. Having a winch is certainly comforting when you see a difficult section of road ahead and have to decide whether to risk it or turn back. Also, major obstacles can appear when you least expect them, even on trails that are otherwise easy.

Owning a winch is not a panacea to all your recovery problems. Winching depends on the availability of a good anchor point, and electric winches may not work if they are submerged in a stream. Despite these constraints, no accessory is more useful than a high-quality, powerful winch when you get into a difficult situation.

If you acquire a winch, learn to use it properly; take the time to study your owner's manual. Incorrect operation can be extremely dangerous and may cause damage to the winch or to your anchor points, which are usually trees.

Navigation by the Global Positioning System (GPS)

Although this book is designed so that each trail can be navigated simply by following the detailed directions provided, nothing makes navigation easier than a GPS receiver.

The global positioning system (GPS) consists of a network of 24 satellites, nearly 13,000 miles in space, in six different orbital paths. The satellites are constantly moving at about 8,500 miles per hour and make two complete orbits around the earth every 24 hours.

Each satellite is constantly transmitting data, including its identification number, its operational health, and the date and time. It also transmits its location and the location of every other satellite in the network.

By comparing the time the signal was transmitted to the time it is received, a GPS receiver calculates how far away each satellite is. With a sufficient number of signals, the receiver can then triangulate its location. With three or more satellites, the receiver can determine latitude and longitude coordinates. With four or more, it can calculate elevation. By constantly making these calculations, it can determine speed and direction. To facilitate these calculations, the time data broadcast by GPS is accurate to within 40 billionths of a second.

The U.S. military uses the system to provide positions accurate to within half an inch. When the system was first established, civilian receivers were deliberately fed slightly erroneous information in order to effectively deny military applications to hostile countries or terrorists—a practice called selective availability (SA). However on May 1, 2000, in response to the growing importance of the system for civilian applications, the U.S. government stopped intentionally downgrading GPS data. The military gave its support to this change once new technology made it possible to selectively degrade the system within any defined geographical area on demand. This new feature of the system has made it safe to have higher-quality signals available for civilian use. Now, instead of the civilian-use signal having a margin of error between 20 and 70 yards, it is only about one-tenth of that.

A GPS receiver offers the four-wheeler numerous benefits:

■ You can track to any point for which you know the longitude and latitude coordinates with no chance of heading in the wrong direction or getting lost. Most receivers provide an extremely easy-to-understand graphic display to keep you on track.

■ It works in all weather conditions.

■ It automatically records your route for easy backtracking.

■ You can record and name any location, so that you can relocate it with ease. This may include your campsite, a fishing spot, or even a silver mine you discover!

■ It displays your position, enabling you to pinpoint your location on a map.

■ By interfacing the GPS receiver directly to a portable computer, you can monitor and record your location as you travel (using the appropriate map software) or print the route you took.

However, remember that GPS units can fail, batteries can go flat, and tree cover and tight canyons can block the signals. Never rely entirely on GPS for navigation. Always carry a compass for backup.

Special 4WD Equipment

Tires

When 4WD touring, you will likely encounter a variety of terrain: rocks, mud, talus, slickrock, sand, gravel, dirt, and bitumen. The immense array of tires on the market includes many specifically targeted at one or another of these types of terrain, as well as tires designed to adequately handle a range of terrain.

Every four-wheel driver seems to have a preference when it comes to tire selection, but most people undertaking the 4WD trails in this book will need tires that can handle all of the above types of terrain adequately.

The first requirement is to select rugged, light-truck tires rather than passenger-vehicle tires. Check the size data on the sidewall: it should have "LT" rather than "P" before the number. Among light-truck tires, you must choose between tires that are designated "all-terrain" and more-aggressive, wider-tread mud tires. Either type will be adequate, especially on rocks, gravel, talus, or dirt. Although mud tires have an advantage in muddy conditions and soft snow, all-terrain tires perform better on slickrock, in sand, and particularly on ice and paved roads.

When selecting tires, remember that they affect not just traction but also cornering ability, braking distances, fuel consumption, and noise levels. It pays to get good advice before making your decision.

Global Positioning System Receivers

GPS are rapidly becoming indispensable navigational tools. Many cars now offer integrated GPS receivers, and will become available on most models.

Battery-powered, hand-held units that meet the needs of off-highway driving currently range from less than $100 to a little over $300 and continue to come down in price. Some high-end units feature maps that are incorporated in the display, either from a built-in database or from interchangeable memory cards. Currently, only a few of these maps include 4WD trails.

If you are considering purchasing a GPS unit, keep the following in mind:

■ Price. The very cheapest units are likely outdated and very limited in their display features. Expect to pay from $125 to $300.

■ The display. Compare the graphic display of one unit with another. Some are much easier to decipher or offer more alternative displays.

■ The controls. GPS receivers have many functions, and they need to have good, simple controls.

■ Vehicle mounting. To be useful, the unit needs to be placed where it can be read easily by both the driver and the navigator. Check that the unit can be conveniently located in your vehicle. Different units have different shapes and different mounting systems.

■ Map data. More and more units have map data built in. Some have the ability to download maps from a computer. Such maps are normally sold on a CD-ROM. GPS units have a finite storage capacity and having the ability to download maps covering a narrower geographical region means that the amount of data relating to that specific region can be greater.

■ The number of routes and the number of sites (or "waypoints") per route that can be stored in memory. For off-highway use, it is important to be able to store plenty of waypoints so that you do not have to load coordinates into the machine as frequently. Having plenty of memory also ensures that you can automatically store your present location without fear that the memory is full.

■ Waypoint storage. The better units store up to 500 waypoints and 20 reversible routes of up to 30 waypoints each. Also consider the number of characters a GPS receiver allows you to use to name waypoints. When you try to recall a waypoint, you may have difficulty recognizing names restricted to only a few characters.

■ Automatic route storing. Most units automatically store your route as you go along and enable you to display it in reverse to make backtracking easy.

After you have selected a unit, a number of optional extras are also worth considering:

■ A cigarette lighter electrical adapter. Despite GPS units becoming more power efficient, protracted in-vehicle use still makes this accessory a necessity.

■ A vehicle-mounted antenna, which will improve reception under difficult conditions. (The GPS unit can only "see" through the windows of your vehicle; it cannot monitor satellites through a metal roof.) Having a vehicle-mounted antenna also means that you do not have to consider reception when locating the receiver in your vehicle.

■ An in-car mounting system. If you are going to do a lot of touring using the GPS, consider attaching a bracket on the dash rather than relying on a Velcro mount.

■ A computer-link cable and digital maps. Data from your GPS receiver can be downloaded to your PC; maps and waypoints can be downloaded from your PC; or if you have a laptop computer, you can monitor your route as you go along, using one of a number of inexpensive map software products on the market.

Yank Straps

Yank straps are industrial-strength versions of the flimsy tow straps carried by the local discount store. They are 20 to 30 feet long and 2 to 3 inches wide, made of heavy nylon, rated to at least 20,000 pounds, and have looped ends.

Do not use tow straps with metal hooks in the ends (the hooks can become missiles in the event the strap breaks free). Likewise, never join two yank straps together using a shackle.

CB Radios

If you are stuck, injured, or just want to know the conditions up ahead, a citizen's band (CB) radio can be invaluable. CB radios are relatively inexpensive and do not require an Federal Communications Comission license. Their range is limited, especially in very hilly country, as their transmission patterns basically follow lines of sight. Range can be improved using single sideband (SSB) transmission, an option on more expensive units. Range is even better on vehicle-mounted units that have been professionally fitted to ensure that the antenna and cabling are matched appropriately.

Winches

There are three main options when it comes to winches: manual winches, removable electric winches, and vehicle-mounted electric winches.

If you have a full-size 4WD vehicle—which can weigh in excess of 7,000 pounds when loaded—a manual winch is of limited use without a lot of effort and considerable time. However, a manual winch is a very handy and inexpensive accessory if you have a small 4WD. Typically, manual winches are rated to pull about 5,500 pounds.

An electric winch can be mounted to your vehicle's trailer hitch to enable it to be removed, relocated to the front of your vehicle (if you have a hitch installed), or moved to another vehicle. Although this is a very useful feature, a winch is heavy, so relocating one can be a two-person job. Consider that 5,000-pound-rated winches weigh only about 55 pounds, while 12,000-pound-rated models weigh around 140 pounds. Therefore, the larger models are best permanently front-mounted. Unfortunately, this position limits their ability to winch the vehicle backward.

When choosing among electric winches, be aware that they are rated for their maximum capacity on the first wind of the cable around the drum. As layers of cable wind onto the drum, they increase its diameter and thus decrease the maximum load the winch can handle. This decrease is significant: A winch rated to pull 8,000 pounds on a bare drum may only handle 6,500 pounds on the second layer, 5,750 pounds on the third layer, and 5,000 pounds on the fourth. Electric winches also draw a high level of current and may necessitate upgrading the battery in your 4WD or adding a second battery.

There is a wide range of mounting options—from a simple, body-mounted frame that holds the winch to heavy-duty winch bars that replace the original bumper and incorporate brush bars and mounts for auxiliary lights.

If you buy a winch, either electric or manual, you will also need quite a range of additional equipment so that you can operate it correctly:

- at least one choker chain with hooks on each end,
- winch extension straps or cables,
- shackles,
- a receiver shackle,
- a snatch block,
- a tree protector,
- gloves.

Grill/Brush Bars and Winch Bars

Brush bars protect the front of the vehicle from scratches and minor bumps; they also provide a solid mount for auxiliary lights and offer high-lift jacking points. The level of protection they provide depends on how solid they are and whether they are securely mounted onto the frame of the vehicle. Lighter models attach in front of the standard bumper, but the more substantial units replace the bumper. Prices range from about $150 to $450.

Winch bars replace the bumper and usually integrate a solid brush bar with a heavy-duty winch mount. Some have the brush bar as an optional extra to the winch bar component. Manufacturers such as Warn, ARB, and TJM offer a wide range of integrated winch bars. These are significantly more expensive, starting at about $650.

Remember that installing heavy equipment on the front of the vehicle may necessitate increasing the front suspension rating to cope with the additional weight.

Portable Air Compressors

Most portable air compressors on the market are flimsy models that plug into the cigarette lighter and are sold at the local discount store. These are of very limited use for four-wheel driving. They are very slow to inflate the large tires of a 4WD vehicle; for instance, to reinflate from 15 to 35 pounds typically takes about 10 minutes for each tire. They are also unlikely to be rated for continuous use, which means that they will overheat and cut off before completing the job. If you're lucky, they will start up again when they have cooled down, but this means that you are unlikely to reinflate your tires in less than an hour.

The easiest way to identify a useful air compressor is by the price—good ones cost $200 or more. Many of the quality units feature a Thomas-brand pump and are built to last. Another good unit is sold by ARB. All these pumps draw between 15 and 20 amps and thus should not be plugged into the cigarette lighter socket but attached to the vehicle's battery with clips. The ARB unit can be permanently mounted under the hood.

Quick-Air makes a range of units including a 10-amp compressor that can be plugged into the cigarette lighter socket and performs well.

Auxiliary Driving Lights

There is a vast array of auxiliary lights on the market today and selecting the best lights for your purpose can be a confusing process.

Auxiliary lights greatly improve visibility in adverse weather conditions. Driving lights provide a strong, moderately wide beam to supplement headlamp high beams, giving improved lighting in the distance and to the sides of the main beam. Fog lamps throw a wide-dispersion, flat beam; and spots provide a high-power, narrow beam to improve lighting range directly in front of the vehicle. Rear-mounted auxiliary lights provide greatly improved visibility for backing up.

For off-highway use, you will need quality lights with strong mounting brackets. Some high-powered off-highway lights are not approved by the U.S. Department of Transportation for use on public roads.

Roof Racks

Roof racks can be excellent for storing gear, as well as providing easy access for certain weatherproof items. However, they raise the center of gravity on the vehicle, which can substantially alter the rollover angle. A roof rack is best used for lightweight objects that are well-strapped down. Heavy recovery gear and other bulky items should be packed low in the vehicle's interior to lower the center of gravity and stabilize the vehicle.

A roof rack should allow for safe and secure packing of items and be sturdy enough to withstand knocks.

Packing Checklist

Before embarking on any 4WD adventure, whether a lazy Sunday drive on an easy trail or a challenging climb over rugged terrain, be prepared. The following checklist will help you gather the items you need.

Essential

- ❏ Rain gear
- ❏ Small shovel or multipurpose ax, pick, shovel, and sledgehammer
- ❏ Heavy-duty yank strap
- ❏ Spare tire that matches the other tires on the vehicle
- ❏ Working jack and base plate for soft ground
- ❏ Maps
- ❏ Emergency medical kit, including sun protection and insect repellent
- ❏ Bottled water
- ❏ Blankets or space blankets
- ❏ Parka, gloves, and boots
- ❏ Spare vehicle key
- ❏ Vehicle jump starter/Smart charger
- ❏ Heavy-duty LED flashlight with emergency signalling
- ❏ Multipurpose tool, such as a Leatherman™
- ❏ Emergency food—high-energy bars or similar

Worth Considering

- ❏ Global Positioning System (GPS) receiver
- ❏ Cell phone
- ❏ A set of light-truck, off-highway tires and matching spare
- ❏ High-lift jack
- ❏ Additional tool kit
- ❏ CB radio
- ❏ Portable air compressor
- ❏ Tire gauge
- ❏ Tire-sealing kit
- ❏ Tire chains
- ❏ Handsaw and ax
- ❏ Binoculars
- ❏ Firearms
- ❏ Whistle
- ❏ Flares
- ❏ Vehicle fire extinguisher
- ❏ Gasoline, engine oil, and other vehicle fluids
- ❏ Portable hand winch
- ❏ Electric cooler

If Your Credit Cards Aren't Maxed Out

- ❏ Electric, vehicle-mounted winch and associated recovery straps, shackles, and snatch blocks
- ❏ Auxiliary lights
- ❏ Locking differential(s)

Trails in the West Region

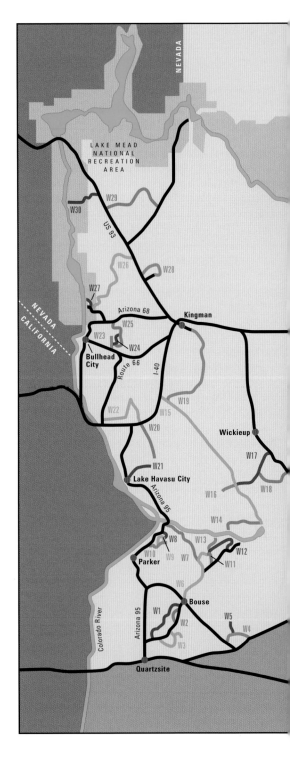

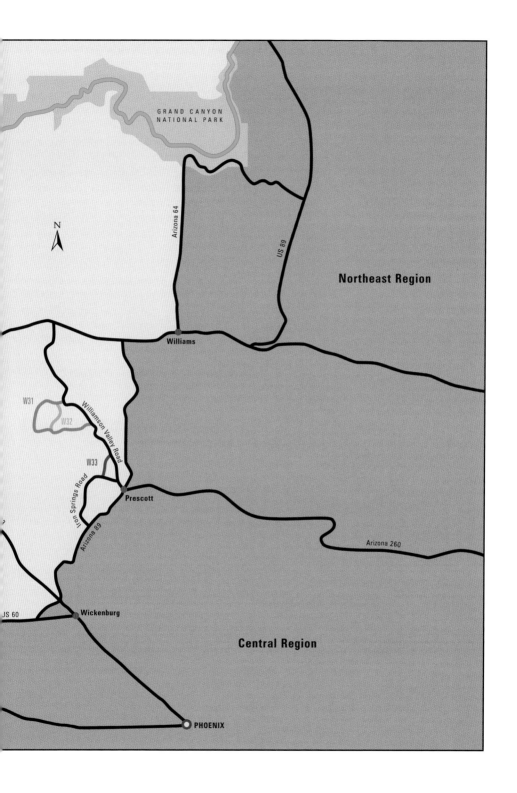

GRAND CANYON
NATIONAL PARK

N

Arizona 64

US 89

Northeast Region

Williams

W31

W32

Williamson Valley Road

W33

Iron Springs Road

Prescott

Arizona 89

Arizona 260

US 60

Wickenburg

Central Region

PHOENIX

Four Peaks Mountain Trail

STARTING POINT Plomosa Road, 3.3 miles south of Bouse
FINISHING POINT Plomosa Road, 0.5 miles north of mile marker 7
TOTAL MILEAGE 14.8 miles
UNPAVED MILEAGE 14.8 miles
DRIVING TIME 2 hours
ELEVATION RANGE 1,100–1,600 feet
USUALLY OPEN Year-round
BEST TIME TO TRAVEL Fall to spring
DIFFICULTY RATING 4
SCENIC RATING 8
REMOTENESS RATING +0

Special Attractions

- Rockhounding for jasper and hematite.
- Four Peaks Mountain and Plomosa Range scenery.
- Access to a network of 4WD trails.

- Many sand dunes to cross at the lower end of the trail.

History

Bouse, first settled in 1906, was originally named Brayton, after John Brayton, the owner of the nearby Harquahala Mine. It became Bouse when an official misread the application and accidentally registered the community as Bouse, which was the name of the person filing the form.

Thomas Bouse, after whom the town was accidentally named, arrived in the area in 1889. His wife, Katherine, and daughter joined him in 1892 after he had built the first two rooms of his home. More children were added to the family and more rooms to the house until the simple cabin he first built became a large, two-story home. Thomas Bouse died of a rattlesnake bite in 1929 and is buried in Bouse Cemetery. The homestead site, located a short distance out of Bouse on the Plomosa Road, is marked by a historical plaque.

Four Peaks Mountain

The Plomosa Range (*plomosa* means "lead bearing") has had much mining activity over the years, mainly for gold. Early mines date back as far as the 1860s.

Description

To reach the start of the trail from the middle of Bouse, turn southwest on the paved Plomosa Road at the sign for the Bouse Community Park. This road is also known as the Quartzsite Scenic Route. Follow the paved road for 3.3 miles to the start of the trail.

The first part of the trail is well used because its smooth, gravelly surface attracts a lot of winter visitors in RVs. Consequently, there are many turnouts, small side trails, and areas used for RV parking in the first couple of miles. The route directions only list the major tracks to the left and right for the first few miles as new small tracks appear all the time. Remain on the main trail.

Two miles from the start, the trail passes through some low hills that are frequented by rockhounds. Chunks of hematite and rusty-colored jasper can be found around the slopes of the hills and the creek beds on either side of the trail.

From here the trail winds through the low hills of the Plomosa Range past many small mine workings. It passes along the eastern side of Four Peaks Mountain—the four distinct peaks are most visible from this side, the highest to the south end. After 3.8 miles a short track on the right climbs steeply to a mine shaft and tailings. The deep, perfectly square shaft is lined with timber as far as the eye can see.

From the junction with West #2: Plomosa Range Trail, the navigation becomes tricky. There are some well-used side trails along the south side of Four Peaks Mountain and it is easy to overshoot a turn. Keep a close eye on the directions and GPS coordinates to ensure you don't go wrong.

The scenery as the trail crosses through the Plomosa Range is very rugged and spectacular, with red soil, large saguaro cacti, and the southernmost peak of Four Peaks Mountain. The trail runs along a wash for a couple of miles and then leaves the wash to swing down through the sand dunes on the western side of the range. The right turn, 8.1 miles from the start of the trail, is easy to miss as there are no distinguishing features to mark it, and the trail straight ahead is well used. If you overshoot and continue past this point, it is possible to exit to Plomosa Road by heading generally south, but it is an absolute maze of trails. Many tracks are used mainly by ATVs, and many are dead ends with brushy vegetation.

The final few miles of the trail cross through some sand dunes that have collected on the eastern side of the Plomosa Range. The sand is deep and loose, but the dunes are not high enough to cause many problems. In the warmer months you may need to deflate your tires. Watch for oncoming vehicles on the crests. The dunes are covered with saguaro and ocotillo and are exceptionally photogenic, especially in spring when the desert flowers are blooming. There are many small washes to cross and many faint tracks on the right and left on this final part of the trail. Only the major washes and tracks are noted in the route directions.

For the most part the trail is moderate. The surface is loose, especially in the washes and around the southern end of Four Peaks Mountain, but it lacks the fist-sized, rubbly boulders that make a lot of trails in the area more difficult.

The trail ends on Plomosa Road, 0.5 miles north of mile marker 7. Neither the topographic nor the BLM maps accurately show the trail on the east side of the Plomosa Range.

Current Road Information

Bureau of Land Management
Lake Havasu Field Office
1785 Kiowa Avenue
Lake Havasu City, AZ 86403
(928) 505-1200

Bureau of Land Management
Yuma Field Office
7341 E. 30th Street
Yuma, AZ 85365
(928) 317-3200

An easy sandy section of the trail

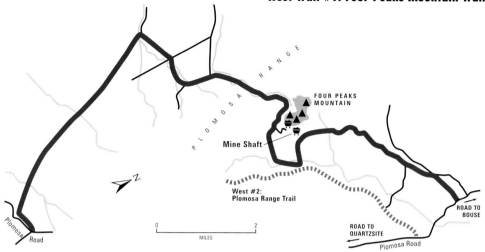

Map References

BLM   Blythe
USGS   1:24,000   Bouse, Ibex Peak,
           Bouse SW
           1:100,000 Blythe
Arizona Atlas & Gazetteer, pp. 40, 41
Arizona Road & Recreation Atlas, p. 71

Route Directions

▼ 0.0   From Plomosa Road, 3.3 miles south of
                 Bouse and the intersection with
                 Arizona 72, turn west onto unmarked,
                 single-lane dirt road. The turn is just
                 south of a cattle guard. Zero trip meter.

4.3 ▲   Trail ends back on Plomosa Road, 3.3
                 miles south of Bouse. Turn left for
                 Bouse; turn right for Quartzsite.
                 GPS: N33°53.67′ W114°01.95′

▼ 0.3   SO Track on left. The start of the trail is a
                 popular RV winter parking area. Many
                 small tracks and turnouts for the first
                 2.1 miles. Remain on the main trail.

4.0 ▲   SO Track on right.

▼ 0.4   SO Track on left.

3.9 ▲   SO Track on right.
                 GPS: N33°53.62′ W114°02.38′

▼ 0.6   BL Crossroads with well-used tracks

coming in from the right; keep to the
major left-hand track. Followed by
track on left.

3.7 ▲   BR Track on right, then crossroads with
                 well-used tracks coming in from left.
                 Keep to the major right-hand track.
                 GPS: N33°53.57′ W114°02.65′

▼ 1.0   SO Track on left.

3.3 ▲   SO Track on right.

▼ 2.1   SO Trail passes through some low hills.
                 Hematite and jasper can be found
                 scattered in the hills on both sides of
                 the trail.

2.2 ▲   SO Trail passes through some low hills.
                 Hematite and jasper can be found scat-
                 tered in the hills on both sides of the
                 trail. Many small tracks and turnouts
                 for the next 2.1 miles as the trail pass-
                 es through a popular RV winter parking
                 area. Remain on the main trail.
                 GPS: N33°52.88′ W114°03.95′

▼ 2.9   SO Cross through wash.

1.4 ▲   SO Cross through wash.
                 GPS: N33°52.51′ W114°04.41′

▼ 3.0   SO Cross through wash.

1.3 ▲   SO Cross through wash.

ATVs crossing a sand ridge on the trail

▼ 3.1 SO Track on right. Four Peaks Mountain is ahead.

1.2 ▲ SO Track on left.
GPS: N33°52.39′ W114°04.51′

▼ 3.2 SO Cross through wash.

1.1 ▲ SO Cross through wash.

▼ 3.5 SO Faint tracks on left and right; then cross through wash.

0.8 ▲ SO Cross through wash; then faint tracks on left and right.

▼ 3.6 SO Faint track on left; then cross through wash.

0.7 ▲ SO Cross through wash; then faint track on right.

▼ 3.7 SO Faint track on left.

0.6 ▲ SO Faint track on right.

▼ 3.8 SO Track on right goes to mine shaft and tailings. The four distinct peaks of Four Peaks Mountain are clearly visible to the right.

0.5 ▲ BR Track on left goes to mine shaft and tailings. The four distinct peaks of Four Peaks Mountain are clearly visible to the left.
GPS: N33°51.80′ W114°04.74′

▼ 4.1 SO Track on right.

0.2 ▲ SO Track on left.
GPS: N33°51.69′ W114°04.45′

▼ 4.2 SO Cross through wash; then faint track on left. Then cross through larger wash with tracks on left and right up and down wash.

0.1 ▲ SO Cross through large wash with tracks on left and right up and down the wash. Then faint track on right. Cross through second wash.

▼ 4.3 TR Track on left and track straight ahead immediately lead to West #2: Plomosa Range Trail. Zero trip meter.

0.0 ▲ Continue to the northwest.
GPS: N33°51.60′ W114°04.27′

▼ 0.0 Continue to the southwest.

4.1 ▲ TL Two tracks on right immediately lead to West #2: Plomosa Range Trail. Zero trip meter.

▼ 0.1 BR Track on left; then cross through wash.

4.0 ▲ SO Cross through wash; then track on right.

▼ 0.3 SO Track on right to old vehicle.

3.8 ▲ SO Track on left to old vehicle.

▼ 0.5 SO Track on left.

3.6 ▲ BL Track on right.
GPS: N33°51.29′ W114°04.67′

▼ 0.8 BR Cross through wash; then track on left.

3.3 ▲ SO Track on right; then cross through wash.
GPS: N33°51.30′ W114°04.93′

▼ 1.0 BR Track on left.

3.1 ▲ BL Track on right. The largest peak of Four Peaks Mountain is ahead.

▼ 1.1 SO Track on left; cross through small wash.

3.0 ▲ SO Cross through small wash; track on right.

▼ 1.2 TR Cross through wash; then turn right; main track continues straight ahead. After the right turn, immediately bear left up red soil trail.

2.9 ▲ TL Track on left; continue straight ahead; then immediately turn left at T-intersection and cross through wash.
GPS: N33°51.51′ W114°05.19′

▼ 1.3 TR Mine with deep wooden shaft and concrete foundation on right at southern end of Four Peaks Mountain; then turn right again to rejoin main trail.

2.8 ▲ TL Turn left to pass by mine with deep wooden shaft and concrete foundation on left; then turn left again to rejoin main trail.
GPS: N33°51.60′ W114°05.18′

▼ 1.6 SO Cross through wash—there are many small washes to cross in this section.

2.5 ▲ SO Cross through wash.

▼ 1.8   SO   Track on right. Main trail follows alongside wash.

2.3 ▲   BR   Track on left.

    GPS: N33°51.87′ W114°05.44′

▼ 2.3   SO   Enter wash.

1.8 ▲   SO   Exit wash.

▼ 2.5   SO   Exit wash; then track on left. Many small wash crossings for the next 1.6 miles.

1.6 ▲   SO   Track on right; then enter wash.

    GPS: N33°51.52′ W114°05.99′

▼ 3.5   BL   Cross through wash; then track on right; then cross through small wash.

0.6 ▲   SO   Cross through small wash; then track on left; then cross through wash.

    GPS: N33°51.08′ W114°06.76′

▼ 3.6   SO   Track on right.

0.5 ▲   SO   Track on left.

▼ 4.1   TR   Cross through wash; then turn right. Zero trip meter.

0.0 ▲   Continue to the north. Many small wash crossings for the next 1.6 miles.

    GPS: N33°50.54′ W114°06.87′

▼ 0.0   Continue to the west.

6.4 ▲   TL   T-intersection. Zero trip meter.

▼ 0.2   SO   Cross through wash.

6.2 ▲   SO   Cross through wash.

▼ 0.4   SO   Cross through wash.

6.0 ▲   SO   Cross through wash.

▼ 0.5   SO   Cross through wash.

5.9 ▲   SO   Cross through wash.

▼ 0.6   TL   Crossroads.

5.8 ▲   TR   Crossroads.

    GPS: N33°50.51′ W114°07.48′

▼ 0.7   BL   Small track on right goes to some diggings.

5.7 ▲   SO   Small track on left is second entrance to diggings.

    GPS: N33°50.47′ W114°07.54′

▼ 0.8   SO   Track on right is second entrance to diggings. Survey marker on left.

5.6 ▲   BR   Track on left goes to some diggings. Survey marker on right.

▼ 1.4   TL   Track swings sharp left; faint track straight on.

5.0 ▲   TR   Track swings sharp right; faint track on left.

    GPS: N33°50.24′ W114°08.27′

▼ 1.5   SO   Cross through wash. Tracks on right down wash.

4.9 ▲   SO   Cross through wash. Tracks on left down wash.

▼ 1.9   SO   Cross sand ridge.

4.5 ▲   SO   Cross sand ridge.

▼ 2.7   SO   Cross double sand ridge.

3.7 ▲   SO   Cross double sand ridge.

    GPS: N33°49.18′ W114°07.70′

▼ 3.1   SO   Cross sand ridge.

3.3 ▲   SO   Cross sand ridge.

▼ 3.3   SO   Cross through wash.

3.1 ▲   SO   Cross through wash.

▼ 3.6   SO   Cross through wash.

2.8 ▲   SO   Cross through wash.

▼ 4.1   SO   Faint track on left; then cross through deep wash.

2.3 ▲   SO   Cross through deep wash; then faint track on right.

    GPS: N33°48.01′ W114°07.40′

▼ 4.2   SO   Faint track on left.

2.2 ▲   SO   Faint track on right.

▼ 4.3   SO   Cross sand ridge.

2.1 ▲   SO   Cross sand ridge.

    GPS: N33°47.86′ W114°07.23′

▼ 4.4   SO   Track on left.

2.0 ▲   SO   Track on right.

▼ 4.7   SO   Cross through wash.

1.7 ▲	SO	Cross through wash.
▼ 4.9	SO	Track on right.
1.5 ▲	SO	Track on left.
		GPS: N33°47.42' W114°06.92'
▼ 5.0	SO	Track on left.
1.4 ▲	SO	Track on right.
▼ 5.1	SO	Cross through wash.
1.3 ▲	SO	Cross through wash.
▼ 5.2	SO	Cross through wash; tracks on right and left up and down wash.
1.2 ▲	SO	Cross through wash; tracks on right and left up and down wash.
▼ 5.5	SO	Cross through wash.
0.9 ▲	SO	Cross through wash.
▼ 5.9	TL	T-intersection at graded dirt Old Plomosa Road.
0.5 ▲	TR	Turn onto unmarked, small, ungraded trail heading to the northwest. This turn is easy to miss.
		GPS: N33°46.79' W114°06.32'
▼ 6.0	SO	Small track on left; then cross through wash.
0.4 ▲	SO	Cross through wash; then small track on right.
▼ 6.4		Trail ends at the junction with the paved Plomosa Road, 0.5 miles north of mile marker 7. Turn is unmarked but numbered trail 822 is opposite the turn.
0.0 ▲		Trail commences on the paved Plomosa Road, 0.5 miles north of mile marker 7. The turn is unmarked, but numbered trail 822 is opposite the turn. Turn southwest on the graded Old Plomosa Road, which parallels the paved new road. Zero trip meter.
		GPS: N33°46.95' W114°05.87'

Plomosa Range Trail

STARTING POINT Plomosa Road, 0.4 miles north of mile marker 15

FINISHING POINT Plomosa Road, 0.1 miles south of mile marker 12

TOTAL MILEAGE 6.4 miles

UNPAVED MILEAGE 6.4 miles

DRIVING TIME 1 hour

ELEVATION RANGE 1,100–1,400 feet

USUALLY OPEN Year-round

BEST TIME TO TRAVEL Fall to spring

DIFFICULTY RATING 3

SCENIC RATING 8

REMOTENESS RATING +0

Special Attractions

■ Views of Four Peaks Mountain.
■ Popular winter RV parking and camping area.

Description

This easy trail runs along the eastern edge of the Plomosa Range, giving views across the Plomosa Mountains.

To get to the start of the trail from the middle of Bouse, turn southwest on the paved Plomosa Road at the sign for the Bouse Community Park. The road is also known as the Quartzsite Scenic Route. Follow the paved road for 4.7 miles, then turn west on the narrow unmarked trail. The turn is 0.4 miles north of mile marker 15. The first couple of miles of the trail are smooth and wide enough that large RVs are able to traverse it. This aspect of the trail, and the many flat areas, make it a popular winter camping area for RVs, although there is a 14-day limit. There are many narrow trails and turnouts in the first few miles. Remain on the main trail.

The trail intersects with the rougher West #1: Four Peaks Mountain Trail, which crosses the range. The main trail then runs along a ridge top, which is easy and smooth. One nice thing about this trail is the absence of the fist-sized, rubbly rocks that make many of Arizona's trails difficult. The surface is

The Plomosa Range

loose in places, and has some minor ruts, but is well within the capabilities of a stock SUV. A couple of the descents through the dry washes are slightly rougher.

The trail, which then rejoins the paved Plomosa Road, is a pleasant alternative route for exploring the area around the range.

Current Road Information
Bureau of Land Management
Lake Havasu Field Office
1785 Kiowa Avenue
Lake Havasu City, AZ 86403
(928) 505-1200

Map References
BLM Blythe
USGS 1:24,000 Bouse, Ibex Peak
       1:100,000 Blythe
Arizona Atlas & Gazetteer, p. 41
Arizona Road & Recreation Atlas, p. 71

Route Directions

▼ 0.0   On Plomosa Road, 0.4 miles north of
            mile marker 15, 4.7 miles south of
            Bouse, turn west on small, ungraded,
            unmarked dirt road and zero trip meter.
            There is a small track opposite. Many
            small trails on the right and left; remain
            on main trail for the first 2.5 miles.
2.5 ▲   Trail finishes back on Plomosa Road.
            Turn left for Bouse; turn right for
            Quartzsite.
            GPS: N33°52.76′ W114°01.70′

▼ 2.5   BL Track on right leads to West #1: Four
            Peaks Mountain Trail. Zero trip meter.
0.0 ▲   Continue to the northeast. Many small
            trails on the right and left; remain on
            the main trail for the final 2.5 miles.
            GPS: N33°51.66′ W114°04.19′

▼ 0.0   Continue to the southeast.
2.4 ▲   BR Track on left leads to West #1: Four

West Trail #2: Plomosa Range Trail

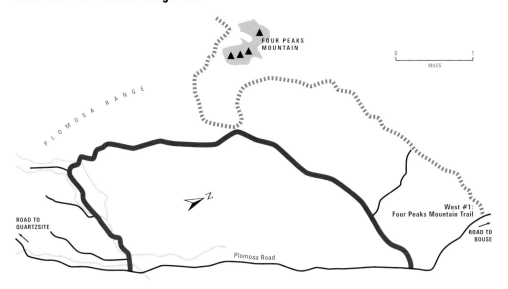

The trail is smooth and easygoing

Peaks Mountain Trail. Zero trip meter.

▼ 0.1   SO   Faint track on left.
2.3 ▲   BL   Faint track on right.
     GPS: N33°51.48′ W114°04.23′

▼ 0.4   SO   Track on left.
2.0 ▲   SO   Track on right.
     GPS: N33°51.27′ W114°04.29′

▼ 0.6   SO   Track on left.
1.8 ▲   BR   Track on right.

▼ 1.4   SO   Track on right.
1.0 ▲   BR   Track on left.
     GPS: N33°50.37′ W114°04.64′

▼ 2.2   SO   Cross through wash.
0.2 ▲   SO   Cross through wash.
     GPS: N33°49.84′ W114°04.73′

▼ 2.3   SO   Track on right.
0.1 ▲   BR   Track on left.
     GPS: N33°49.74′ W114°04.73′

▼ 2.4   SO   Track on right. Zero trip meter.
0.0 ▲   Continue to the northwest.
     GPS: N33°49.67′ W114°04.68′

▼ 0.0   Continue to the east.
1.5 ▲   BR   Track on left. Zero trip meter.

▼ 0.3   SO   Track on right.
1.2 ▲   SO   Track on left.

▼ 0.4   SO   Faint track on left and right.
1.1 ▲   SO   Faint track on left and right.

▼ 0.6   BL   Cross through wash; then track on right.
0.9 ▲   BR   Track on left; then cross through wash.
     GPS: N33°49.76′ W114°04.04′

▼ 0.9   SO   Track on left; then cross through wash.
0.6 ▲   BL   Cross through wash; then track on right.

▼ 1.2   SO   Cross through wide wash.
0.3 ▲   SO   Cross through wide wash.

▼ 1.3   SO   Two tracks on right.

0.2 ▲   BR   Two tracks on left.

▼ 1.4   SO   Cross through wash.
0.1 ▲   SO   Cross through wash.

▼ 1.5   Trail ends at the junction with the paved Plomosa Road. Turn right for Quartzsite; turn left for Bouse.
0.0 ▲   Trail commences on the paved Plomosa Road, 0.1 miles south of mile marker 12. Turn west on unmarked, ungraded dirt road and zero trip meter. There is a turnout opposite.
     GPS: N33°49.89′ W114°03.19′

South Plomosa Range Trail

STARTING POINT   Plomosa Road, mile marker 8
FINISHING POINT   Plomosa Road, 0.3 miles northeast of mile marker 3
TOTAL MILEAGE   16.2 miles
UNPAVED MILEAGE   16.2 miles
DRIVING TIME   2.5 hours
ELEVATION RANGE   1,000–2,000 feet
USUALLY OPEN   Year-round
BEST TIME TO TRAVEL   October to May
DIFFICULTY RATING   4
SCENIC RATING   9
REMOTENESS RATING   +0

Special Attractions
- Remains of the Southern Cross Mine.
- Views of Haystack Peak and Ibex Peak.
- Winding, remote desert trail through the Plomosa Range.
- Bouse Fisherman intaglio.

History
Quinn Pass, located approximately 1.5 miles north of the northern end of this trail, was for many years the home of Thomas Quinn. Originally from New Jersey, Quinn prospected in the Plomosa Range and lived north of the pass that bears his name in a cabin.

A stone ruin at Southern Cross Mine with Ibex Peak (on right) and Haystack Peak in the background

The Bouse Fisherman is an intaglio, or geoglyph, an etching in the desert floor by Native Americans many years ago. It is one of a series of geoglyphs that can be found along the Colorado River. The most well known is at Blythe; there are others south of Quartzsite and near Yuma. The Bouse Fisherman is thought to represent Kumastamho, the creator, as he plunges his spear into the desert to create the Colorado River. The ancient story tells of Kumastamho as he made his way north through the desert, searching for water. His first attempts were unsuccessful; the water drained away to the more fertile, well-watered lands to the north. On his third attempt he struck water that drained to the south and the desert areas. With his spear tip, he made a path for the water, creating the Colorado River.

The intaglio is large and has been fenced off by the BLM to protect it. At first, it can be difficult to see the lighter-colored edges against the desert pavement, but it is still possible to make out most of the figure, the spear raised above his head, and two fish in the water below.

The Bouse Fisherman is 0.2 miles southwest of the northern end of the trail and is marked by a small sign. There is a large parking area. To reach the intaglio, hike 0.2 miles along the old vehicle trail. Coordinates for the intaglio are GPS: N33°47.45' W114°05.57'.

Description

This highly scenic trail winds through the southern end of the Plomosa Range, south of the paved Plomosa Road. The well-formed, ungraded trail is well-used and easy to follow. A fairly deep wash at the start of the trail forms a natural barrier to RVs, so this trail does not have the large network of faint trails and campsites that make navigation tricky on many of the other trails in the Plomosa Range.

The trail winds through a pathway in the range, passing close to dramatic, steep red walls as it climbs into the hills. Close to the northern end, a spur trail leads 2.8 miles to the remains of the Southern Cross Mine. There are a few small stone ruins, extensive diggings, adits, shafts, and a large wooden ore hopper—all located near the foot of Ibex Peak.

Climax Mine shaft with the trail behind

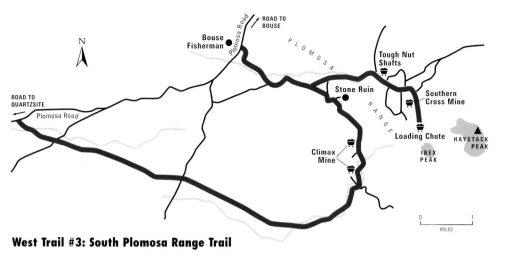

West Trail #3: South Plomosa Range Trail

The main trail climbs through a tight, scenic canyon past the many diggings of the Climax Mine before exiting the south side of the range onto the wide, gently sloping bajada. The trail finishes back on the paved Plomosa Road. If you drive the route in the reverse direction, take care not to miss the start of the formed trail where it turns southeast off the old graded, gravel Plomosa Road.

Current Road Information
Bureau of Land Management
Lake Havasu Field Office
1785 Kiowa Avenue
Lake Havasu City, AZ 86403
(928) 505-1200

Map References
BLM   Blythe
USGS 1:24,000   Ibex Peak, Plomosa Pass,
          Bouse SW
          1:100,000 Blythe
Arizona Atlas & Gazetteer, pp. 40, 41
Arizona Road & Recreation Atlas, p. 71

Route Directions

▼ 0.0   From the center of Bouse, proceed south
         on Plomosa Road for 11 miles to mile
         marker 8. The start of trail is immedi-
         ately north of mile marker 8. Zero trip

meter and turn northeast on unmarked,
formed, well-used trail. Cross through
wash.

1.7 ▲   Trail finishes at the intersection with
         the paved Plomosa Road. Turn right for
         Bouse; turn left for Quartzsite.
         GPS: N33°47.45′ W114°05.40′

▼ 0.3   SO Cross through wash.
1.4 ▲   SO Cross through wash.

▼ 0.5   SO Track on left.
1.2 ▲   SO Track on right.

▼ 0.6   SO Cross through wash.
1.1 ▲   SO Cross through wash.

▼ 0.8   BL Track on right.
0.9 ▲   BR Track on left.

▼ 1.1   SO Cross through wash.
0.6 ▲   SO Cross through wash.

▼ 1.2   SO Cross through wash.
0.5 ▲   SO Cross through wash.

▼ 1.7   BR Track straight on is the spur trail to the
            Southern Cross Mine. Zero trip meter.
0.0 ▲   Continue to the northwest.
         GPS: N33°46.95′ W114°04.08′

Spur to Southern Cross Mine

▼ 0.0   1.7 miles from the north end of the trail, zero trip meter and proceed to the east on the formed trail.

▼ 0.2   SO   Cross through wash.

▼ 0.3   SO   Track on right returns to main trail.
       GPS: N33°47.04' W114°03.80'

▼ 0.5   SO   Cross through wash.

▼ 0.7   SO   Faint track on right.

▼ 0.9   SO   Cross through wash.

▼ 1.0   SO   Faint track on left.

▼ 1.2   SO   Two tracks on left. Tough Nut Shafts are on the left. Ibex Peak is ahead on the right. Haystack Peak is ahead on the left.
       GPS: N33°47.17' W114°02.99'

▼ 1.3   SO   Cross through wash; tracks on left and right in wash.

▼ 1.4   SO   Two tracks on left.

▼ 1.5   SO   Track on right.

▼ 1.6   SO   Track on left on ridge.

▼ 1.7   SO   Cross through wash; then track on right; then bear right at track on left.
       GPS: N33°46.98' W114°02.48'

▼ 1.8   BL   Cross through wash; then track on right; then stone ruin straight ahead. Bear left at stone ruin. This is the Southern Cross Mine. Concrete foundations on left; diggings and tailings on right.
       GPS: N33°46.93' W114°02.41'

▼ 1.9   BR   Concrete foundations on left; then bear right. Track on left.

▼ 2.0   TR   T-intersection. Turn right and cross through wash.

▼ 2.2   SO   Track on left and track on right to concrete foundations and mine diggings.
       GPS: N33°46.90' W114°02.26'

▼ 2.3   SO   Two tracks on left to tailings.

▼ 2.4   SO   Deep shaft on left immediately beside trail.
       GPS: N33°46.75' W114°02.23'

▼ 2.5   TL   Track on right to adits and diggings.
       GPS: N33°46.64' W114°02.20'

▼ 2.6   SO   Cross through wash.

▼ 2.8   Spur ends at the wooden loading chute and shaft near the base of Ibex Peak.
       GPS: N33°46.46' W114°02.17'

Continuation of Main Trail

▼ 0.0   Continue around the loop.
5.5 ▲   BL   Track on right is the spur trail to the Southern Cross Mine. Zero trip meter.
       GPS: N33°46.95' W114°04.08'

▼ 0.3   BR   Second entrance to spur trail on left.
5.2 ▲   BL   First entrance to spur trail on right.
       GPS: N33°46.80' W114°03.78'

▼ 0.4   SO   Cross through wash.
5.1 ▲   SO   Cross through wash.

▼ 0.5   BR   Track on left goes to stone ruin and wooden memorial marker on hillside above.
5.0 ▲   BL   Track on right goes to stone ruin and memorial marker on hillside above.
       GPS: N33°46.76' W114°03.68'

▼ 0.7   SO   Cross through wash.
4.8 ▲   SO   Cross through wash.

▼ 0.9   SO   Cross through wash.
4.6 ▲   SO   Cross through wash.

▼ 1.0   SO   Cross through wash.
4.5 ▲   SO   Cross through wash.

▼ 1.1   SO   Cross through wash.
4.4 ▲   SO   Cross through wash.

▼ 1.4   SO   Timber-braced adit of the Climax Mine on right of trail; then saddle.
4.1 ▲   SO   Saddle; then timber-braced adit of the Climax Mine on left of trail. Ibex Peak is ahead.
       GPS: N33°46.15' W114°03.21'

▼ 1.5   BL   Faint track on right.
4.0 ▲   SO   Faint track on left.

▼ 1.6   SO Cross through wash.
3.9 ▲   SO Cross through wash.

▼ 1.7   SO Cross through wash.
3.8 ▲   SO Cross through wash.

▼ 1.8   SO Cross through two washes.
3.7 ▲   SO Cross through two washes.

▼ 1.9   SO Track on right goes into Climax Mine.
3.6 ▲   SO Track on left goes into Climax Mine.
        GPS: N33º45.75' W114º03.19'

▼ 2.0   SO Cross through wash; then track on
            right to Climax Mine.
3.5 ▲   SO Track on left to Climax Mine; then
            cross through wash.

▼ 2.1   SO Track on right goes to mine workings.
            There is a deep shaft on right at inter-
            section.
3.4 ▲   SO Track on left goes to mine workings.
            There is a deep shaft on left at inter-
            section.

▼ 2.2   TR Intersection. Well-used track on left
            crosses through wash, faint track
            straight on. Turn right and cross
            through wash.
3.3 ▲   TL Cross through wash; then intersection.
            Well-used track ahead crosses through
            wash, faint track on right.

▼ 2.5   SO Cross through wash.
3.0 ▲   SO Cross through wash.
        GPS: N33º45.26' W114º03.32'

▼ 2.8   SO Faint track on right.
2.7 ▲   SO Faint track on left.

▼ 2.9   SO Faint track on right; then cross through
            wash.
2.6 ▲   SO Cross through wash; then faint track
            on left.

▼ 3.0   SO Track on left.
2.5 ▲   SO Track on right.

▼ 3.4   SO Cross through wash.

2.1 ▲   SO Cross through wash.

▼ 3.5   SO Track on left.
2.0 ▲   SO Track on right.

▼ 3.6   SO Cross through wash; then track on left.
1.9 ▲   SO Track on right; then cross through wash.

▼ 5.5   SO Intersection. Equally used tracks on left,
            right, and straight on over open area of
            desert pavement. Zero trip meter.
0.0 ▲   Continue to the east.
        GPS: N33º45.48' W114º06.27'

▼ 0.0   Continue to the west.
3.4 ▲   SO Intersection. Equally used tracks on
            left, right, and straight on over open
            area of desert pavement. Zero trip
            meter.

▼ 2.1   SO Cross wide, graded dirt road.
1.3 ▲   SO Cross wide, graded dirt road.
        GPS: N33º45.91' W114º08.56'

▼ 2.6   SO Cross through wide wash.
0.8 ▲   SO Cross through wide wash.

▼ 2.8   TL Turn left onto graded dirt road running
            parallel to paved Plomosa Road, which
            is just beyond.
0.6 ▲   TR Turn right onto small, unmarked, well-
            used, formed trail to the northeast.
            There is a "No Camping" marker at the
            turn.
        GPS: N33º46.18' W114º09.22'

▼ 3.4   Trail ends at intersection with the
            paved Plomosa Road. Turn left for
            Quartzsite; turn right for Bouse.
0.0 ▲   Trail starts on the paved Plomosa
            Road, 3.2 miles northeast of Arizona
            95, 0.3 miles northeast of mile marker
            3. Turn east on wide, graded gravel Old
            Plomosa Road, which runs parallel to
            the paved road, and zero trip meter.
        GPS: N33º46.07' W114º09.78'

The loading hopper at the Desert Queen Mine

Desert Queen Mine Trail

STARTING POINT Arizona 72 in Vicksburg
FINISHING POINT US 60 in Salome
TOTAL MILEAGE 9.9 miles
UNPAVED MILEAGE 7.5 miles
DRIVING TIME 1.5 hours
ELEVATION RANGE 1,400–2,200 feet
USUALLY OPEN Year-round
BEST TIME TO TRAVEL September to May
DIFFICULTY RATING 3
SCENIC RATING 8
REMOTENESS RATING +0

Special Attractions

■ Remains of the historic Desert Queen
Mine. Connects to Central Region Trail
#11.

History

This trail passes through, or close to, the site
of three interesting settlements of the past
and present. The first is Vicksburg. Situated
on Arizona 72, the town was named after
Victor Satterdahl, a storekeeper in the 1890s
who set up a post office in his store in 1906.
Wells Fargo had a stage station in Vicksburg
in 1907. Today Vicksburg has a small, year-
round population that swells every winter
with visiting "snowbirds" from the north.

Winchester Peak, situated to the southeast of the trail, is named after Josiah Winchester, who owned the Desert Mine just
southeast of the Desert Queen Mine around
1910. He was also the founder of the nearby,
short-lived town of Winchester. Dick Wick
Hall can also lay claim to the founding of
Winchester, having set off the major rush for
the region by announcing his assay returns of
between $117 and $338 per ton of gold on
the streets of Phoenix in 1909.

Winchester boomed! Approaching a population of 2,000 in just the first month, the town
boasted two restaurants, a saloon, an accom-
modation house, various stores (including a
lumberyard), and a telephone line to Vicksburg. Through zealous promotion, Josiah Winchester sold $2,500 worth of town lots on the
first day of sales, and the town was soon the

An old cabin at the Desert Spring Mine

The Calcite Mine shafts

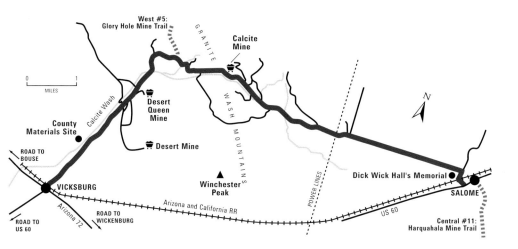

largest settlement on the Arizona & California Railroad. However, after only two months the gold ran out and the town was abandoned.

Salome, at the east end of the trail, was established in 1904 by "Dick Wick" Hall (see page 49), his brother Ernest, and Charles W. Pratt as a speculative venture; they were counting on the probable route of the new railroad going through the town. Visitors will enjoy checking out the Salome Restaurant and viewing their collection of newspaper clippings and memorabilia about the eccentric town founders, including Dick Wick's famous creation, the Salome frog.

In an effort to improve the rutted roads for the new automobiles of the early 1900s, organizers held road races (one of which was called the Cactus Derby) from Los Angeles to Phoenix as early as 1905. Salome was on the route. Drivers averaged an amazing 15 to 17 miles an hour and carried extra gas and spare parts strapped to every conceivable part of their vehicles. Promoters predicted that one day there would be an all-weather surfaced road through the desert.

Description

This moderate, narrow trail runs north from Vicksburg, close to the town site of Winchester, and past the Desert Queen Mine—one of the major gold-producing mines of the area. Initially, the trail is a graded road, but after it passes the county materials site it drops to a small, formed trail. It follows along Calcite Wash, passing close to the Desert Queen Mine after 2.3 miles. The mine is listed as being privately owned, but there appears to be no restrictions on access. Like all mining claims, its status may change.

A small track on the right leads 0.4 miles into the site of the mine, past an old cabin, and along a narrow section of shelf road to the mine hole and wooden loading hopper. Be careful as you approach the hopper: There is a big shaft on the left just as the trail opens out at the mine. Some workings of the mine are also visible to the right.

Past the Desert Queen Mine, the trail winds through the Granite Wash Mountains. There are a few ditchy gullies and washes to cross, and the trail is rough in spots, but it is mainly easy. Close to the Calcite Mine, navigation can be difficult as there are so many side tracks, but generally speaking the main trail is the correct one. The trail follows Calcite Wash, running along the small ridge above the wash but dropping down to cross through it often. Past the mine the trail crosses the open plain of McMullen Valley to reach Salome. A memorial to Dick Wick Hall is passed just before the end of the trail.

Current Road Information

Bureau of Land Management
Lake Havasu Field Office
1785 Kiowa Avenue
Lake Havasu City, AZ 86403
(928) 505-1200

Map References

BLM   Salome
USGS 1:24,000   Vicksburg, Hope,
          Harcuvar, Salome
          1:100,000 Salome
Arizona Atlas & Gazetteer, p. 41
Arizona Road & Recreation Atlas, p. 71

Route Directions

▼ 0.0   From Arizona 72 in Vicksburg, zero trip
          meter and turn north on unmarked
          gravel road that immediately crosses
          the railroad. The turn is opposite the
          paved road that cuts across back to
          US 60.
1.2 ▲   Trail ends on Arizona 72 in Vicksburg.
          Turn right for Bouse; turn left for
          Wickenburg.
          GPS: N33°44.66' W113°45.12'

▼ 0.2 BL Graded gravel road on right.
1.0 ▲ SO Graded gravel road on left.

▼ 1.1 SO Cross through Calcite Wash.
0.1 ▲ SO Cross through Calcite Wash.

▼ 1.2 BR Bear right on smaller graded road
          immediately before La Paz County
          Materials Site. Zero trip meter.
0.0 ▲   Continue to the southwest.
          GPS: N33°45.68' W113°44.51'

▼ 0.0   Continue to the northeast.
1.2 ▲ SO Continue past La Paz County Materials
          Site onto wider graded road. Zero trip
          meter.

▼ 0.3 SO Enter Calcite Wash.
0.9 ▲ SO Exit Calcite Wash.

▼ 0.4 BR Fork in wash; keep to the right.
0.8 ▲ SO Track on right in wash.

▼ 0.8 SO Track on right and track on left.
0.4 ▲ SO Track on right and track on left.
          GPS: N33°46.34' W113°44.10'

▼ 0.9 SO Track on right.
0.3 ▲ SO Track on left.

▼ 1.0 SO Two tracks on right.
0.2 ▲ SO Two tracks on left.

▼ 1.1 SO Track on right goes into the remains of
          the Desert Queen Mine.
0.1 ▲ SO Track on left goes into the remains of
          the Desert Queen Mine.
          GPS: N33°46.61' W113°43.96'

▼ 1.2 BR Well-used track on left. Zero trip meter.
0.0 ▲   Continue to the south.
          GPS: N33°46.71' W113°43.93'

▼ 0.0   Continue to the north.
1.3 ▲ SO Well-used track on right. Zero trip meter.

▼ 0.4 BL Bear left and dip down to cross
          through wash.
0.9 ▲ SO Dip down to cross through wash.
          GPS: N33°47.04' W113°43.75'

▼ 0.7 BR Bear right up Calcite Wash.
0.6 ▲ BL Bear left out of Calcite Wash.
          GPS: N33°47.30' W113°43.80'

▼ 0.8 BR Fork in wash; track on left; keep to
          the right.
0.5 ▲ SO Track on right.

▼ 0.9 BR Rise up out of wash.
0.4 ▲ BL Drop down to travel along wash.
          GPS: N33°47.38' W113°43.64'

▼ 1.0 SO Cross through wash.
0.3 ▲ SO Cross through wash.

▼ 1.3 SO Track on left is West #5: Glory Hole
          Mine Trail, which turns sharply back.
          Turn is unmarked. Zero trip meter.
0.0 ▲   Continue to the west.
          GPS: N33°47.41' W113°43.23'

"DICK WICK" HALL AND SALOME

Born in 1877, Deforest "Dick Wick" Hall became one of Arizona's most notable humorists. At the age of 21, Hall traveled west from Iowa to the Arizona Territory. Settling in the Wickenburg area, Hall worked as a U.S. Bureau of the census counter on the Hopi reservations, as a rancher, and as a construction worker. It wasn't until he became editor of the *Wickenburg News-Herald* that he earned the nickname Dick Wick.

When Dick and a friend struck gold a few miles west of Wickenburg, a new settlement arose around the Glory Mine. Named for the wife of Hall's friend and business partner, Salome grew into a small but substantial town. Dick penned the city's motto: "Salome, Arizona—Where She Danced." He respectfully declined credit for the phrase saying that it wasn't his fault that Mrs. Grace Salome Pratt (for whom the town was named) took her shoes off and tried to walk through the desert.

Dick Hall wanted his town to be well known, so he opened a gas station in hopes of bringing in business. He loved to make fun of the town that he helped found. He once wrote across the front of his gas station, "Smile, you don't have to stay here but we do." He further demonstrated his wit in *The Salome Sun,* which was distributed in the early 1920s. In the *Sun,* Hall sketched local figures, punned, exaggerated, satirized, and revealed his unique crackerbarrel philosophy. The paper received national attention, and national magazines solicited his work. However, Hall is best known for Salome's cartoon mascot, a 7-year-old desert frog that regretted never learning how to swim. With help from the *Saturday Evening Post,* the Salome frog became famous.

Dick Wick Hall was both honored and revered by those who knew him. After his death on April 28, 1926, friends, writers, miners, and cowboys created a monument to him made out of nuggets of the choicest ore. Although the town dwindled years ago after Dick Wick's death, Salome still "dances" one night out of the year. Commemorators gather annually to feast on barbecue, to square dance, and to celebrate Salome and its unforgotten heritage.

▼ 0.0   Continue to the southeast. Small diggings on hill to the left and right on saddle at intersection.

2.2 ▲   BL Track on right is West #5: Glory Hole Mine Trail. Turn is unmarked. Small diggings on hill to the left and right on saddle at intersection. Zero trip meter.

▼ 0.1   SO Cross through wash.
2.1 ▲   SO Cross through wash.

▼ 0.2   SO Track on left.
2.0 ▲   SO Track on right.

▼ 0.5   SO Track on right enters wash.
1.7 ▲   SO Track on left enters wash.
        GPS: N33°47.24' W113°42.72'

▼ 0.6   SO Cross diagonally through wash.

1.6 ▲   SO Cross diagonally through wash.
        GPS: N33°47.29' W113°42.66'

▼ 0.7   SO Track on left.
1.5 ▲   SO Track on right.

▼ 0.8   SO Cross through Calcite Wash.
1.4 ▲   SO Cross through Calcite Wash.

▼ 0.9   SO Cross through Calcite Wash.
1.3 ▲   SO Cross through Calcite Wash.

▼ 1.0   SO Cross through Calcite Wash.
1.2 ▲   SO Cross through Calcite Wash.

▼ 1.3   SO Cross through Calcite Wash.
0.9 ▲   SO Cross through Calcite Wash.
        GPS: N33°47.38' W113°42.03'

▼ 1.5   SO   Enter wash. Calcite Mine is on the left. Some workings on the left; then track on left climbs the hill to mine shafts.

0.7 ▲   BL   Calcite Mine is on the right. Track on right climbs hill to mine shafts; then workings on the right. Exit wash.
GPS: N33°47.31' W113°41.86'

▼ 1.55   TR   Exit wash; track on left and track straight on. Turn right, staying close to the wash and then cross through wash.

0.65 ▲   TL   Cross through wash; then turn left and enter wash. Tracks on right and straight on.
GPS: N33°47.26' W113°41.81'

▼ 1.6   BR   Bear right and enter wash; track on left out of wash.

0.6 ▲   BL   Bear left out of wash. Track on right out of wash.
GPS: N33°47.25' W113°41.71'

▼ 1.7   SO   Cross through wash.
0.5 ▲   SO   Cross through wash.

▼ 1.8   SO   Cross through wash. More diggings of the Calcite Mine on the left, and track on right; then cross through wash.

0.4 ▲   SO   Cross through wash; then track on left. Diggings of the Calcite Mine on right; then cross through wash a second time.
GPS: N33°47.19' W113°41.53'

▼ 1.9   SO   Cross through wash; then track on left.
0.3 ▲   SO   Track on right; then cross through wash.
GPS: N33°47.12' W113°41.39'

▼ 2.2   SO   Track on left and well-used track on right. Zero trip meter.
0.0 ▲   Continue to the west.
GPS: N33°47.09' W113°41.16'

▼ 0.0   Continue toward Salome.
1.6 ▲   SO   Track on right and well-used track on left. Zero trip meter.

▼ 0.3   SO   Cross through wash.
1.3 ▲   SO   Cross through wash.

▼ 0.7   SO   Cross through wash.
0.9 ▲   SO   Cross through wash.

▼ 0.8   SO   Cross through wash.
0.8 ▲   SO   Cross through wash.

▼ 1.1   SO   Well-used track on left.
0.5 ▲   BL   Well-used track on right.
GPS: N33°46.98' W113°40.05'

▼ 1.3   SO   Tracks on right and left along power lines; continue straight on and cross through wash.

0.3 ▲   SO   Cross through wash; then tracks on left and right along power lines.

▼ 1.5   SO   Cross through wash.
0.1 ▲   SO   Cross through wash.

▼ 1.6   TR   Track on left; then junction with paved road. Turn right onto paved road and zero trip meter.
0.0 ▲   Continue west on dirt road.
GPS: N33°46.99' W113°39.45'

▼ 0.0   Continue on paved road, ignoring turns on right and left.
2.4 ▲   TL   Turn left off paved road at right-hand bend and head west on unmarked, single-track trail; then track on right.

▼ 2.2   TR   Turn onto paved Center Street in Salome. Dick Wick Hall's memorial is immediately on the right.
0.2 ▲   TL   Dick Wick Hall's memorial is on the left; then turn left at T-intersection onto Hall Avenue. Continue due west, ignoring turns on right and left.
GPS: N33°47.00' W113°37.03'

▼ 2.4   Cross over railroad. Trail ends at the junction with US 60 in Salome.
0.0 ▲   From the western edge of Salome, turn north on paved Center Street at the sign for the historical marker on US 60 and zero trip meter. Immediately cross over railroad.
GPS: N33°46.76' W113°37.00'

Glory Hole Mine Trail

STARTING POINT West #4: Desert Queen Mine Trail, 3.6 miles north of Vicksburg
FINISHING POINT Glory Hole Mine
TOTAL MILEAGE 2.1 miles
UNPAVED MILEAGE 2.1 miles
DRIVING TIME 45 minutes (one-way)
ELEVATION RANGE 2,000–2,400 feet
USUALLY OPEN Year-round
BEST TIME TO TRAVEL September to May
DIFFICULTY RATING 5
SCENIC RATING 8
REMOTENESS RATING +0

Special Attractions

■ Scenic section of narrow shelf road.
■ Short trail to the Glory Hole Mine.

Description

This short spur trail from West #4: Desert Queen Mine Trail travels 2 miles to the Glory Hole Mine, was historically one of the more productive mines of the region. The trail's main difficulty comes from the very narrow section of shelf road that climbs out of the wash to a saddle and descends down the far side to the mine. It is steep and has some loose sections, but it should not cause too many problems for most high-clearance 4WD vehicles. Very large SUVs and pickups may find this trail rather tight—there are some ditchy gullies along the way that can catch a long overhang.

Shortly after passing a small timber cabin, the trail reaches the Glory Hole Mine. The final 200 yards of the trail are washed out and are too narrow for vehicles, although ATVs are able to continue to the mine. There is a small turning point at the 2-mile mark—be prepared to do a many point turn, especially if you are in a long vehicle.

There are tailings piles, shafts, adits, and concrete foundations to the left at the Glory Hole Mine, which is set in a very pretty, small, tight valley.

A view of the saguaros along the spur trail to Glory Hole Mine

West Trail #5: Glory Hole Mine Trail

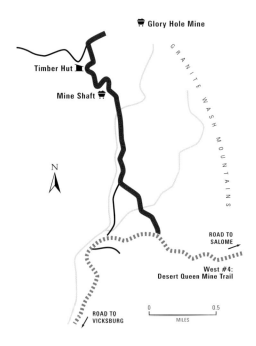

- Glory Hole Mine
- Timber Hut
- Mine Shaft
- GRANITE WASH MOUNTAINS
- N
- ROAD TO SALOME
- West #4: Desert Queen Mine Trail
- ROAD TO VICKSBURG
- 0 ... 0.5 MILES

Current Road Information

Bureau of Land Management
Lake Havasu Field Office
1785 Kiowa Avenue
Lake Havasu City, AZ 86403
(928) 505-1200

Map References

BLM   Salome
USGS 1:24,000   Harcuvar
          1:100,000 Salome
Arizona Atlas & Gazetteer, p. 41

Route Directions

▼ 0.0   From West #4: Desert Queen Mine
             Trail, 3.6 miles north of Vicksburg,
             zero trip meter and turn northwest on
             unmarked, rough, single-track trail.
             There is no sign or marking at the inter-
             section, but it is on a small saddle.
             GPS: N33°47.41' W113°43.23'

▼ 0.2   SO   Cross through wash with pour off to thc lcft.
▼ 0.5   BR   Enter wash. Tracks on left down wash.
             GPS: N33°47.74' W113°43.58'

A timber hut near the Glory Hole Mine

▼ 1.0	BL	Bear left out of wash (turn can be hard to spot, but track is visible farther up rise to the left). **GPS: N33°48.16' W113°43.56'**
▼ 1.2	SO	Trail climbs up narrow, rough shelf road. Mine shaft on left of trail. **GPS: N33°48.30' W113°43.64'**
▼ 1.3	SO	Saddle, with views to the north. **GPS: N33°48.38' W113°43.65'**
▼ 1.6	SO	Bottom of descent. Stone marker on left, recording a mining claim filed in 1968. Small timber hut on left and concrete foundations. **GPS: N33°48.44' W113°43.87'**
▼ 1.8	SO	Track on left. **GPS: N33°48.58' W113°43.87'**
▼ 2.0	SO	Final turning point. **GPS: N33°48.63' W113°43.76'**
▼ 2.1		Trail ends approximately 200 yards before the Glory Hole Mine. **GPS: N33°48.69' W113°43.68'**

WEST REGION TRAIL #6

Swansea Road

STARTING POINT Arizona 72 in Bouse
FINISHING POINT Swansea Ghost Town
TOTAL MILEAGE 24.6 miles
UNPAVED MILEAGE 23.8 miles
DRIVING TIME 1.5 hours
ELEVATION RANGE 900–1,900 feet
USUALLY OPEN Year-round
BEST TIME TO TRAVEL November to April
DIFFICULTY RATING 1
SCENIC RATING 9
REMOTENESS RATING +1

Special Attractions
■ Extensive remains of the buildings and mines of Swansea town site.

■ Access to and views of the sand dunes of the East Cactus Plain Wilderness Area.
■ Access to a network of 4WD and ATV trails.
■ Remote, lightly traveled trail through rugged desert scenery.

History
The history of Swansea (originally called Signal, see Signal p. 105) began in 1886, when three prospectors in search of silver explored the region between the Buckskin and Rawhide Mountains. They found some silver, but most of the ore body was copper. At the time, copper was not worth mining, so they moved on, hoping for better luck elsewhere.

When copper prices climbed in the early 1900s, there was renewed interest in the Swansea region, which was further spurred by the construction of a line being built by the Arizona & California Railroad west from Phoenix. With the railroad running through Bouse, Swansea's location enabled the town to profit from the nearby railroad.

In 1907, Swansea was a company town, with three owners in the company: Newton Evans, Thomas Carrigan, and George Mitchell. Mitchell was added to the group when, in 1907, Evans and Carrigan approached the Welsh-born metallurgist and opportunist with the prospect of investing in the mines.

Mitchell, who had arrived in the United States in the 1880s with his brother Robert, had been involved with developing mines in Alaska and Mexico. His ethics were questionable; he appeared to profit handsomely from his dealings but others were not so lucky. His previous venture, the Mitchell Mining Company of Mexico, went bankrupt, but he personally gained more than $200,000.

Seeing the potential of the site, Mitchell threw himself into the development of Swansea with great enthusiasm. In 1908 he consolidated claims as the Clara Consolidated Gold and Copper Mining Company and started selling shares. His dreams were grandiose, and initially prospects seemed rosy.

The old dust chamber at Swansea ghost town

Using the money raised, Mitchell built an electricity plant, grand houses for the mine managers, and small cottages for the workers. He also piped in water from the Bill Williams River. Swansea, with a population of 500, boasted a newspaper, restaurants, saloons, and a movie house. It also had insurance salesmen and a car dealership. What the hardworking, poorly paid miners thought of these businesses is not recorded.

When the post office was registered, the name of the town was changed from Signal to Swansea, after Mitchell's hometown in Wales. Mitchell continued attracting outside investors. He took a profitable and much-publicized trip to France on which he raised $2 million. He had a taste for the high life, and although he was able to bring in outside money, he was also pretty good at spending it. His lavish 3,600-square-foot adobe home with its palm-lined entranceway and luxury French car testified to his ability to spend money.

With the completion of the railroad extension from Bouse to Swansea in 1910, Mitchell was able to start the next phase of his plans. Machinery was brought in to construct a 700-ton capacity smelter. Ironically, rather than cementing Swansea's status as a prosperous boomtown, the huge smelter hastened its demise. The smelter was so inefficient that it cost three cents more to produce a pound of copper than it could be sold for. Although the ore body was good, Mitchell had invested more money in the surface and amenities of Swansea than he did underground and the smelter was never run at full capacity, rendering it even less cost-effective.

In 1911 the company was declared bankrupt with debts of $71,200. Mitchell left Swansea and went on to become the manager of the Jerome Superior Copper Company, which also went bankrupt after four years of his management.

Rising copper prices caused a brief revival of interest in the region, and Swansea was worked under different owners until 1937 when the falling prices associated with the depression led to its closure. It had produced more than $5 million in copper.

Description

This road offers easy access into a remote and highly scenic area of southwestern Arizona. Swansea town site at the end of the trail should be on every ghost town aficionado's list of places to visit. The town site is extensive and well preserved, with many buildings and mine remains.

The wide road is graded gravel all the way and suitable for passenger vehicles in dry weather. The major hazards are patches of soft road and a couple of loose, deep sand traps that are impassable in wet weather. The road can also be washboardy. It leaves Bouse and follows close to the line of the old Bouse to Swansea railroad. The railroad property is closed to vehicles, but a keen eye will see the old grade where it crosses the road on a couple of occasions.

The trail initially crosses Cactus Plain, with panoramic views north to the Buckskin Mountains. There are many wash crossings along the road; only the major ones are mentioned in the route directions. There are also many small 4WD trails that lead off in both directions. Again, only the major ones are mentioned; many of the others go just a short distance to campsites. The BLM Arizona Access Guide–Cactus Plain map shows all of these small trails in detail.

The trail runs alongside the East Cactus Plain Wilderness Area. There is a parking area and hiking access immediately after the aqueduct. The wilderness area encompasses more than 14,000 acres of sand dunes with dense desert vegetation.

Swansea is one of the best-preserved and most extensive ghost towns in Arizona. The BLM has marked designated trails through the town site to avoid multiple trails that would scar the landscape. The setting is perfect for photographers and ghost town aficionados to explore. The town is located in a very scenic spot, with low hills set against the backdrop of the larger Buckskin and Rawhide Mountains. You can drive or hike around many of the remains on the marked trails. Many visitors frequent it on weekends and weekdays during the winter, but in sum-

Tailings and workers' cottages at Swansea Ghost Town

mer it is deserted. Extreme summer temperatures keep most people away.

The BLM publishes a free brochure on Swansea, which includes a detailed map of the town site. It is available at BLM offices or at the information boards at Swansea. It is also included on the map, Arizona Access Guide–Cactus Plain. Facilities are limited in Swansea. There are a couple of campsites that have picnic tables under shade ramadas 0.3 miles past the end of the trail, but there is no water.

Passenger vehicles can make the trip with care; the final section of the road, as it climbs over the ridge and then drops down to Swansea, is slightly rough, but still reasonable. Watch your vehicle's temperature over this section. Trails past the town site are for high-clearance or 4WD vehicles only.

If you are planning to do much exploration around Swansea and the surrounding trails, you may need to carry extra fuel. Note that fuel is not available in Bouse; the nearest gas stations are approximately 27 miles away at either Quartzsite or Hope.

Current Road Information

Bureau of Land Management
Lake Havasu Field Office
1785 Kiowa Avenue
Lake Havasu City, AZ   86403
(928) 505-1200

Map References

BLM   Blythe, Salome, Alamo Lake
USGS 1:24,000   Bouse, Bouse Hills West, Powerline Well, Planet, Swansea
      1:100,000 Blythe, Salome, Alamo Lake
Arizona Atlas & Gazetteer, p. 41
Arizona Road & Recreation Atlas, p. 71
Recreational Map of Arizona

Route Directions

▼ 0.0   From the center of Bouse, at mile marker 27 on Arizona 72, turn northeast on paved Main Street opposite Plomosa Road and immediately cross over railroad. Turn is signposted to the Museum Assay Office. Continue straight on and pass the museum on the right. Zero trip meter.

2.4 ▲ Cross over railroad; trail ends on Arizona 72 in Bouse. Turn right for Parker; turn left for Wickenburg; continue straight on for Quartzsite.
GPS: N 33º55.93' W 114º00.29'

▼0.2 TL Turn onto the paved Rayder Drive. Remain on Rayder Drive, ignoring turns to the right and left.

2.2 ▲ TR Turn onto Main Street and continue south to Arizona 72, passing the Museum Assay Office on the left.
GPS: N33º55.93' W114º00.29'

▼0.8 SO Paved road on left is Saguaro Drive at the edge of Bouse. Continue straight ahead on graded dirt road.

1.6 ▲ SO Edge of Bouse; pavement begins. Paved road on right is Saguaro Drive. Continue straight ahead on Rayder Drive, ignoring turns to the right and left.
GPS: N33º56.56' W114º00.37'

▼2.0 SO Faint track on right goes to Barber Gene Mine.

0.4 ▲ SO Faint track on left goes to Barber Gene Mine.
GPS: N33º57.48' W113º59.91'

▼2.4 BL Graded road on right is Butler Valley Road. Information board at junction. This is Bouse Y Limited Use Area. Zero trip meter.

0.0 ▲ Continue to the southwest. Road is now Rayder Drive.
GPS: N33º57.80' W113º59.85'

▼0.0 Continue to the northwest. Road is now Swansea Road.

5.2 ▲ BR Graded road on left is Butler Valley Road. Information board at junction. This is Bouse Y Limited Use Area. Zero trip meter.

▼0.3 SO Private drive on left. Old railroad grade crosses road, driveway follows it on left.

4.9 ▲ SO Private drive on right. Old railroad grade crosses road, driveway follows it on right.
GPS: N33º58.07' W113º59.86'

▼0.5 SO Cross through wash; then track on left.

4.7 ▲ SO Track on right; then cross through wash.

▼1.0 SO Track on left and small track on right to Thompson Well.

4.2 ▲ SO Track on right and small track on left to Thompson Well.
GPS: N33º58.65' W113º59.70'

▼3.1 SO Track on right.

2.1 ▲ SO Track on left.

▼3.9 SO Old railroad grade crosses road.

1.3 ▲ SO Old railroad grade crosses road.
GPS: N34º00.30' W113º57.56'

▼5.0 SO Old railroad grade crosses road. Track on right.

0.2 ▲ SO Old railroad grade crosses road. Track on left.

▼5.2 SO Cross over large Central Arizona Canal Project Aqueduct on concrete bridge. Zero trip meter.

0.0 ▲ Continue to the southwest.
GPS: N34º01.04' W113º56.52'

▼0.0 Continue to the northeast on Swansea Road.

4.8 ▲ SO Cross over large Central Arizona Canal Project Aqueduct on concrete bridge. Zero trip meter.

▼0.2 SO Information board on left for East Cactus Plain Wilderness Area.

4.6 ▲ SO Information board on right for East Cactus Plain Wilderness Area.

▼0.4 SO Track on right is government property.

4.4 ▲ SO Track on left is government property.

▼0.8 SO Cross through wash.

4.0 ▲ SO Cross through wash.

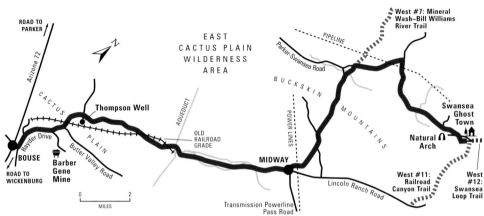

West Trail #6: Swansea Road

▼ 3.4   SO   Cross through wash.
1.4 ▲   SO   Cross through wash.

▼ 4.3   SO   Cross through wash.
0.5 ▲   SO   Cross through wash.

▼ 4.8   BL   Midway. BLM information board at intersection. Graded road on right is Transmission Powerline Pass Road over Butler Pass. Immediately left off this road is Lincoln Ranch Road. Zero trip meter.
0.0 ▲   Continue to the southwest.
       GPS: N34°04.21′ W113°53.19′

▼ 0.0   Continue to the north and immediately cross through wide wash.
5.3 ▲   BR   Cross through wide wash; then arrive at Midway. BLM information board at intersection. Graded road on left is Transmission Powerline Pass Road over Butler Pass. Immediately left off this road is Lincoln Ranch Road. Zero trip meter.

▼ 0.3   SO   Pass underneath power lines; tracks on right and left underneath power lines.
5.0 ▲   SO   Pass underneath power lines; tracks on left and right underneath power lines.

▼ 1.5   SO   Faint track on left.
3.8 ▲   SO   Faint track on right.

▼ 1.6   SO   Track on right.
3.7 ▲   SO   Track on left.
       GPS: N34°05.58′ W113°53.48′

▼ 2.1   SO   Track on left.
3.2 ▲   SO   Track on right.

▼ 4.6   SO   Track on left.
0.7 ▲   SO   Track on right.

▼ 4.8   SO   Cross through wash.
0.5 ▲   SO   Cross through wash.

▼ 5.3   TR   Intersection of graded gravel road. Turn right, remaining on Swansea Road. Graded gravel road ahead and on left. West #7: Mineral Wash–Bill Williams River Trail is straight ahead; Parker–Swansea Road is on left. Zero trip meter.
0.0 ▲   Continue to the south, passing a sign—"Bouse 20 miles."
       GPS: N34°08.25′ W113°55.59′

▼ 0.0   Continue to the northeast.
6.6 ▲   TL   Intersection of graded gravel road. Turn left, remaining on Swansea Road. Graded gravel road ahead and on right. West #7: Mineral Wash–Bill Williams River Trail is on the right; Parker–

Swansea Road is straight on. Zero trip meter.

▼ 1.3   SO   Aboveground gas pipeline crosses road; tracks on right and left along pipeline.
5.3 ▲   SO   Aboveground gas pipeline crosses road; tracks on right and left along pipeline.

▼ 2.0   SO   Track on left.
4.6 ▲   SO   Track on right.
        GPS: N34°09.85′ W113°54.72′

▼ 2.2   SO   Faint track on left.
4.4 ▲   SO   Faint track on right.

▼ 2.4   SO   Aboveground gas pipeline crosses road; tracks on right and left along pipeline.
4.2 ▲   SO   Aboveground gas pipeline crosses road; tracks on right and left along pipeline.

▼ 2.7   SO   Track on left.
3.9 ▲   SO   Track on right.
        GPS: N34°09.53′ W113°54.13′

▼ 4.5   SO   Cross over wash on bridge.
2.1 ▲   SO   Cross over wash on bridge.
        GPS: N34°09.44′ W113°52.48′

▼ 5.1   SO   Views ahead to the tailings piles at Swansea.
1.5 ▲   SO   Final views back to Swansea.

▼ 5.9   SO   Track on left; then cross over wash.
0.7 ▲   SO   Cross over wash; then track on right.

▼ 6.0   SO   Natural arch on right of trail.
0.6 ▲   SO   Natural arch on left of trail.
        GPS: N34°09.89′ W113°51.30′

▼ 6.4   SO   Cross through wash.
0.2 ▲   SO   Cross through wash.

▼ 6.5   SO   Track on right.
0.1 ▲   SO   Track on left.

▼ 6.6   SO   Swansea town site information board.

Track on left. Zero trip meter.
0.0 ▲   Continue to the southwest.
        GPS: N34°10.23′ W113°50.73′

▼ 0.0   Continue into Swansea town site.
0.3 ▲   SO   Swansea town site information board. Track on right. Zero trip meter.

▼ 0.1   SO   Remains of adobe and concrete Company Store on left with the workers' cottages behind. The General Office is at the left-hand bend.
0.2 ▲   SO   The General Office is at the right-hand bend; remains of adobe and concrete Company Store on right with the workers' cottages behind.
        GPS: N34°10.14′ W113°50.61′

▼ 0.2   SO   Workers' cottages on left.
0.1 ▲   SO   Workers' cottages on right.

▼ 0.3   SO   Trail finishes at the information board on left. Continuing straight ahead at this point leads 0.1 miles to the start of West #11: Railroad Canyon Trail and West #12: Swansea Loop Trail.
0.0 ▲   Trail commences at the information board on right, 0.1 miles south of the end of West #11: Railroad Canyon Trail and West #12: Swansea Loop Trail.
        GPS: N34°10.24′ W113°50.50′

WEST REGION TRAIL #7

Mineral Wash–Bill Williams River Trail

STARTING POINT 4-way intersection with West #6: Swansea Road, Parker–Swansea Road, and Mineral Wash Road
FINISHING POINT Arizona 95, 2.8 miles north of Parker Dam Road
TOTAL MILEAGE 16.2 miles
UNPAVED MILEAGE 16.2 miles
DRIVING TIME 2 hours
ELEVATION RANGE 500–1,800 feet

BILL WILLIAMS

Even though a town, a stream, and a mountain in Arizona are named after this bold explorer, there is little known about Bill Williams. Born in 1787 in North Carolina, William Shirley "Old Bill" Williams spent his early years in St. Louis. As a young man, he was a Methodist preacher. When he proposed to a young lady in his congregation, not only was he summarily turned down, but he was humiliated when the woman laughed in his face. Williams left St. Louis and headed west. So great was his faith that he became a missionary to the Osage Indians, translating part of the Bible into their language. He set up a trading post within their village and there he got this first taste of trapping and trading. Williams grew accustomed to and had great respect for the Indian culture, but realized that his faith was increasingly dissolving into their paganism. He eventually married an Osage woman who bore him two daughters.

His wife died at a young age, and Williams became increasingly reclusive. He turned to the mountains for solace, working as a trapper. He moved farther and farther west, traveling through the northern Arizona mountains as he did so. He worked for a while as a guide on the Santa Fe Trail and accompanied Colonel John C. Frémont on one of his expeditions. Wild Bill's nickname was well earned. He is most often described as a tall, gangly red-headed man, eccentric to the point of insanity, with wild woolly hair, a luxuriant beard, and questionable hygiene.

Much of his solitary life is unrecorded and given to legend. After a very successful period of trapping, he would engage in wild stunts that were said to be astounding. At times he was known to drink and gamble his fortune away. He would wager a $100 on his marksmanship, and there is a rumor that he lost nearly $1,000 in just one game of seven up. While in Taos, New Mexico, he tried setting up another trading post. But when he grew tired of the selling, he dumped his wares in the middle of town and took off for the wilderness. Before going, it is said that he stood by and watched merrily as the women of the town scrambled for the choicest pieces of calico cloth.

On one expedition through Arizona, Williams met up with another notable trapper, Antoine Leroux. Later, in 1851, in tribute to "Old Bill," Leroux and Richard H. Kern named Bill Williams Mountain and Bill Williams Fork after him.

Bill Williams's last expedition occurred in 1849. He led a party of 32 explorers into the Rockies and was besieged by terrible weather. Deep snow ended any possibility of travel and freezing temperatures chilled the party. In the end, starvation claimed 11 members. Williams, John C. Frémont, and the remainder of the ill-fated party straggled into Taos. Ignoring the rumors of cannibalism and murderous intentions, Williams struck back out in the spring to recover the party's lost scientific equipment. Somewhere between Pueblo, Colorado, and Taos, New Mexico, Bill Williams was killed by Ute Indians. His final resting place remains a mystery. Some accounts say he lies in an unmarked grave in the mountains that bear his name, the Bill Williams Mountains, in northwest Arizona.

USUALLY OPEN Year-round
BEST TIME TO TRAVEL October to May
DIFFICULTY RATING 5
SCENIC RATING 9
REMOTENESS RATING +0

Special Attractions
- Fording the Bill Williams River many times.
- Bird-watching in the Bill Williams River National Wildlife Refuge.
- Varied, remote desert scenery from arid mountains to riparian valleys.

History
The Bill Williams River National Wildlife Refuge, dedicated in January 1941, protects

Looking into Mineral Wash with its striking red-rock formations

Crossing through a pool of water along the trail

a part of the dwindling native riparian habitat in Arizona. It follows a 9-mile stretch of the Bill Williams River to the confluence with the Colorado River. Today the Bill Williams River is not free flowing. The Alamo Dam, constructed in 1968, regulates the flow.

The refuge is named after William Shirley Williams, known as Bill Williams, a reclusive mountain man who wandered extensively in the Southwest.

Description

Most people who visit the Swansea region will travel via the well-used West #6: Swansea Road or Parker–Swansea Road. However, for those with high-clearance 4WDs who want a little more driving excitement, there are two alternative routes into and out of the region. One is from the north, via West #14: Rawhide Mountains Trail; the other is through the Bill Williams River National Wildlife Refuge and along Mineral Wash.

The Mineral Wash–Bill Williams River Trail leaves from the intersection of the graded Parker-Swansea Road and West #6: Swansea Road. Initially, it is a well-graded road as it travels to join Planet Ranch Road. It runs along a wide, gravelly wash in a canyon (a branch of Mineral Wash), passing alongside Planet Peak and the smaller Squaw Peak. This first part of the trail is also known as the Swansea Cutoff Road. After 6.8 miles, the trail enters the main Mineral Wash and travels down an extremely pretty canyon with high, red walls that contrast with the green paloverde growing along the sides.

The trail then enters into Bill Williams River National Wildlife Refuge. No camping or campfires are permitted within the reserve, so if you plan on camping along the trail you will need to take this into account. There are some suitable sites near the south end of the trail outside of the refuge; once you start to enter the wash, sites are very limited.

The difficulty rating for this trail comes from the many deep crossings of the Bill Williams River. The trail runs alongside the river, passing through dense vegetation, so

that, at first, the river channel is not seen at all. The initial water crossings are offshoots of the river that have flowed into depressions in the riverbed. Under normal conditions they can be up to 24 inches deep, but local conditions can alter the depths. The crossings are wide, in some cases extending out of sight around a bend, and the muddy water obscures the bottom. The bottom is generally firm, so if you are satisfied that the depth of the water is within safe limits for your vehicle, you can proceed. If in doubt, consider walking through first, although this idea is not particularly appealing given the muddy water! At the very least, use a long stick to determine the depth in a few places before proceeding. There are normally six distinct crossings within 0.6 miles. In between the water crossings, the trail is sandy and continues through the tamarisks, cottonwoods, and willows. Tamarisk, the curse of Arizona waterways, started to take hold in the region with the damming of the Colorado River. Also known as salt cedar, tamarisk was used as a quick fix to stabilize riverbanks. However, it has gotten out of control and has spread rapidly within the region. Active management within the refuge has kept the spread of tamarisk to a minimum and it is less prevalent there than in other riparian areas.

After the first stretch of river crossings, the trail opens out and runs along a sandy trail past some red rock formations—the most attractive stretch of scenery along this part of the trail. There are two more crossings of the main channel of the Bill Williams River before you leave the refuge, but these are generally shallow. They are also out in open areas and the water is clear so it is easy to assess the depth.

The trail finishes on Arizona 95, 0.8 miles north of the NWR headquarters. The headquarters has information on the refuge; for bird-watchers, there are detailed lists of the 288 species of birds that you can expect to see in the refuge. The refuge is one of the premier bird-watching locations in Arizona. In addition to birds, you may be lucky enough to spot beaver, raccoon, bobcat, gray fox, mountain lion, coyote, desert bighorn sheep, javelina, and mule deer. Hunting in season is permitted south of the trail for dove, quail, cottontail, and desert bighorn sheep.

The Bill Williams River is dammed upstream at Alamo Lake, but the river flows year-round. In summer it may go underground for a while, but the constant flow is responsible for the lush vegetation. The regulated flow is also partly responsible for the decline in the native fish, which do not thrive in these conditions. Summer travelers will need to take extra care—Mineral Wash often washes out following summer storms and may be impassable. In spring and summer, be very careful before proceeding across the river; the depth may be deceptive.

Current Road Information

Bureau of Land Management
Lake Havasu Field Office
1785 Kiowa Avenue
Lake Havasu City, AZ 86403
(928) 505-1200

Bill Williams National Wildlife Refuge
60911 Hwy 95
Parker, AZ 85344
(928) 667-4144

Map References

BLM   Alamo Lake, Parker
USGS 1:24,000 Planet, Osborne Well,
      Monkeys Head
      1:100,000 Alamo Lake, Parker
Arizona Atlas & Gazetteer, p. 41
Arizona Road & Recreation Atlas, p. 71
Recreational Map of Arizona

Route Directions

▼ 0.0   From West #6: Swansea Road, 17.7
           miles from Bouse, 6.9 miles from
           Swansea, zero trip meter and turn
           northwest on graded gravel road
           signed to Mineral Wash 8 miles.
1.2 ▲   Trail ends at the intersection with West
           #6: Swansea Road and the Parker–
           Swansea Road. Continue straight ahead
           for Bouse; turn left to continue to
           Swansea; turn right to exit to Parker.
           GPS: N34°08.26′ W113°55.58′

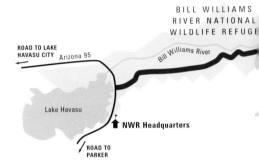

ROAD TO LAKE HAVASU CITY Arizona 95

BILL WILLIAMS RIVER NATIONAL WILDLIFE REFUGE

Bill Williams River

Lake Havasu

↑ NWR Headquarters

ROAD TO PARKER

▼ 0.4   SO Cross over gas pipeline. Track on right
              and track on left along pipeline.
0.8 ▲   SO Cross over gas pipeline. Track on right
              and track on left along pipeline.

▼ 1.0   SO Enter wash.
0.2 ▲   SO Exit wash.

▼ 1.2   SO Exit wash; track on right up wash goes
              0.4 miles to a mine. Zero trip meter.
0.0 ▲   Continue to the southeast.
              GPS: N34°09.40′ W113°55.99′

▼ 0.0   Continue to the northwest.
3.5 ▲   SO Enter wash; track on sharp left goes
              up wash for 0.4 miles to mine. Zero
              trip meter.

▼ 0.3   SO Track on right is the second entrance
              to mine.
3.2 ▲   SO Track on left is the first entrance to
              mine.

▼ 0.8   SO Enter wash.
2.7 ▲   SO Exit wash.

▼ 1.0   SO Exit wash.
2.5 ▲   SO Enter wash.

▼ 1.1   SO Two tracks on right.

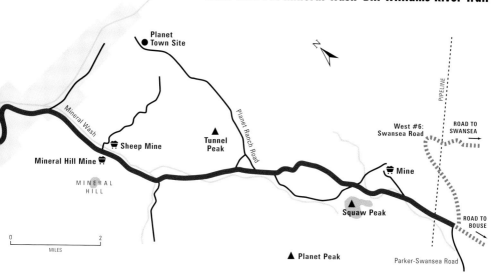

2.4 ▲   SO   Two tracks on left.
      GPS: N34°10.20' W113°56.60'

▼ 1.2   SO   Track on left.
2.3 ▲   SO   Track on right.

▼ 1.4   SO   Enter wash.
2.1 ▲   SO   Exit wash.

▼ 3.2   SO   Track on left.
0.3 ▲   SO   Track on right.
      GPS: N34°11.47' W113°57.84'

▼ 3.4   SO   Small track on left; then small track on right.
0.1 ▲   SO   Small track on left; then small track on right.

▼ 3.5   BL   Graded road on right is Planet Ranch Road. Zero trip meter.
0.0 ▲   Continue up wash to the southeast.
      GPS: N34°11.66' W113°58.09'

▼ 0.0   Continue down wash to the northwest.
2.1 ▲   BR   Graded road on left is Planet Ranch Road. Zero trip meter.

▼ 0.5   BL   Track on right down side wash. Remain in main wash.
1.6 ▲   SO   Track on left down side wash. Remain in main wash.

      GPS: N34°12.03' W113°58.48'

▼ 1.5   SO   Exit wash. Track on right continues in wash.
0.6 ▲   SO   Enter wash. Track on left in wash.

▼ 2.1   TR   Turn right and immediately cross through Mineral Wash. Zero trip meter.
0.0 ▲   Continue on Mineral Wash Road to the south.
      GPS: N34°12.87' W113°59.85'

▼ 0.0   Continue on Mineral Wash Road to the north.
2.4 ▲   TL   Cross through Mineral Wash and turn left on rise. Zero trip meter.

▼ 0.2   SO   Drop down and enter Mineral Wash.
2.2 ▲   SO   Exit Mineral Wash up rise.

▼ 0.3   SO   Track on right in side canyon.
2.1 ▲   SO   Track on left in side canyon.

▼ 0.9   SO   Track on right leaves wash to the Sheep Mine and gives a rewarding view over Mineral Hill. Continue in wash.
1.5 ▲   SO   Continue in wash; then track on left goes to Sheep Mine and gives a rewarding view over Mineral Hill.
      GPS: N34°13.59' W114°00.08'

| ▼ 1.0 | SO | Entrance to Mineral Hill Mines on left—no admittance. |
| 1.4 ▲ | SO | Second entrance to Mineral Hill Mines on right. |

| ▼ 1.1 | BR | Second entrance to Mineral Hill Mines on left. |
| 1.3 ▲ | BL | Entrance to Mineral Hill Mines on right—no admittance. |

| ▼ 1.3 | SO | Track on right; then track on left; then second track on right. |
| 1.1 ▲ | SO | Track on left; then track on right; then second track on left. |

| ▼ 1.6 | SO | Track on right. |
| 0.8 ▲ | SO | Track on left. |

GPS: N34°14.21′ W114°00.36′

| ▼ 2.4 | SO | Entering Bill Williams River National Wildlife Refuge. Information board at boundary. Zero trip meter. |
| 0.0 ▲ | | Continue up Mineral Wash into BLM land. |

GPS: N34°14.95′ W114°00.44′

| ▼ 0.0 | | Continue into Bill Williams River National Wildlife Refuge. Small arch on right at top of cliff. |
| 3.8 ▲ | SO | Exiting Bill Williams River National Wildlife Refuge into BLM land. Information board at boundary. Small arch on left at top of cliff. Zero trip meter. |

| ▼ 0.2 | SO | Track on right to power lines (opposite old pipeline remains) and track on left. |
| 3.6 ▲ | SO | Track on left to power lines (opposite old pipeline remains) and track on right. |

| ▼ 0.3 | BL | Track on left is dead end. |
| 3.5 ▲ | SO | Track on right is dead end. |

| ▼ 0.5 | BL | Bear left and run alongside river. |
| 3.3 ▲ | BR | Bear right and leave river. |

| ▼ 0.8 | SO | Start of river crossings. |
| 3.0 ▲ | SO | End of river crossings. |

GPS: N34°15.53′ W114°00.96′

| ▼ 1.4 | SO | End of first stretch of crossings. |
| 2.4 ▲ | SO | Start of multiple river crossings. |

GPS: N34°15.90′ W114°01.29′

| ▼ 2.5 | SO | Ford Bill Williams River. |
| 1.3 ▲ | SO | Ford Bill Williams River. |

| ▼ 2.6 | SO | Ford Bill Williams River. |
| 1.2 ▲ | SO | Ford Bill Williams River. |

| ▼ 3.2 | SO | Cross through wash. |
| 0.6 ▲ | SO | Cross through wash. |

| ▼ 3.8 | SO | Gate. Zero trip meter. |
| 0.0 ▲ | | Continue to the south. |

GPS: N34°16.40′ W114°03.16′

| ▼ 0.0 | | Continue to the north. |
| 3.2 ▲ | SO | Gate. Zero trip meter. |

| ▼ 3.1 | SO | Information board on left. |
| 0.1 ▲ | SO | Information board on right. |

| ▼ 3.2 | | Trail ends at intersection with Arizona 95. Turn left for Parker; turn right for Lake Havasu City. |
| 0.0 ▲ | | Trail commences on Arizona 95 at the intersection with Bill Williams Highway, 0.8 miles north of the Bill Williams River National Wildlife Refuge Headquarters and 2.8 miles north of the intersection with Parker Dam Road. Zero trip meter and turn southeast on graded dirt road into the Bill Williams River National Wildlife Refuge. |

GPS: N34°17.68′ W114°05.78′

WEST REGION TRAIL #8

Red Mountain Trail

STARTING POINT Arizona 95, 2.9 miles south of the turn to Parker Dam
FINISHING POINT Gray Eagle Mine
TOTAL MILEAGE 3.8 miles
UNPAVED MILEAGE 3.8 miles
DRIVING TIME 1 hour

ELEVATION RANGE 400–1,200 feet
USUALLY OPEN Year-round
BEST TIME TO TRAVEL Fall to spring
DIFFICULTY RATING 6
SCENIC RATING 8
REMOTENESS RATING +1

Special Attractions

- Challenging trail through a rugged mountain range.
- Rockhounding around mine tailings dumps.
- Gray Eagle Mine.

Description

This short trail starts on Arizona 95, 2.9 miles south of the turn to Parker Dam. The turn is unsigned and easy to miss. It is opposite the Castle Rock Shores RV Park, immediately south of the Gas Market. Turning south, the trail runs alongside the RV storage fence line. There are many turns off the trail but generally the most used trail is the correct one; however, it pays to follow the directions closely. The trail initially passes through Buckskin Mountain State Park, but neither the trail nor the park are marked or signed in any way. Also, the trail is not shown in its entirety on the topographic maps of the region.

The trail winds along a well-used road, running along the western boundary of the Gibraltar Mountain Wilderness Area through the Buckskin Mountains. It then swings sharp right and climbs up the side of a hill. At this point, a disused jeep trail goes a short distance to an old mine. There are tailings and shafts nearby on the hillside, and rock hounds will enjoy picking up small, colorful specimens of copper rock.

An open mine adit beside the trail

The trail twists and turns around Giers Mountain

The scenery is rugged, and the area is sparsely vegetated with paloverde, creosote bush, and the occasional saguaro.

The climbs present the greatest challenge of the trail. Although the trail is not long or particularly steep, the surface is very loose and rubbly, and it is hard to get adequate traction in places. This is not the place for road tires! Some of the wash crossings can be gully-like, and some sections of the trail, which are normally narrow, are made narrower by washouts; even so, this trail should be suitable for all but the very longest or very widest vehicles. The newer, lower-to-the ground, super-sized SUVs may struggle a bit. Experienced drivers, well versed in picking a line for their vehicles will enjoy the trail, but there are tight spots and often the best line takes you close to the edge of the drop.

The hardest section comes after the mine, as the trail climbs up the edge of the hill to a saddle before dropping to the Gray Eagle Mine. Run in reverse, the climb from the Gray Eagle Mine may halt some vehicles as it has some difficult ledges. The ledge surfaces are extremely loose and gravelly, challenging the driver with the worst traction of the trail.

The trail finishes at the junction of West #9: Gray Eagle Mine Trail. The mine is at the junction—a small stone cabin remains, and many tailings and workings are scattered around nearby.

Current Road Information
Bureau of Land Management
Lake Havasu Field Office
1785 Kiowa Avenue
Lake Havasu City, AZ 86403
(928) 505-1200

Map References
BLM   Parker
USGS 1:24,000   Gene Wash, Cross Roads
       1:100,000 Parker
Arizona Atlas & Gazetteer, pp. 40, 41

West Trail #8: Red Mountain Trail

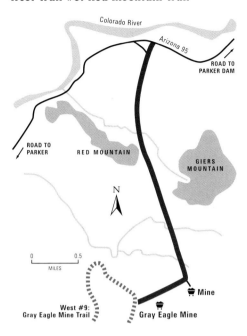

Route Directions

▼ 0.0   From Arizona 95, 2.9 miles south of the turn to Parker Dam, turn south immediately south of the Gas Market on the well-used, narrow trail alongside the RV storage fence line. Zero trip meter.

3.8 ▲   Trail finishes on Arizona 95 at the Gas Market. Turn right for the Parker Dam; turn left for Parker.

           GPS: N34°15.41′ W114°08.82′

▼ 0.1   BL   Track on right; then trail heads up wash.
3.7 ▲   BR   Trail leaves wash; then track on left.

▼ 0.2   TL   Track on right; climb out of wash.
3.6 ▲   TR   Track on left; enter wash.

▼ 0.6   BR   Two faint tracks on left.
3.2 ▲   BL   Two faint tracks on right.

▼ 0.8   BL   Track on right.
3.0 ▲   BR   Track on left.

           GPS: N34°14.80′ W114°09.06′

A tough and rocky section of trail

▼ 0.9	SO	Track on left.
2.9 ▲	SO	Track on right.

▼ 1.1	BR	Faint track on left goes toward arch.
2.7 ▲	SO	Faint track on right goes toward arch.

GPS: N34°14.58′ W114°09.04′

▼ 1.2	SO	Cross through wash. Loose, rutted terrain for difficult climb out of wash.
2.6 ▲	SO	Loose, rutted terrain for the descent; then cross through wash.

▼ 1.6	SO	Cross through wash. Giers Mountain is on the left.
2.2 ▲	SO	Cross through wash. Giers Mountain is on the right.

▼ 1.7	BR	Trail enters wash.
2.1 ▲	BL	Exit wash.

▼ 1.8	SO	Exit wash. Loose, scrabbly descent into wash.
2.0 ▲	SO	Enter wash. Loose, scrabbly climb out of wash.

▼ 1.9	SO	Crest of rise.
1.9 ▲	SO	Crest of rise.

▼ 2.3	SO	Start to cross through wide wash. Vehicles travel to the right down wash.
1.5 ▲	SO	Exit wash crossing.

GPS: N34°13.71′ W114°08.75′

▼ 2.5	SO	Exit wash crossing.
1.3 ▲	SO	Start to cross through wide wash. Vehicles travel to the left down wash.

▼ 2.8	SO	Cross through wash.
1.0 ▲	SO	Cross through wash.

▼ 2.9	SO	Cross through wash.
0.9 ▲	SO	Cross through wash.

▼ 3.0	SO	Cross through wash.
0.8 ▲	SO	Cross through wash.

▼ 3.1	TR	Turn sharp right and start to climb up ridge. Disused track straight ahead goes short distance to mine.
0.7 ▲	TL	End of descent from ridge; turn sharp left on main trail. Disused track on right goes short distance to mine.

GPS: N34°13.08′ W114°08.48′

▼ 3.3	SO	Crest of ridge; turnout on right and views in both directions. Mine shafts at crest. Difficult descent ahead from crest with large boulders and a tight line.
0.5 ▲	SO	Crest of ridge; turnout on left and views in both directions. Mine shafts at crest. Descend from ridge.

GPS: N34°13.04′ W114°08.65′

▼ 3.8		Trail ends at the junction with West #9: Gray Eagle Mine Trail at the Gray Eagle Mine. Remains of a small stone cabin, shafts, and tailings on the left. Turn left for the quickest exit to the county road (West #10: Nellie Mine Road); turn right to continue around the Gray Eagle Mine Trail.
0.0 ▲		Trail commences along West #9: Gray Eagle Mine Trail, 1.2 miles from the western end of the trail at the Gray Eagle Mine. Zero trip meter and turn northeast on the rough trail. Trail immediately climbs a ridge with large boulders and a tight line.

GPS: N34°12.84′ W114°09.10′

WEST REGION TRAIL #9

Gray Eagle Mine Trail

STARTING POINT West #10: Nellie Mine Road, 3 miles from Arizona 95

FINISHING POINT West #10: Nellie Mine Road, 4.1 miles from Arizona 95

TOTAL MILEAGE 3.6 miles

UNPAVED MILEAGE 3.6 miles

DRIVING TIME 45 minutes

ELEVATION RANGE 800–900 feet

USUALLY OPEN Year-round

BEST TIME TO TRAVEL Fall to spring

DIFFICULTY RATING 4

SCENIC RATING 8

REMOTENESS RATING +1

An off-camber section of trail as it exits the wash

Special Attractions

■ Gray Eagle Mine.
■ Rugged, remote trail through the spectacular Buckskin Mountains.
■ Rockhounding in old mine sites.

Description

This is a short, winding trail that travels through the very rugged terrain of Billy Mack Mountain. It offers good views of the area and is an easy, undulating trail suitable for all stock vehicles. The trail starts and finishes on the graded West #10: Nellie Mine Road. The eastern entrance to the trail is easier to find as it has a small marker post at the junction. The western entrance is unmarked.

Much of the trail travels in a narrow, gravelly, smooth wash. Part of the time it runs in a narrow canyon with paloverde trees growing up the sides. There are a few rocky sections, but the formed trail is generally easygoing, if a bit rough in places. This is an easier trail than West #8: Red Mountain Trail, but it runs through similar scenery.

The Gray Eagle Mine is located 2.4 miles along the trail. The remains of an old stone cabin can be seen at the junction with West #8: Red Mountain Trail; a short distance farther along, a short spur leads to more mining remains.

From the mine, the trail climbs up a narrow shelf road out of the wash and then wraps back and rejoins West #10: Nellie Mine Road.

Current Road Information

Bureau of Land Management
Lake Havasu Field Office
1785 Kiowa Avenue
Lake Havasu City, AZ 86403
(928) 505-1200

Map References

BLM   Parker
USGS 1:24,000   Cross Roads
         1:100,000 Parker
Arizona Atlas & Gazetteer, p. 40

West Trail #9: Gray Eagle Mine Trail

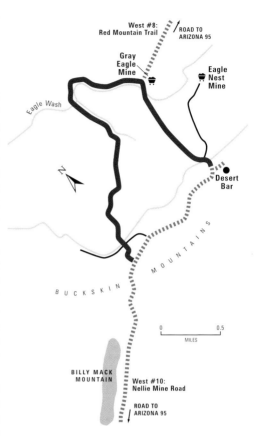

Route Directions

▼ 0.0		Trail commences on West #10: Nellie Mine Road, 3 miles east of Arizona 95. Zero trip meter and turn north on unmarked trail.
2.4 ▲		Trail finishes on West #10: Nellie Mine Road. Turn right to return to Arizona 95. **GPS: N34°11.98' W114°10.27'**
▼ 0.1	SO	Two tracks on left; track on right; then cross through wash. Vehicles travel up and down wash.
2.3 ▲	SO	Cross through wash; track on left; then two tracks on right. Vehicles travel up and down wash.
▼ 0.2	SO	Faint track on left.
2.2 ▲	SO	Faint track on right.

The loading chute at Gray Eagle Mine

▼ 0.3   SO   Cross through wash; then track on left.
2.1 ▲   SO   Track on right; then cross through wash.
         GPS: N34°12.24′ W114°10.25′

▼ 0.6   SO   Cross through wash.
1.8 ▲   SO   Cross through wash.

▼ 0.9   SO   Cross through wash; track on left down wash.
1.5 ▲   SO   Cross through wash; track on right down wash.
         GPS: N34°12.56′ W114°09.76′

▼ 1.1   BL   Enter wash canyon; track on right in wash.
1.3 ▲   BR   Track on left; bear right and exit wash.

▼ 1.6   BR   Second wash joins; bear right up wash.
0.8 ▲   BL   Bear left follows vehicle tracks dow wash.

▼ 1.8   BR   Exit wash.
0.6 ▲   SO   Re-enter wash.
         GPS: N34°13.22′ W114°09.57′

▼ 1.9   SO   Re-enter wash.
0.5 ▲   BL   Bear left on formed trail and exit wash.

▼ 2.3   SO   Exit wash.

0.1 ▲   SO   Enter wash.

▼ 2.4   BR   Track on left is West #8: Red Mountain Trail. The Gray Eagle Mine is directly ahead—remains of old stone cabin and tailings on the left. Zero trip meter.
0.0 ▲   Continue toward West #10: Nellie Mine Road.
         GPS: N34°12.84′ W114°09.11′

▼ 0.0   Continue past the Gray Eagle Mine. Immediately, small track on left to mine, followed by large adit on left.
1.2 ▲   BL   Large adit on right, followed by small track on right to mine. Track on right is West #8: Red Mountain Trail. The Gray Eagle Mine is on the right— remains of an old stone cabin and tailings. Zero trip meter.

▼ 0.1   BR   Track on left goes to mining remains. Bear right and descend to wash.
1.1 ▲   SO   Exit from wash; then track on right goes to mining remains.

▼ 0.2   SO   Cross through wash.

1.0 ▲	SO	Cross through wash.

▼ 0.6	SO	Track on right.
0.6 ▲	SO	Track on left.

▼ 0.7	SO	Track on left; then faint track on right.
0.5 ▲	SO	Faint track on left; then track on right.
		GPS: N34°12.36' W114°09.22'

▼ 0.9	BR	Track on left; bear right and cross through wash.
0.3 ▲	BL	Cross through wash; then track on right.
		GPS: N34°12.19' W114°09.21'

▼ 1.0	SO	Enter wash.
0.2 ▲	SO	Exit wash.

▼ 1.1	TR	Wash forks. Track on left goes to Eagle Nest Mine.
0.1 ▲	TL	Wash forks. Track on right goes to Eagle Nest Mine.
		GPS: N34°12.13' W114°09.15'

▼ 1.2		Trail ends on West #10: Nellie Mine Road, near the end of the trail. Turn right for Arizona 95.

0.0 ▲		Trail commences at the junction with West #10: Nellie Mine Road, 4.1 miles from the junction with Arizona 95. Turn northwest on roughly graded dirt road at the BLM sign for Gray Eagle Mine Trail. Zero trip meter.
		GPS: N34°12.06' W114°09.15'

Nellie Mine Road

STARTING POINT Arizona 95
FINISHING POINT Desert Bar
TOTAL MILEAGE 4.2 miles
UNPAVED MILEAGE 4.2 miles
DRIVING TIME 30 minutes
ELEVATION RANGE 400–900 feet
USUALLY OPEN Year-round
BEST TIME TO TRAVEL Fall to spring
DIFFICULTY RATING 1
SCENIC RATING 7
REMOTENESS RATING +0

A church front at the Desert Bar at the end of the trail

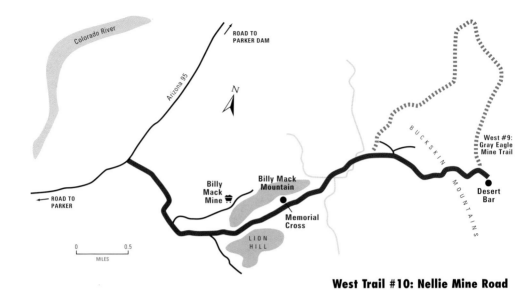

West Trail #10: Nellie Mine Road

Special Attractions
■ Rockhounding sites.
■ Cienega Mining District.
■ The Desert Bar.

Description
This short county road gives access to additional, more difficult 4WD trails as well as to the Cienega Mining District. But the major attraction of this trail could be the unmarked, unadvertised Desert Bar, situated at the very end of the trail. It only operates on weekends and is closed in summer, but it is a popular watering hole for locals and travelers alike. During the week, there is no access to the property. In addition to the bar, the owner has built a "church" (which is nothing more than a board front) on his property. It is hard to miss as you come down the wash.

Nellie Mine Road goes past an area popular with RV travelers in the winter and past the active Billy Mack Mine. There are numerous old mining claims in these hills, and many are popular areas for rock hounds. West #9: Gray Eagle Mine Trail leads off from this route and loops around to rejoin Nellie Mine Road.

Current Road Information
Bureau of Land Management
Lake Havasu Field Office
1785 Kiowa Avenue
Lake Havasu City, AZ 86403
(928) 505-1200

Map References
BLM   Parker
USGS 1:24,000   Cross Roads
        1:100,000 Parker
Arizona Atlas & Gazetteer, p. 40
Arizona Road & Recreation Atlas, p. 71

Route Directions

▼ 0.0   Trail commences on Arizona 95, 1 mile north of the Riverside Drive stoplight on the northern edge of Parker. The turn is unmarked; turn southeast on the graded road and zero trip meter.

3.0 ▲   Trail ends at junction with Arizona 95. Turn left for Parker; turn right for Parker Dam.
        GPS: N34°11.43′ W114°12.55′

▼ 0.6   BR Graded dirt road on left is Cienega Springs Road, which goes to Billy Mack Mine. Bear right, following the

An old abandoned truck along the trail

A cross standing along the trail

sign pole for Nellie Mine Road. Many small tracks on right and left; remain on main graded road.

2.4 ▲ BL Graded dirt road on right is Cienega Springs Road, which goes to Billy Mack Mine.

▼ 0.9 SO Two tracks on left and two tracks on right at information board. Mining adits on the right are the start of the Cienega Mining District.

2.1 ▲ SO Two tracks to left and two tracks on right at information board. Mining adits on left. Many small tracks on right and left; remain on main road.
GPS: N34°11.04′ W114°11.98′

▼ 1.1 SO Cross through wash; then track on right.
1.9 ▲ SO Track on left; then cross through wash.

▼ 1.4 BL Track on right.
1.6 ▲ SO Track on left.
GPS: N34°10.99′ W114°11.53′

▼ 1.6 SO Track on right goes to diggings on Lion Hill.
1.4 ▲ SO Track on left goes to diggings on Lion Hill.

▼ 1.8 SO Track on left.

1.2 ▲ SO Track on right.

▼ 1.9 SO Memorial cross on the flank of Billy Mack Mountain on left.
1.1 ▲ SO Memorial cross on the flank of Billy Mack Mountain on right.

▼ 2.3 BR Track on left.
0.7 ▲ SO Track on right.
GPS: N34°11.57′ W114°10.72′

▼ 2.6 SO Track on left; then cross through wash.
0.4 ▲ SO Cross through wash; then track on right.

▼ 2.7 SO Two tracks on left.
0.3 ▲ SO Two tracks on right.

▼ 2.8 SO Cross through wash; then track on left.
0.2 ▲ SO Track on right; then cross through wash.

▼ 3.0 SO Track on left is West #9: Gray Eagle Mine Trail. Zero trip meter.
0.0 ▲ Continue to the west.
GPS: N34°11.99′ W114°10.27′

▼ 0.0 Continue to the east and cross through wash.
1.2 ▲ SO Cross through wash; then track on

right is the other end of West #9: Gray Eagle Mine Trail. Zero trip meter.

▼ 0.2   SO   Three tracks on left. One goes to a cross on top of a hillock.
1.0 ▲   SO   Three tracks on right. One goes to a cross on top of a hillock.

▼ 0.7   SO   Track on left.
0.5 ▲   SO   Track on right.

▼ 1.1   SO   Track on left is the other end of West #9: Gray Eagle Mine Trail; there is a post marking the route.
0.1 ▲   SO   Track on right is West #9: Gray Eagle Mine Trail; there is a post marking the route.
     GPS: N34°12.06′ W114°09.15′

▼ 1.2   Track on right; then trail ends in wash at the Desert Bar.
0.0 ▲   Trail commences at the end of the public access road to the Desert Bar. This property is only open on weekends; please do not trespass at other times. Zero trip meter and proceed west along the graded road.
     GPS: N34°12.06′ W114°08.99′

Railroad Canyon Trail

STARTING POINT Lincoln Ranch Road, 5.4 miles from Midway and 4.7 miles southwest of junction with Johnson Ranch Road
FINISHING POINT West #12: Swansea Loop Trail in Swansea
TOTAL MILEAGE 4.1 miles
UNPAVED MILEAGE 4.1 miles
DRIVING TIME 30 minutes
ELEVATION RANGE 1,400–1,600 feet
USUALLY OPEN Year-round
BEST TIME TO TRAVEL November to April
DIFFICULTY RATING 3
SCENIC RATING 7
REMOTENESS RATING +1

Special Attractions
■ Final section of historic railroad grade from Bouse to Swansea.
■ Can be driven as part of a loop drive from Swansea.

The old railroad grade running beside the wash in Railroad Canyon

Description

This short trail follows part of the railroad grade from Bouse to Swansea. The train operated from 1910 to 1937, transporting workers, copper ore, and supplies to and from Swansea.

The trail leaves Lincoln Ranch Road and runs along an undulating ridge, with views of Clara Peak to the east. It enters the gravelly wash of Railroad Canyon and immediately the railroad grade can be seen built up on an embankment, running around the edge of the canyon. The original grade is washed out in several places. The original wooden trestle bridges that crossed over the wash at several points are gone, leaving only the built-up embankments on either side.

The trail is an easy, fairly smooth drive. The section after it leaves Johnson Ranch Road has some interesting moguls and can become very greasy in wet weather. The trail ends in Swansea at the junction with West #12: Swansea Loop Trail, 0.1 miles north of the end of West #6: Swansea Road.

Current Road Information

Bureau of Land Management
Lake Havasu Field Office
1785 Kiowa Avenue
Lake Havasu City, AZ 86403
(928) 505-1200

Map References

BLM Alamo Lake
USGS 1:24,000 Swansea
        1:100,000 Alamo Lake
Arizona Atlas & Gazetteer, p. 41
Arizona Road & Recreation Atlas, p. 71

Route Directions

▼ 0.0   From Lincoln Ranch Road, 4.7 miles southwest of the junction with Johnson Ranch Road and 5.4 miles northeast of Midway, turn northeast on the small, well-used, formed trail. Trail is marked with a wooden marker post for Railroad Canyon; zero trip meter. Cross through wash.

4.1 ▲   Cross through wash; trail ends at the junction with Lincoln Ranch Road. Turn right for Midway; turn left to return to Swansea via West #12: Swansea Loop Trail.
        GPS: N34°07.56' W113°49.28'

▼ 0.7   SO Cross through wash.
3.4 ▲   SO Cross through wash.

▼ 0.9   SO Cross through wash.
3.2 ▲   SO Cross through wash.

▼ 1.6   SO Views ahead into Railroad Canyon. Clara Peak is on the right.
2.5 ▲   SO Clara Peak is on the left.

▼ 1.8   BR Enter Railroad Canyon wash and bear right down wash. Lesser-used track on left in wash.
2.3 ▲   BL Lesser-used track on right in wash; keep to the left in wash; then exit wash and bear left up to ridge. Marker post at junction.
        GPS: N34°08.89' W113°49.70'

▼ 2.2   SO Railroad grade enters on left.
1.9 ▲   SO Railroad grade leaves on right.
        GPS: N34°09.04' W113°49.82'

▼ 3.5   SO Two small adits on left.
0.6 ▲   SO Two small adits on right.

▼ 3.6   BL Bear left out of wash; trail ahead in wash joins West #12: Swansea Loop Trail; G. Mitchell Camp on left with picnic table and shade ramada.
0.5 ▲   BR G. Mitchell Camp on right with picnic table and shade ramada; then drop down into wash and bear right up wash. Track on left in wash joins West #12: Swansea Loop Trail.
        GPS: N34°10.28' W113°50.00'

▼ 3.7   BL Adobe railroad depot on left. Bear left past the depot. Track on right.
0.4 ▲   BR Adobe railroad depot on right. Bear right past the depot. Track on left.
        GPS: N34°10.34' W113°50.13'

An old railroad foundation in Railway Canyon

West Trail #11: Railroad Canyon Trail

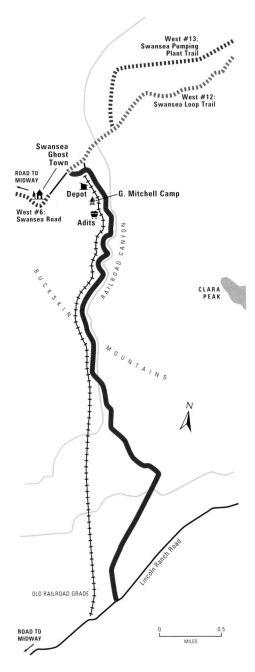

▼ 3.9	BL	Bear left at fork; then small track on left down wash.
0.2 ▲	BR	Small track on right down wash; then bear right at fork.
		GPS: N34°10.43′ W113°50.26′

▼ 4.0	SO	Cross through wash.
0.1 ▲	SO	Cross through wash.

▼ 4.1		Trail ends at the junction with West #12: Swansea Loop Trail, 0.1 miles south of the information board in Swansea. Turn left for Midway; turn right to continue around the Swansea Loop Trail.
0.0 ▲		Trail commences 0.1 miles south of the information board in Swansea. Zero trip meter and turn northeast on well-used, formed trail. There is a marker post for Railroad Canyon at the junction. The left fork at this intersection is West #12: Swansea Loop Trail signed for Swansea Pumping Plant.
		GPS: N34°10.38′ W113°50.40′

Swansea Loop Trail

STARTING POINT Swansea Ghost Town
FINISHING POINT Lincoln Ranch Road
TOTAL MILEAGE 12 miles
UNPAVED MILEAGE 12 miles
DRIVING TIME 1.5 hours
ELEVATION RANGE 800–1,400 feet
USUALLY OPEN Year-round
BEST TIME TO TRAVEL November to April
DIFFICULTY RATING 3
SCENIC RATING 9
REMOTENESS RATING +1

Special Attractions

■ The Bill Williams River.
■ Spectacular views to the Rawhide Mountains.
■ Access to a network of 4WD trails.

Description

When combined with part of the graded gravel Lincoln Ranch Road and West #11:

Railroad Canyon Trail, this trail makes a complete loop. The trail runs through some wild and rugged country south of the Bill Williams River, coming within 0.1 miles of the river at the apex of the trail.

The trail is marked from Swansea as going to the Swansea Pumping Plant, a spur trail (West #13: Swansea Pumping Plant Trail) that leads off from the main loop trail. The trail is well formed and easy to follow. It has some scrabbly sections and some moderately steep grades as it descends to cross through a large wash; but it is well within the capabilities of most high-clearance 4WDs.

For the first few miles the trail runs along a ridge top, offering great views to the north over the Rawhide Mountains and the Bill Williams River Valley. It descends toward the river, traveling in a gravelly wash between high, red canyon walls. Closer to the Bill Williams River, the vegetation gets denser, and the short sandy section running parallel to the river can be quite brushy because of the close-growing tamarisk.

The trail loops back to join Lincoln Ranch Road by following the El Paso Gas Pipeline Road. This part of the trail is wider and more frequently used, and for a couple of miles it follows a roller-coaster ride over the ridge tops and down to cross through the washes.

The trail joins the graded Johnson Ranch Road, called Rankin Ranch Road on some maps, 3.1 miles after leaving the river. The left turn at this point goes a couple of miles back to the river and the Johnson Ranch. Some maps show a small trail that goes past this point and then doubles back to run close to the river, eventually joining West #14: Rawhide Mountains Trail. This trail is becoming very overgrown and is seldom used. Camping opportunities close to the river are extremely limited and not particularly appealing.

The trail follows the graded Johnson Ranch Road out to join Lincoln Ranch Road. From here it is 4.7 miles to the south end of West #11: Railroad Canyon Trail. This trail takes you back to Swansea or to Midway (10.1 miles) to join the graded West #6: Swansea Road to exit the region to Bouse or Parker.

Red rock formations contrast with the white wash trail as it approaches Bill Williams River

Current Road Information

Bureau of Land Management
Lake Havasu Field Office
1785 Kiowa Avenue
Lake Havasu City, AZ 86403
(928) 505-1200

Map References

BLM   Alamo Lake
USGS 1:24,000 Swansea, Reid Valley
          1:100,000 Alamo Lake
Arizona Atlas & Gazetteer, p. 41
Arizona Road & Recreation Atlas, p. 71

Route Directions

▼ 0.0   From the northern end of West #6:
        Swansea Road, at the information board,
        zero trip meter and continue along the
        road for another 0.1 miles. At the fork in
        the trail, zero trip meter and bear left
        onto the Swansea Loop Trail, signed to
        the Swansea Pumping Plant. To the right
        is West #11· Railroad Canyon Trail.
        Continue to the northeast. Table and
        shade ramada immediately on right is
        J. W. Johnson Campsite. Swansea
        company houses are on the left.
0.5 ▲   Trail ends in Swansea, 0.1 miles north
        of the information board at the end of
        West #6: Swansea Road. The track on
        left is West #11: Railroad Canyon Trail.
        Continue south to exit to Bouse or
        Parker via graded dirt road.
        GPS: N34°10.39′ W113°50.41′

▼ 0.1   TR Intersection. Track on left; track ahead
            goes to T. J. Carrigan Campsite and pic-
            nic table with shade ramada. Turn right
            following marker for Swansea Pumping
            Plant and cross through wash.
0.4 ▲   TL Cross through wash; then intersection.
            Track on right goes to T. J. Carrigan
            Campsite and picnic table with shade
            ramada. Track ahead.

▼ 0.2   TL Track on right goes to railroad depot.
0.3 ▲   TR Track on left goes to railroad depot.
            GPS: N34°10.48′ W113°50.28′

▼ 0.4   SO Cross through wash.
0.1 ▲   SO Cross through wash.

▼ 0.5   SO Track on left is West #13: Swansea
            Pumping Plant Trail. Zero trip meter
            and follow marker for Bill Williams
            River.
0.0 ▲   Continue toward Swansea.
            GPS: N34°10.75′ W113°50.09′

▼ 0.0   Continue to the northeast.
5.5 ▲   Track on right is West #13: Swansea
            Pumping Plant Trail. Zero trip meter.

▼ 0.3   SO Cross through wash.
5.2 ▲   SO Cross through wash.

▼ 0.4   SO Track on right; then faint track on left.
5.1 ▲   SO Faint track on right; then track on left.

▼ 0.6   SO Enter wash.
4.9 ▲   SO Exit wash.

▼ 1.1   SO Exit wash.
4.4 ▲   SO Enter wash.

▼ 1.4   SO Gas pipeline crosses trail; track on
            right and track on left along pipeline.
4.1 ▲   SO Gas pipeline crosses trail; track on
            right and track on left along pipeline.
            GPS: N34°11.57′ W113°49.10′

▼ 1.5   SO Cross through wash; track on right in
            wash follows pipeline.
4.0 ▲   SO Cross through wash; track on left in
            wash follows pipeline.

▼ 1.7   SO Cross through wash.
3.8 ▲   SO Cross through wash.

▼ 2.1   SO Cross through wash; gas pipeline
            crosses trail; tracks on left and right
            along pipeline.
3.4 ▲   SO Cross through wash; gas pipeline
            crosses trail; tracks on left and right
            along pipeline.

▼ 2.5   SO Trail starts to descend to cross wide
            wash. Views to the right over the
            wash canyon.

A view of the dry landscape as the trail descends to cross a wash

West Trail #12: Swansea Loop Trail

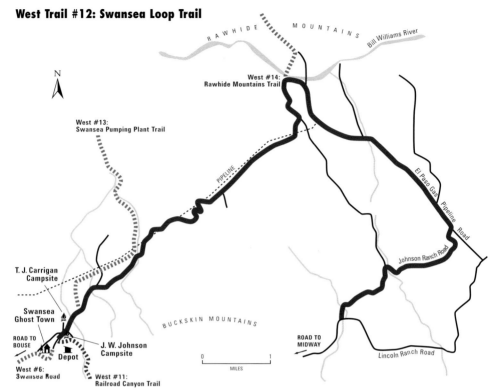

3.0 ▲	SO	End of climb out of wash; views to the left over the wash canyon. **GPS: N34°11.99′ W113°48.28′**

▼ 2.6	TR	Two tracks on left along pipeline.
2.9 ▲	BL	Two tracks on right along pipeline.

▼ 2.7	BL	Enter wash and bear left down wash; track on right in wash; track on left along pipeline.
2.8 ▲	BR	Exit wash; track straight on continues in wash; second track on right follows pipeline. **GPS: N34°12.09′ W113°48.26′**

▼ 2.8	TR	Turn right and exit wash up ridge.
2.7 ▲	TL	Enter wash and turn left up wash.

▼ 3.0	SO	Top of climb out of wash; continue alongside pipeline.
2.5 ▲	SO	Descend into wash; views ahead and to the right down wash.

▼ 3.2	SO	Cross through wash; then faint track on left. Trail crosses through many washes for the next 1.7 miles.
2.3 ▲	SO	Faint track on right; then cross through wash. **GPS: N34°12.31′ W113°47.87′**

▼ 4.6	BL	Bear left on crest; track continues straight ahead. Views down to wash and then over toward Bill Williams River and the Rawhide Mountains.
0.9 ▲	BR	At top of crest bear right; track on left along pipeline.

▼ 4.9	TL	Enter wash and turn left down wash. Track on right up wash.
0.6 ▲	TR	Exit wash to the right; track continues in wash straight ahead. Trail crosses through many washes for the next 1.7 miles. **GPS: N34°13.25′ W113°46.71′**

▼ 5.5	TR	Track on right in wash is private property; then second track on right is El Paso Gas Pipeline Road. Turn sharp right onto this road and zero trip meter. Track straight on is the start of West #14:

Rawhide Mountains Trail; the Bill Williams River is 0.1 miles along the start of it.

0.0 ▲   Proceed to the south.
GPS: N34°13.72′ W113°46.94′

▼ 0.0   Proceed to the southeast through dense vegetation.

2.9 ▲   TL   Track ahead is the start of West #14: Rawhide Mountains Trail; the Bill Williams River is 0.1 miles along the start of it. Zero trip meter and turn sharp left. The track on left in wash is private property.

▼ 0.2   BR   Two tracks on left.
2.7 ▲   SO   Two tracks on right.

▼ 0.3   TR   Track on left goes to pipeline bridge.
2.6 ▲   TL   Track straight on goes to pipeline bridge.

▼ 0.9   SO   Track on right beside gas pressure valves.
2.0 ▲   SO   Track on left beside gas pressure valves.

▼ 1.3   SO   Cross through wash.
1.6 ▲   SO   Cross through wash.

▼ 1.6   BR   Cross over wash on causeway; then track on left. Tracks rejoin almost immediately; left-hand fork has track on left leading off from it.
1.3 ▲   SO   Tracks rejoin; cross over wash on causeway.

▼ 1.7   SO   Tracks rejoin.
1.2 ▲   BL   Track on right; tracks rejoin almost immediately; right-hand fork has track on right leading off from it.
GPS: N34°12.99′ W113°45.58′

▼ 2.2   SO   Cross through wash.
0.7 ▲   SO   Cross through wash.

▼ 2.5   SO   Cross over wash.
0.4 ▲   SO   Cross over wash.

▼ 2.6   SO   Cross over wash.
0.3 ▲   SO   Cross over wash.

▼ 2.9   SO   Graded road on left. Trail now joins the wider Johnson Ranch Road. Zero trip meter.
0.0 ▲   Continue northwest, following the pipeline.
GPS: N34°12.19′ W113°44.58′

▼ 0.0   Continue to the southeast.
3.1 ▲   SO   Graded road on right. Trail leaves the wider Johnson Ranch Road. Zero trip meter.

▼ 0.4   BR   Track on left is El Paso Gas Pipeline Road; bear right away from pipeline.
2.7 ▲   SO   Track on right is El Paso Gas Pipeline Road. Trail now follows close to the pipeline.
GPS: N34°11.88′ W113°44.32′

▼ 0.6   SO   Cross through wash.
2.5 ▲   SO   Cross through wash.

▼ 0.8   SO   Cross through wash.
2.3 ▲   SO   Cross through wash.

▼ 1.0   SO   Cross through wash.
2.1 ▲   SO   Cross through wash.

▼ 1.9   BL   Enter wash. Track on right down wash.
1.2 ▲   BR   Track on left down wash. Exit wash.
GPS: N34°11.32′ W113°45.34′

▼ 2.1   SO   Exit wash.
1.0 ▲   SO   Enter wash.

▼ 2.3   SO   Cross through wash.
0.8 ▲   SO   Cross through wash.

▼ 2.4   SO   Enter wash.
0.7 ▲   SO   Exit wash.

▼ 2.6   SO   Exit wash.
0.5 ▲   SO   Enter wash.

▼ 2.9   SO   Cross through wash.
0.2 ▲   SO   Cross through wash.

▼ 3.1   Trail ends at the junction with the graded gravel Lincoln Ranch Road.

Track on left is marked with a wooden marker post—Lincoln Ranch Road. Turn right for Midway.

0.0 ▲ From Lincoln Ranch Road, 4.7 miles past the south end of West #11: Railroad Canyon Trail and 10.1 miles northwest of Midway, zero trip meter and turn northwest onto graded gravel road. Lincoln Ranch Road continues east at this point and is marked with a marker post. The road you take is unmarked except for a primitive road sign.
GPS: N34°10.70′ W113°46.03′

Swansea Pumping Plant Trail

STARTING POINT West #12: Swansea Loop Trail, 0.5 miles northeast of Swansea
FINISHING POINT Swansea Pumping Plant
TOTAL MILEAGE 3.8 miles
UNPAVED MILEAGE 3.8 miles
DRIVING TIME 45 minutes (one-way)
ELEVATION RANGE 900–1,300 feet
USUALLY OPEN Year-round
BEST TIME TO TRAVEL November to April
DIFFICULTY RATING 4
SCENIC RATING 9
REMOTENESS RATING +1

Special Attractions
■ Historic Swansea Pumping Plant.
■ Scenic trail in deep, red-walled canyon.
■ Access to the Bill Williams River.

Description
This short trail runs down an extremely pretty canyon to the Bill Williams River and the site of the Swansea Pumping Plant. The pump supplied Swansea with water from the Bill Williams River.

The trail's main difficulty comes from a loose, moderately steep descent down to wash and then the very deep gravel in the wash that runs down to the river. In hotter weather especially, watch engine temperatures on the return trip when you are climbing up the wash.

The wide wash has no close vegetation but is lined with palo verde trees. In April, the mass of yellow blossoms against the red walls of the canyon makes for a very colorful scene. Small barrel cacti grow precariously on the sheer rock walls.

The trail ends at a turnaround, 0.1 miles before the Bill Williams River. You can hike the short distance down the wash to the river. The river normally flows year-round but can disappear into the sand in the hotter months. The wash is lined with dense vegetation.

To reach the pumping plant, walk through the fence and after about 20 yards, bear right out of the wash. You will need to scramble up the bank on a small foot track. The pump is on the rise on the north side of the wash. A concrete tank and some footings remain.

Current Road Information
Bureau of Land Management
Lake Havasu Field Office
1785 Kiowa Avenue
Lake Havasu City, AZ 86403
(928) 505-1200

Map References
BLM Alamo Lake
USGS 1:24,000 Swansea
        1:100,000 Alamo Lake
Arizona Atlas & Gazetteer, p. 41

Route Directions

▼ 0.0 From West #12: Swansea Loop Trail, 0.5 miles northeast of Swansea, turn north on the Swansea Pumping Plant Trail at the marker and zero trip meter. Trail is well used and formed.

A view of the trail dropping down into the wash

A view of the climb out of the wash

West Trail #13: Swansea Pumping Plant Trail

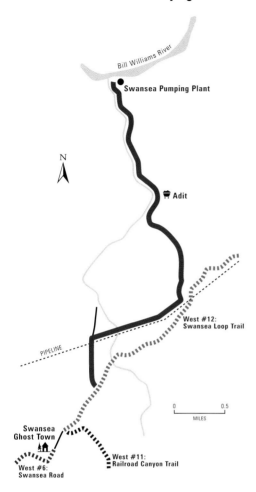

Bill Williams River

● **Swansea Pumping Plant**

N

☗ **Adit**

West #12:
Swansea Loop Trail

PIPELINE

|—————————| 0   0.5
MILES

Swansea
Ghost Town
🏚

West #6:
Swansea Road

West #11:
Railroad Canyon Trail

GPS: N34°10.75′ W113°50.07′

▼ 0.4   SO   Cross through wash.
▼ 0.5   TR   Track on left follows along pipeline. Turn right and follow alongside pipeline.
          GPS: N34°11.16′ W113°50.13′

▼ 0.6   SO   Cross through wash.
▼ 0.7   SO   Cross through wash.
▼ 1.4   TL   Enter wash and turn left down wash at the marker for Swansea Pumping Plant. Trail continues ahead along pipeline. Zero trip meter.
          GPS: N34°11.49′ W113°49.18′

▼ 0.0   Continue down wash to the northwest.
▼ 0.9   SO   Exit wash up rise.
▼ 1.1   BR   Enter wash and bear right down wash. Mine adit on right.
          GPS: N34°12.37′ W113°49.46′

▼ 2.4   Trail ends at a turning circle in the wash. From here, hike down the wash to the Bill Williams River and from there to Swansea Pumping Plant.
          GPS: N34°13.30′ W113°49.95′

WEST REGION TRAIL #14

Rawhide Mountains Trail

STARTING POINT   West #12: Swansea Loop Trail, 6 miles from Swansea, 2.9 miles from junction with JW Ranch Road
FINISHING POINT   West #15: Alamo Lake Road
TOTAL MILEAGE   16.3 miles
UNPAVED MILEAGE   16.3 miles
DRIVING TIME   1.5 hours
ELEVATION RANGE   800–2,400 feet
USUALLY OPEN   Year-round
BEST TIME TO TRAVEL   November to April
DIFFICULTY RATING   3 (5 at river crossing)
SCENIC RATING   9
REMOTENESS RATING   +1

Special Attractions

■ Fording the Bill Williams River.
■ Trail connecting two major travel areas—Cactus Plain and the Rawhide Mountains.
■ Varied scenery through the Rawhide Mountains.

Description

The trail commences along West #12: Swansea Loop Trail, 6 miles from Swansea. It immediately crosses the wide, sandy wash of the Bill Williams River and fords the river. The crossing in normal conditions is about 100 yards wide and it can be up to 24 inches deep. The bottom is firm. The river depth can vary, and it has the potential to be much higher in winter and after summer flooding. If in doubt, walk the crossing first.

Once over the crossing, the trail takes a roller-coaster ride alongside the pipeline for a few miles before turning off to proceed up a wide, sandy wash. Although unmarked, the turn is relatively easy to spot as it will be the only very wide wash encountered since you crossed the river. Once you are in the wash, navigation becomes tricky for the next few miles. There are many branching tracks in the wash, and the most-used trail is not necessarily the correct one. Keep to the left in the wash so that you don't miss the exit—up the bank to the left, 1.2 miles from the entry point. The trail remains faint as it winds through creosote bushes, and there are a few side trails to confuse the navigator.

After the next major intersection (where the trail turns east), it is well defined and easy to follow as it runs along a ridge with a deep wash on each side. From there it remains well defined to the end of the trail;

however, if you take one of the unmarked turns you will be convinced to follow the directions closely. A GPS unit is extremely handy on this trail.

The trail offers attractive views along its length: over Fools Peak and the Rawhide Mountains, and from the top of the saddle farther afield to the Arrastra Mountains to the east and the Bill Williams Mountains to the west. For those with more time to explore, there are a number of side trails that lead to some of the old mines in the region. The trail surface and difficulty rates a 3. It is rated a 5 at the initial crossing of the Bill Williams River, which must be negotiated to complete the trail.

The eastern end of trail is called McGuffie Mine Road on some maps.

Current Road Information

Bureau of Land Management
Lake Havasu Field Office
1785 Kiowa Avenue
Lake Havasu City, AZ 86403
(928) 505-1200

The trail climbs through the Rawhide Mountains as seen from West #12: Swansea Loop Trail

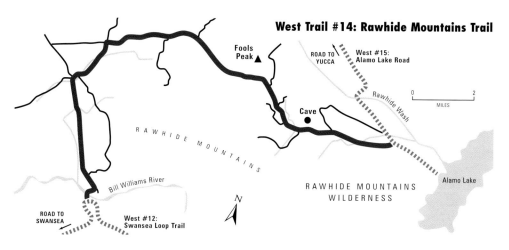

Map References

BLM   Alamo Lake
USGS 1:24,000   Swansea, Centennial
        Wash, Rawhide Wash, Artillery Peak
        1:100,000 Alamo Lake
Arizona Atlas & Gazetteer, p. 41
Arizona Road & Recreation Atlas, p. 71

Route Directions

▼ 0.0   From West #12: Swansea Loop Trail,
           6 miles from Swansea, zero trip meter
           and continue northwest along the
           sandy trail toward the Bill Williams
           River. Trail enters the sandy river
           channel. There are many tracks on
           right and left. Continue northwest
           toward the river.
3.8 ▲   Trail ends at the intersection with
           West #12: Swansea Loop Trail. Bear
           right to continue to Swansea; bear left
           to exit via Lincoln Ranch Road.
           GPS: N34°13.72' W113°46.94'

▼ 0.1   SO Ford through Bill Williams River.
3.7 ▲   SO Ford through Bill Williams River; then
              many tracks up and down wide wash.

▼ 0.2   SO Track on left to private property.
3.6 ▲   SO Track on right to private property.

▼ 0.4   TL Track on right along pipeline.
3.4 ▲   TR Track straight on along pipeline.
              GPS: N34°14.07' W113°46.72'

▼ 0.8   SO Track on left.
3.0 ▲   SO Track on right.

▼ 0.9   SO Track on right.
2.9 ▲   SO Track on left.

▼ 1.6   SO Cross through wash.
2.2 ▲   SO Cross through wash.

▼ 2.4   SO Cross over wash.
1.4 ▲   SO Cross over wash.

▼ 2.9   SO Cross through wash.
0.9 ▲   SO Cross through wash.

▼ 3.8   TR At wide wash crossing, turn right up
              wash, following vehicle tracks. Track
              on left down wash; trail along the
              pipeline continues straight on. This is
              the first turn off the pipeline trail for a
              few miles. Zero trip meter.
0.0 ▲   Continue to the southeast.
              GPS: N34°16.88' W113°48.00'

▼ 0.0   Continue to the northeast along the wash.
4.7 ▲   TL Exit wash and turn onto well-used formed
              trail along the pipeline. Zero trip meter.

▼ 0.2   BL Trail forks in wash.
4.5 ▲   SO Track on left in wash.

▼ 1.2   BL Keep to the left in wash. Bear left and
              exit wash.
3.5 ▲   BR Enter wash and bear right.
              GPS: N34°17.66' W113°47.22'

Checking the depth and soundness of the Bill Williams River before driving across is always a good idea

▼ 1.4   SO Cross through wash.
3.3 ▲   SO Cross through wash.

▼ 1.6   SO Faint track on right.
3.1 ▲   SO Faint track on left.

▼ 1.7   TR Crossroads. Turn right onto equally used, small, formed trail. Immediately track on right.
3.0 ▲   TL Track on left; then crossroads. Turn left at the crossroads onto equally used, small, formed trail.
         GPS: N34°18.08' W113°47.05'

▼ 1.9   SO Cross through wash.
2.8 ▲   SO Cross through wash.

▼ 2.1   SO Cross through wash and enter a gap in the hills.
2.6 ▲   SO Leaving the hills; cross through wash.

▼ 2.4   SO Cross through wash.
2.3 ▲   SO Cross through wash.

▼ 3.6   BR Enter wash and bear right, crossing wash.
1.1 ▲   BL Bear left and exit wash; tracks contin-

ue down wash.
GPS: N34°18.49' W113°45.15'

▼ 3.8   SO Exit wash; then well-used track on right.
0.9 ▲   BR Well-used track on left; bear right and enter wash.
         GPS: N34°18.48' W113°44.91'

▼ 3.9   SO Faint track on right; cross through wash.
0.8 ▲   SO Cross through wash; faint track on left.

▼ 4.2   SO Cross through wash.
0.5 ▲   SO Cross through wash.

▼ 4.3   SO Cross through wash.
0.4 ▲   SO Cross through wash.

▼ 4.7   SO Well-used track on left opposite abandoned trailer. Zero trip meter.
0.0 ▲   Continue to the west.
         GPS: N34°18.55' W113°43.99'

▼ 0.0   Continue to the east.
2.9 ▲   SO Well-used track on right opposite abandoned trailer. Zero trip meter.

▼ 0.3   SO Cross through wash.
2.6 ▲   SO Cross through wash.

▼ 0.8   SO   Cross through wash.
2.1 ▲   SO   Cross through wash.

▼ 1.2   SO   Cross through wash.
1.7 ▲   SO   Cross through wash.

▼ 1.4   SO   Saddle. The dark-colored cone of Fools Peak is on the left. Views ahead to the Arrastra Mountain Wilderness on the far side of the Alamo Lake Valley.
1.5 ▲   SO   Saddle. The dark-colored cone of Fools Peak is on the right. Views ahead to the Aubrey Peak Wilderness, with the Bill Williams Mountains in distance and the closer Rawhide Mountains.
         GPS: N34°17.73' W113°42.84'

▼ 1.7   SO   Cross through wash.
1.2 ▲   SO   Cross through wash.

▼ 2.1   SO   Cross through wash.
0.8 ▲   SO   Cross through wash.

▼ 2.5   SO   Cross through wash.
0.4 ▲   SO   Cross through wash.

▼ 2.7   SO   Cross through wash.
0.2 ▲   SO   Cross through wash.

▼ 2.9   SO   Well-used trail on left. Zero trip meter.
0.0 ▲   Continue to the northwest.
         GPS: N34°17.56' W113°41.43'

▼ 0.0   Continue to the south.
4.9 ▲   BL   Well-used trail on right. Zero trip meter.

▼ 0.3   SO   Cross through wash.
4.6 ▲   SO   Cross through wash.

▼ 0.4   SO   Cross through wash.
4.5 ▲   SO   Cross through wash.

▼ 0.6   SO   Track on right and track on left.
4.3 ▲   SO   Track on right and track on left.

▼ 0.7   SO   Cross through wash.
4.2 ▲   SO   Cross through wash.

▼ 1.3   BL   Track on right.

3.6 ▲   BR   Track on left.
         GPS: N34°16.60' W113°40.72'

▼ 1.6   SO   Cross through wash.
3.3 ▲   SO   Cross through wash.

▼ 1.7   SO   Cross through wash; then track on right. Rawhide Mountains Wilderness is now on the right of the trail.
3.2 ▲   SO   Track on left; then cross through wash; end of Rawhide Mountains Wlderness.
         GPS: N34°16.46' W113°40.22'

▼ 1.9   SO   Cross through wash.
3.0 ▲   SO   Cross through wash.

▼ 2.2   SO   Large cave on left set back from trail.
2.7 ▲   SO   Large cave on right set back from trail.
         GPS: N34°16.47' W113°39.76'

▼ 2.4   SO   Cross through wash.
2.5 ▲   SO   Cross through wash.

▼ 2.8   SO   Track on left.
2.1 ▲   BL   Track on right.
         GPS: N34°16.52' W113°39.09'

▼ 3.7   BL   Enter wash and bear left down main wash channel.
1.2 ▲   BR   Bear right out of wash.
         GPS: N34°16.27' W113°38.21'

▼ 4.2   SO   Exit wash.
0.7 ▲   SO   Enter wash.

▼ 4.9   Trail ends on West #15: Alamo Lake Road, 1.5 miles west of Alamo Lake. Continue east to Alamo Lake; turn left to exit to Yucca or Wickenburg via West #17: Signal Road.
0.0 ▲   Trail commences on West #15: Alamo Lake Road, 1.5 miles west of the end of the trail at Alamo Lake. The road is unmarked, but there is a "Rawhide Mountains Wilderness Area" sign at the junction. Zero trip meter and turn west on well-used, formed dirt trail.
         GPS: N34°16.44' W113°36.92'

Alamo Lake Road

STARTING POINT I-40 at exit 25 (Yucca)
FINISHING POINT Alamo Lake
TOTAL MILEAGE 53.9 miles
UNPAVED MILEAGE 50.9 miles
DRIVING TIME 1.25 hours
ELEVATION RANGE 1,200–3,200 feet
USUALLY OPEN Year-round
BEST TIME TO TRAVEL October to May
DIFFICULTY RATING 1
SCENIC RATING 8
REMOTENESS RATING +0

Special Attractions

- Access to Alamo Lake and Alamo Lake National Wildlife Refuge.
- Joshua tree forest.
- Rockhounding for onyx and rhyolite.

Description

This well-used, graded dirt road is the primary access road to the west side of Alamo Lake. Alamo Lake State Park, a popular spot, is on the east side of the lake; however a national wildlife refuge on the west is just as popular with fishermen. It is primarily included as an easy, scenic trail to a seldom-used part of Alamo Lake. Many other 4WD trails in the area start or finish from this road.

The trail leaves Yucca and for several miles travels across Dutch Flat. The first section of the trail passes through a thick Joshua tree forest. Farther down, there are views of Mc-Cracken Peak before the trail starts to wind through the low hills around Rawhide Wash.

For rock hounds, the gullies on the east side of the trail immediately south of the junction with West #17: Signal Road can yield some interesting specimens of onyx and rhyolite. The site has been picked over through the years, but there are still rocks to be found.

The trail is graded dirt all the way and suitable for passenger vehicles in dry weather. As it is heavily used, it can be very wash-boardy, although it is regularly graded. Campers can find some pleasant spots near the McCracken Hills. There are some other popular sites near the lake.

Current Road Information

Bureau of Land Management
Kingman Field Office
2755 Mission Blvd.
Kingman, AZ 86401
(928) 718-3700

Map References

BLM Needles, Bagdad, Alamo Lake
USGS 1:24,000 Yucca, Yucca SE, Creamery Canyon, Dutch Flat NW, Beecher Canyon, Dutch Flat SE, Groom Spring, Signal, Rawhide Wash, Artillery Peak
1:100,000 Needles, Bagdad, Alamo Lake
Arizona Atlas & Gazetteer, pp. 30, 31, 41
Arizona Road & Recreation Atlas, pp. 63, 71
Recreational Map of Arizona

Route Directions

▼ 0.0		From I-40 at exit 25 (Yucca), proceed to east side of freeway and zero trip meter. Follow sign for Alamo Road and immediately turn right on paved road.
2.6 ▲		Trail ends at exit 25 (Yucca) on I-40.
		GPS: N34°51.87′ W114°08.67′
▼ 1.1	SO	Cattle guard.
1.5 ▲	SO	Cattle guard.
▼ 1.2	SO	Track on right.
1.4 ▲	SO	Track on left.
▼ 1.4	SO	Graded road on right is Apache Road.
1.2 ▲	SO	Graded road on left is Apache Road.
▼ 2.0	SO	Graded road on right.
0.6 ▲	SO	Graded road on left.
▼ 2.1	SO	Graded road on right.
0.5 ▲	SO	Graded road on left.
▼ 2.6	SO	Graded road on left is West #19: Flag

Baker Well with a Joshua tree in the foreground

Alamo Lake with the Rawhide Mountains in the distance

		Mine Trail. Zero trip meter.
0.0 ▲		Continue to the west.
		GPS: N34°50.99′ W114°06.60′

▼ 0.0		Continue to the east and cross over Mackenzie Wash.
8.7 ▲	SO	Cross over Mackenzie Wash; then graded road on right is West #19: Flag Mine Trail. Zero trip meter.

▼ 0.4	SO	Road turns to graded dirt.
8.3 ▲	SO	Road is now paved.

▼ 0.7	SO	Graded road on right.
8.0 ▲	SO	Graded road on left.

▼ 1.3	SO	Track on left; then track on right.
7.4 ▲	SO	Track on left; then track on right.

▼ 1.6	SO	Track on left.
7.1 ▲	SO	Track on right.

▼ 2.5	SO	Track on left; then track on right.
6.2 ▲	SO	Track on left; then track on right.

▼ 3.1	SO	Major graded road on left and right is Knox Drive.

5.6 ▲	SO	Major graded road on left and right is Knox Drive.
		GPS: N34°49.13′ W114°03.81′

▼ 4.7	SO	Two tracks on left and track on right; then cattle guard.
4.0 ▲	SO	Cattle guard; then two tracks on right and track on left.

▼ 5.8	SO	Track on right.
2.9 ▲	SO	Track on left.

▼ 6.9	SO	Track on left and track on right. There are many signed subdivision roads on the left and right for the next 11.3 miles.
1.8 ▲	SO	Track on left and track on right.

▼ 8.7	SO	Graded road on left is La Cienega Ranch Road. Zero trip meter.
0.0 ▲		Continue to the northwest.
		GPS: N34°45.99′ W113°58.94′

▼ 0.0		Continue to the southeast.
8.1 ▲	SO	Graded road on right is La Cienega Ranch Road. Zero trip meter.

▼ 1.1   SO   Cross through Cow Creek.
7.0 ▲   SO   Cross through Cow Creek.

▼ 3.6   SO   Track on right.
4.5 ▲   SO   Track on left.

▼ 4.0   SO   Track on right.
4.1 ▲   SO   Track on left.

▼ 4.5   SO   Track on left.
3.6 ▲   SO   Track on right.

▼ 8.1   SO   Well on left; then graded road on right is Cattle Crossing Road. Zero trip meter.
0.0 ▲   Continue to the northwest.
        GPS: N34°40.00' W113°53.47'

▼ 0.0   Continue to the southeast.
7.3 ▲   SO   Graded road on left is Cattle Crossing Road; then well on right. Zero trip meter.

▼ 5.9   SO   Planet Ranch Road on right.
1.4 ▲   SO   Planet Ranch Road on left. There are now many signed subdivision roads on the left and right for the next 11.3 miles.
        GPS: N34°36.36' W113°48.86'

▼ 7.0   SO   Track on right.
0.3 ▲   SO   Track on left.

▼ 7.1   SO   Cross through wash; then track on right to corral.
0.2 ▲   SO   Track on left to corral; then cross through wash.

▼ 7.2   SO   Track on right to Stouts Well.
0.1 ▲   SO   Track on left to Stouts Well.

▼ 7.3   SO   Major graded road on left is Chicken Springs Road to Wickieup. Zero trip meter.
0.0 ▲   Continue to the west.
        GPS: N34°35.46' W113°47.62'

▼ 0.0   Continue to the east toward Alamo Lake.
4.4 ▲   SO   Major graded road on right is Chicken Springs Road to Wickieup. Zero trip meter.

▼ 0.3   SO   Track on left.
4.1 ▲   SO   Track on right.

Rawhide Wash crossing typifies the landscape near Alamo Lake

West Trail #15: Alamo Lake Road

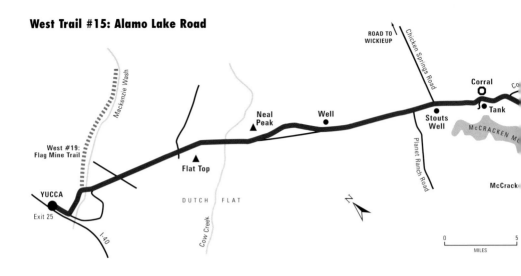

▼ 2.1   SO   Cross through wash.
2.3 ▲   SO   Cross through wash.

▼ 3.3   SO   Corral on left and track on right to tank.
1.1 ▲   SO   Corral on right and track on left to tank.
      GPS: N34°33.10' W113°45.34'

▼ 4.4   SO   Graded road on left is Coyote Wells Road. Zero trip meter.
0.0 ▲   Continue to the northwest.
      GPS: N34°32.25' W113°44.72'

▼ 0.0   Continue to the southeast.
4.9 ▲   SO   Graded road on right is Coyote Wells Road. Zero trip meter.

▼ 1.4   SO   Cross through wash.
3.5 ▲   SO   Cross through wash.

▼ 2.2   SO   Cross through wash.
2.7 ▲   SO   Cross through wash.

▼ 3.4   SO   Cattle guard; then track on right.
1.5 ▲   SO   Track on left; then cattle guard.
      GPS: N34°29.30' W113°43.83'

▼ 4.7   SO   Cross through wash.
0.2 ▲   SO   Cross through wash.

▼ 4.9   SO   Graded road on left is West #17: Signal Road; track on right is West #16: McCracken Peak Trail. Zero trip meter and continue along Alamo Lake Road.
0.0 ▲   Continue to the northwest.
      GPS: N34°28.20' W113°42.93'

▼ 0.0   Continue to the southeast.
4.0 ▲   SO   Graded road on right is West #17: Signal Road; track on left is West #16: McCracken Peak Trail. Zero trip meter and continue along Alamo Lake Road.

▼ 0.1   SO   Track on left.
3.9 ▲   SO   Track on right.
      GPS: N34°28.14' W113°42.94'

▼ 0.2   SO   Cross through wash.
3.8 ▲   SO   Cross through wash.

▼ 1.0   SO   Cross through wash.
3.0 ▲   SO   Cross through wash.

▼ 1.2   SO   Track on left.
2.8 ▲   SO   Track on right.
      GPS: N34°27.22' W113°43.15'

▼ 1.7   SO   Track on left and track on right.
2.3 ▲   SO   Track on left and track on right.
      GPS: N34°26.78' W113°43.36'

▼ 3.8   SO   Cross through wash.
0.2 ▲   SO   Cross through wash.

▼ 0.0   Continue to the southeast.
8.9 ▲   SO Cattle guard. Zero trip meter.

▼ 0.3   SO Cross through wash.
8.6 ▲   SO Cross through wash.

▼ 0.9   SO Cross through Maggie Wash.
8.0 ▲   SO Cross through Maggie Wash.

▼ 2.0   SO Cross through Maggie Wash.
6.9 ▲   SO Cross through Maggie Wash.

▼ 2.5   SO Cross through wash; track on left
              down wash. Trail is following alongside
              Maggie Wash.
6.4 ▲   SO Cross through wash; track on right
              down wash. Trail is following alongside
              Maggie Wash.
              GPS: N34°20.57′ W113°40.89′

▼ 3.3   SO Cross through wash.
5.6 ▲   SO Cross through wash.

▼ 3.5   SO Track on left.
5.4 ▲   SO Track on right.

▼ 3.6   SO Track on right.
5.3 ▲   SO Track on left.
              GPS: N34°19.77′ W113°40.43′

▼ 4.0   SO Cross through wash.
4.9 ▲   SO Cross through wash.

▼ 4.2   SO Tracks on right and left on crest.
4.7 ▲   SO Tracks on right and left on crest.
              GPS: N34°19.45′ W113°39.84′

▼ 5.6   SO Cross through wash.
3.3 ▲   SO Cross through wash.

▼ 6.2   SO Cross through wash.
2.7 ▲   SO Cross through wash.

▼ 6.6   SO Cross through wash.
2.3 ▲   SO Cross through wash.

▼ 6.9   SO Cross through Rawhide Wash.
2.0 ▲   SO Cross through Rawhide Wash.
              GPS: N34°17.74′ W113°38.36′

▼ 4.0   SO Track on right at Baker Well. Well and
              corrals are visible on the right of the
              trail; then track on left. Zero trip meter.
0.0 ▲   Continue toward Yucca.
              GPS: N34°24.92′ W113°44.37′

▼ 0.0   Continue toward Alamo Lake.
3.5 ▲   SO Track on right; then track on left at
              Baker Well. Well and corrals are visible
              on the left of the trail.

▼ 0.1   SO Track on right under power lines. Pass
              under power lines. Aubrey Peak
              Wilderness Area on right.
3.4 ▲   SO Track on left under power lines. Pass
              under power lines. Aubrey Peak
              Wilderness Area on left.
              GPS: N34°24.78′ W113°44.43′

▼ 2.4   SO Cross through wash.
1.1 ▲   SO Cross through wash.

▼ 2.8   SO Cross through wash; then track on right.
0.7 ▲   SO Track on left; then cross through wash.

▼ 2.9   SO Cross through wash.
0.6 ▲   SO Cross through wash.

▼ 3.5   SO Cattle guard. Zero trip meter.
0.0 ▲   Continue to the northwest.
              GPS: N34°22.24′ W113°42.60′

JOSHUA TREE

The Joshua tree, the largest of the yuccas, is a member of the lily family. This picturesque spike-leafed evergreen grows in dry soils on plains, slopes, and mesas, often in groves. Joshua trees range from 15 to 40 feet in height with a diameter of 1 to 3 feet. Flowers are bell-shaped, 1 to 1½ inches long, with six creamy yellow-green sepals. The flowers are crowded into 12- to 18-inch, many-branched clusters that have an unpleasant odor; they blossom mostly in the spring. Not all trees flower annually. Joshua tree fruit is elliptical, green-brown, 2 to 4 inches long,

Joshua tree

and somewhat fleshy. It dries and falls soon after maturity in late spring, revealing many flat seeds. Joshua trees (and most other yuccas) rely on the female pronuba moth (also called the yucca moth) for pollination. No other animal visiting the blooms transfers the pollen from one flower to another. In fact, the female yucca moth has evolved special organs to collect and distribute the pollen onto the surface of the flower. She then lays her eggs in the flower's ovaries, and when the larvae hatch, they feed on the yucca seeds. Without the moth's pollination, the Joshua tree could not reproduce, nor could the moth, whose larvae would have no seeds to eat. Although an old Joshua tree can sprout new plants from its roots, only the seeds produced in pollinated flowers can scatter far enough to establish a new stand. Joshua trees can live to between 100 and 300 years.

▼ 7.1   SO   Cross through wash; then two roads on right and one on left.
1.8 ▲   SO   Two roads on left and one on right; then cross through wash.

▼ 7.3   SO   Cross through wash.
1.6 ▲   SO   Cross through wash.

▼ 7.6   SO   Old road on left.
1.3 ▲   SO   Old road on right.

▼ 8.1   SO   Graded dirt road on left.
0.8 ▲   SO   Graded dirt road on right.
        GPS: N34°17.01' W113°37.58'

▼ 8.2   SO   Cross through wash.
0.7 ▲   SO   Cross through wash.

▼ 8.3   SO   Cross through wash.
0.6 ▲   SO   Cross through wash.

▼ 8.6   SO   Cross through wide wash.
0.3 ▲   SO   Cross through wide wash.

▼ 8.9   SO   Track on right is West #14: Rawhide Mountains Trail. Zero trip meter. Rawhide Mountains Wilderness Area begins on right.
0.0 ▲   Continue to northwest.
        GPS: N34°16.46' W113°36.94'

▼ 0.0   Continue to the east.
1.5 ▲   BR   Track on left is West #14: Rawhide Mountains Trail. Zero trip meter. Rawhide Mountains Wilderness Area ends on left.

▼ 0.1   SO   Track on left.
1.4 ▲   SO   Track on right.

▼ 0.7   SO   Entering Alamo Lake National Wildlife Refuge.
0.8 ▲   SO   Exiting Alamo Lake National Wildlife Refuge.
        GPS: N34°16.23' W113°36.18'

▼ 1.3	SO	Track on left is dead end.
0.2 ▲	SO	Track on right is dead end.

▼ 1.5		Trail ends at the edge of Alamo Lake. There are a couple of trails that lead to the lake's edge through the tamarisk. Some cleared areas are suitable for camping. The exact ending of the trail varies with the water level.
0.0 ▲		From Alamo Lake, zero trip meter and proceed north along the graded dirt road. **GPS: N34°15.85′ W113°35.40′**

McCracken Peak Trail

STARTING POINT Intersection of West #15: Alamo Lake Road and West #17: Signal Road
FINISHING POINT McCracken Peak
TOTAL MILEAGE 4.7 miles
UNPAVED MILEAGE 4.7 miles

DRIVING TIME 1 hour (one-way)
ELEVATION RANGE 2,200–3,400 feet
USUALLY OPEN Year-round
BEST TIME TO TRAVEL November to May
DIFFICULTY RATING 5
SCENIC RATING 8
REMOTENESS RATING +0

Special Attractions
- Historic McCracken Silver Mine.
- Panoramic views from McCracken Peak.
- Rockhounding for quartz crystals.

History
In 1874 a party of prospectors led by "Hassayampa" Jackson McCracken and "Choride Jack" Owens explored the arid and remote hills north of the Bill Williams River. They staked several promising claims, but the richest one was near the top of McCracken Peak; it rewarded them with silver that assayed at $1,000 per ton. As usual, the discovery brought in a rush of people all eager to stake their own

Mine shaft at the top of McCracken Peak with the narrow twisting trail leading back down

claims. The camp of McCracken was a tent city with very few permanent dwellings. The mill at Greenwood City (the site is found along West #18: Seventeen Mile Road) processed the silver, and the nearby settlement of Signal provided most of the supplies for the camp.

The McCracken mines closed in 1879 after producing a reported $1.5 million in silver. They have been worked sporadically since.

Description

The trail up McCracken Peak initially travels on the old, unmaintained graded road to the base of the peak. The road is sufficiently eroded to require a high-clearance 2WD vehicle as far as the base of the peak; past that it is definitely for high-clearance 4WDs only.

The trail climbs steeply up to the peak, winding around on a network of old mining roads. You travel on a narrow shelf road all the way with very few passing places and long drop-offs. Side trails lead to other mine workings. The surface is loose with low traction in places. A couple of the switchbacks are tight enough that drivers will have to back up to complete the turns.

Near the top, the trail passes through a

A close up of quartz crystal seams to be found above the cutting on McCracken Peak

cutting with an adit and large shaft on the right. Those who scramble up to the top of the ridge on the right of the cutting are often rewarded by finding some pretty quartz crystals. A seam of the crystals comes to the surface at this point.

Immediately past the ridge, there is a short section of trail that is extremely narrow and unstable. At the time of writing it was safe to pass, but it may not be in the future. A large boulder on the cliff side forces vehicles close to the edge, and a loose surface, off-camber tilt to the trail increases the difficulty. There is an extremely long drop down from the shelf road at this point, so if you are in any doubt about the safety of passing by the boulder, park your vehicle at the cutting and walk the remaining 0.1 mile to the peak.

There is a small, concrete-block hut at the top of the peak and panoramic views west to the Arrastra Mountain Wilderness and east over the Casteneda Hills to the Bill Williams Mountains.

Current Road Information

Bureau of Land Management
Kingman Field Office
2755 Mission Blvd.
Kingman, AZ 86401
(928) 718-3700

Map References

BLM   Alamo Lake
USGS 1:24,000   Signal, McCracken Peak
       1:100,000 Alamo Lake
Arizona Atlas & Gazetteer, p. 41
Arizona Road & Recreation Atlas, p. 71
(incomplete)

Route Directions

▼ 0.0   SO   At the intersection of West #15: Alamo Lake Road, which is graded dirt, and West #17: Signal Road, zero trip meter and turn southwest on roughly graded dirt road. A landing strip also joins the intersection (at first glance, it resembles a road). The junction is marked with road signs for

A view of an ore hopper along the trail

West Trail #16: McCracken Peak Trail

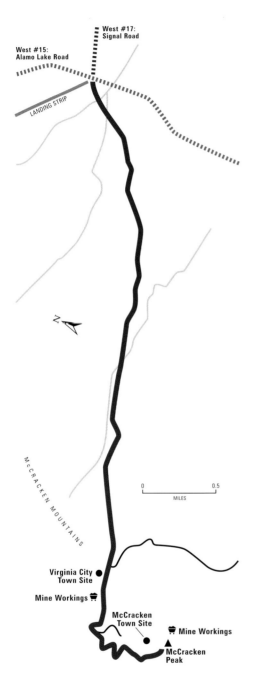

Signal Road and Alamo Road.
GPS: N34°28.17′ W113°42.96′

▼ 0.1	SO	Cross through wash.
▼ 0.2	SO	Cross through wash.
▼ 0.3	SO	Cross through wash.
▼ 0.4	SO	Cross through wash.
▼ 1.9	SO	Cross through wash.

GPS: N34°27.44′ W113°44.82′

▼ 2.3	SO	Gate.
▼ 3.2	SO	Track on left.

GPS: N34°27.14′ W113°46.12′

▼ 3.5 SO Flat area surrounded by mine workings at base of hill. Zero trip meter.
GPS: N34°27.10′ W113°46.34′

▼ 0.0		Continue to the southwest.
▼ 0.2	SO	Track on right.
▼ 0.3	BR	Trail forks; track on left.

GPS: N34°27.04′ W113°46.58′

▼ 0.6 BR Trail forks; track on left goes 0.3 miles to mine adit and continues past it. Bear right and keep climbing.
GPS: N34°26.95′ W113°46.59′

▼ 0.8 SO Timber-supported adit visible down to the left.

▼ 1.0 BR Track on left runs around hill and goes 0.3 miles to more diggings, a stone wall, and a wooden loading hopper and continues past them.
GPS: N34°26.71′ W113°46.58′

▼ 1.1 BL Pass through a cutting with adit and large shaft on the right; then washed-out section on shelf road. This is currently passable, but check before proceeding.
GPS: N34°26.64′ W113°46.56′

▼ 1.2 Top of McCracken Peak. Small, concrete-block hut on top.
GPS: N34°26.66′ W113°46.51′

Signal Road

STARTING POINT West #15: Alamo Lake Road, 36 miles southeast of Yucca

FINISHING POINT US 93, 7 miles south of Wickieup

TOTAL MILEAGE 17.9 miles (including spur to town site)

UNPAVED MILEAGE 17.9 miles

DRIVING TIME 1 hour

ELEVATION RANGE 1,600–2,200 feet

USUALLY OPEN Year-round

BEST TIME TO TRAVEL October to May

DIFFICULTY RATING 1

SCENIC RATING 7

REMOTENESS RATING +0

Special Attractions

■ Ghost town of Signal.
■ The Big Sandy River.
■ Scenic trail through the Poachie Range.

History

The story of Signal is intertwined with that of the McCracken mines, located a few miles away. Signal sprang into existence in 1877 and was quickly established as the milling town for the silver extracted from the mines. The isolated settlement boasted 800 people and 200 buildings, and in its heyday it was a thriving, yet orderly, settlement. The stores supplied not only the people of Signal but the many prospectors and miners working the neighboring McCracken mines, as well as others prospecting in nearby hills. Five stores were needed to supply the population, three restaurants, and thirteen saloons. Signal even had its own brewery. Goods came via rail from San Francisco to Yuma. They were then brought up the Colorado River by barge as far as Aubrey Landing, where they were loaded on to mule teams for the final 35 miles of desert travel to Signal. Storekeepers had to order goods six months in advance; inevitably, fresh goods were scarce.

An old stone ruin at Signal overlook on the Big Sandy River

The town's respectability was mainly attributed to the strictness of the local justice of the peace, Moses Levy, whose legendary sentences had the effect of quelling even the most rambunctious miners.

The mill at Signal operated around the clock while the boom lasted. However, like most mining booms, this one subsided quickly. The ore played out at the McCracken mines and by the mid-1880s, Signal's population had dwindled. About 300 people stayed on, but the number gradually declined over the years.

Today the traveler can see some remains of the mill site as well as a small wooden building. The graveyard, the most noteworthy feature at Signal, can be found a short distance away. There are stories of a second graveyard at Signal. A Chinese cemetery has been said to have existed farther down the wash of the Big Sandy River, but no trace remains of the unmarked site, so these stories cannot be verified.

Description

This graded dirt road connects US 93 with West #15: Alamo Lake Road. After it passes the town site of Signal, the trail follows the course of the Big Sandy River and crosses through the northern end of the Poachie Range.

The site of Signal is just off the main trail, 5.1 miles from the western end. The turn is poorly marked by a hand-painted sign that directs travelers down a side trail. A couple of timber buildings and mining remains are clearly visible. However, a little more exploration and a short hike are required to find the stone ruins and graveyard. It helps to have a handheld GPS unit with the coordinates entered. The fenced graveyard contains several unidentified graves that are marked with piles of rock. There are also some more recent graves in the cemetery.

The entire trail is a reasonable graded road. The crossings of the Big Sandy River usually present no problem to a passenger vehicle. The typical depth of the river is fairly shallow, only a couple of inches. However, conditions can change quickly—do not attempt to cross the wash when it is flooded. The water normally runs in a small channel in the wide, sandy wash.

The final part of the trail rises up to cross the Poachie Range before finishing at US 93.

Current Road Information

Bureau of Land Management
Kingman Field Office
2755 Mission Blvd.
Kingman, AZ 86401
(928) 718-3700

Map References

BLM   Bagdad, Alamo Lake
USGS   1:24,000   Signal, Signal Mountain,
       Greenwood Peak
       1:100,000 Bagdad, Alamo Lake
Arizona Atlas & Gazetteer, pp. 41, 31
Arizona Road & Recreation Atlas, pp. 63, 79
Recreational Map of Arizona

Route Directions

▼ 0.0		From West #15: Alamo Lake Road, at the 4-way intersection with Signal Road and West #16: McCracken Peak Trail, 36 miles southeast of Yucca, zero trip meter and turn northeast on the graded dirt Signal Road at the sign.
5.1 ▲		Trail ends at the 4-way intersection with West #15: Alamo Lake Road and West #16: McCracken Peak Trail. Turn right for Yucca; turn left for Alamo Lake; continue straight ahead to visit McCracken Peak.
		GPS: N34°28.20′ W113°42.96′
▼ 0.9	SO	Track on right.
4.2 ▲	SO	Track on left.
▼ 1.1	SO	Cross through wash.
4.0 ▲	SO	Cross through wash.
▼ 2.6	SO	Pass under power lines; track on right and track on left under power lines.
2.5 ▲	SO	Pass under power lines; track on right and track on left under power lines.
		GPS: N34°28.72′ W113°40.09′

Big Sandy River crossing

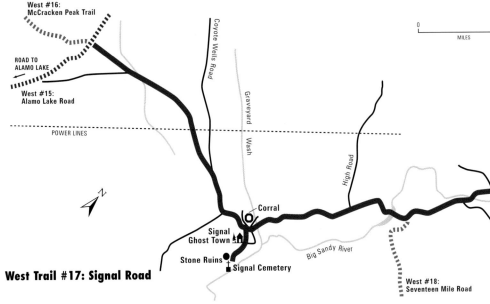

West Trail #17: Signal Road

▼ 3.4	SO	Graded road on left is Coyote Wells Road; then cattle guard.
1.7 ▲	SO	Cattle guard; then graded road on right is Coyote Wells Road.
		GPS: N34°28.49' W113°39.32'

▼ 3.7	SO	Track on left; then cattle guard.
1.4 ▲	SO	Cattle guard; then track on right.

▼ 4.3	SO	Track on right.
0.8 ▲	SO	Track on left.

▼ 4.6	SO	Cattle guard; then track on left.
0.5 ▲	SO	Track on right; then cattle guard.

▼ 5.0	SO	Track on right.
0.1 ▲	SO	Track on left.

▼ 5.1	SO	Track on right goes to Signal town site, marked with old sign board and daubed fence post. Turn is opposite a corral on the left and the entrance to a ranch. Zero trip meter. Also two tracks on left.
0.0 ▲		Continue along graded road to the southwest.
		GPS: N34°28.39' W113°37.81'

Spur to Signal Town Site

▼ 0.0		From Signal Road, at the hand-painted sign to Signal, zero trip meter and turn southeast on small dirt road.
		GPS: N34°28.39' W113°37.81'

▼ 0.1	SO	Two tracks on right.
▼ 0.2	BR	Signal town site. Old corrugated iron cabin and mine workings on hill to the left over wash.
		GPS: N34°28.27' W113°37.58'

▼ 0.3	BL	Two tracks on right and one on left; take major track heading southeast and enter wash at a junction in the wash. Take the right-hand wash.
		GPS: N34°28.19' W113°37.56'

▼ 0.5		Keep right in the wash. The vehicle trail ends where it is washed out and impassable.
		GPS: N34°28.04' W113°37.48'

From here, hike west along the old vehicle trail that leaves the wash. After 0.1 miles you will come to some stone ruins at GPS: N34°28.00' W113°37.58'. From the ruins, the trail is less clear but stay to the left, close

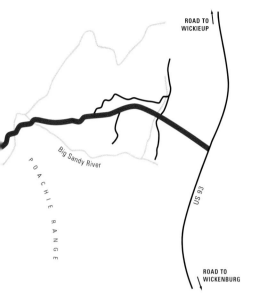

to the wash, and you will reach the
cemetery after another 0.2 miles. The
cemetery is at GPS: N34°27.83'
W113°37.48'.

Continuation of Main Trail

▼ 0.0		Continue along graded road to the northeast.
3.7 ▲	SO	Track on left goes to Signal town site, marked with old sign board and daubed fence post. Turn is opposite a corral on the right and the entrance to a ranch. Zero trip meter. Also two tracks on right.

▼ 0.1	SO	Track on right.
3.6 ▲	SO	Track on left.

▼ 0.2	SO	Cross through Graveyard Wash.
3.5 ▲	SO	Cross through Graveyard Wash.

▼ 0.6	SO	Track on left.
3.1 ▲	SO	Track on right.

▼ 2.3	SO	Graded dirt road, the High Road, on left.
1.4 ▲	SO	Graded dirt road, the High Road, on right.
		GPS: N34°30.06' W113°36.53'

▼ 3.1	SO	Cattle guard.
0.6 ▲	SO	Cattle guard.

▼ 3.2	SO	Start to cross Big Sandy River wash and river channel.
0.5 ▲	SO	Exit Big Sandy River wash.

▼ 3.5	SO	Exit Big Sandy River wash; then small track on right.
0.2 ▲	SO	Small track on left; then start to cross Big Sandy River wash and river channel.
		GPS: N34°30.75' W113°35.70'

▼ 3.6	SO	Track on right.
0.1 ▲	SO	Track on left.

▼ 3.7	SO	Graded road on right is West #18: Seventeen Mile Road. Zero trip meter.
0.0 ▲		Continue to the southwest.
		GPS: N34°30.92' W113°35.57'

▼ 0.0		Continue to the north.
8.1 ▲	SO	Graded road on left is West #18: Seventeen Mile Road. Zero trip meter.

▼ 1.1	SO	Track on right.
7.0 ▲	SO	Track on left.

▼ 1.2	SO	Cross through Big Sandy River wash and river channel.
6.9 ▲	SO	Cross through Big Sandy River wash and river channel.

▼ 1.8	SO	Graded road on left; then track on right.
6.3 ▲	SO	Track on left; then graded road on right.
		GPS: N34°32.35' W113°34.74'

▼ 2.1	SO	Cattle guard.
6.0 ▲	SO	Cattle guard.

▼ 3.1	SO	Track on right is driveway.
5.0 ▲	SO	Track on left is driveway.

▼ 3.4	SO	Cross over pipeline.
4.7 ▲	SO	Cross over pipeline.

▼ 3.6	SO	Track on left; then ford through Big Sandy River.
4.5 ▲	SO	Ford through Big Sandy River; then track on right.
		GPS: N34°33.93' W113°34.53'

| ▼ 3.8 | SO | Track on left; then cattle guard. |
| 4.3 ▲ | SO | Cattle guard; then track on right. |

| ▼ 3.9 | SO | Track on right. |
| 4.2 ▲ | SO | Track on left. |

| ▼ 4.1 | SO | Cross through wash. |
| 4.0 ▲ | SO | Cross through wash. |

| ▼ 4.6 | SO | Two tracks on right. |
| 3.5 ▲ | SO | Two tracks on left. |

| ▼ 4.9 | SO | Track on right. |
| 3.2 ▲ | SO | Track on left. |

| ▼ 5.5 | SO | Track on left. |
| 2.6 ▲ | SO | Track on right. |

▼ 5.9	SO	Track on right.
2.2 ▲	SO	Track on left.
		GPS: N34°35.61' W113°33.34'

| ▼ 6.9 | SO | Cross through wash; track on right and track on left down wash. |
| 1.2 ▲ | SO | Cross through wash; track on right and track on left down wash. |

▼ 8.1		Trail ends at junction of US 93. Turn left for Wickieup; turn right for Wickenburg.
0.0 ▲		Trail commences on US 93, 7 miles south of Wickieup, 0.1 miles south of mile marker 132. Zero trip meter and turn southwest on graded dirt road at the sign for Signal Road.
		GPS: N34°36.57' W113°31.41'

WEST REGION TRAIL #18

Seventeen Mile Road

STARTING POINT West #17: Signal Road, 8.1 miles west of US 93
FINISHING POINT US 93, 0.8 miles northwest of mile marker 144
TOTAL MILEAGE 13.1 miles
UNPAVED MILEAGE 13.1 miles
DRIVING TIME 1 hour

ELEVATION RANGE 1,600–3,300 feet
USUALLY OPEN Year-round
BEST TIME TO TRAVEL October to May
DIFFICULTY RATING 2
SCENIC RATING 8
REMOTENESS RATING +0

Special Attractions
■ Easy trail that passes through spectacular desert scenery.
■ Hiking access to the Arrastra Mountains Wilderness.
■ Greenwood City town site.

History
Like Signal, Greenwood City was founded to process ore from the McCracken mines. A 10-stamp mill was erected, settlers arrived, and there was soon an active town. At its peak, there were 400 inhabitants, a clean and reasonably priced boardinghouse called Davis House, two saloons, a butcher, a physician, a barbershop, and various other stores. For some unknown reason, Greenwood City never had a post office. After a mill was built in Virginia City (adjacent to Signal), Greenwood City declined and was quickly abandoned.

Description
This scenic graded road crosses through the Poachie Range between West #17: Signal Road and US 93. The trail passes very close to the site of Greenwood City. There are some stone foundations, but little is left of this once-thriving town. Much of the trail runs along the ridge tops, giving excellent views over the Arrastra Mountains Wilderness and the Big Sandy River Valley. The vegetation is a diverse combination of ocotillo, yucca, and cholla mixed with small juniper trees.

As the trail enters the Poachie Range, large granite boulders and outcrops dot the landscape. As it descends the range to join US 93, there are views of the Burro Creek Bridge, north toward Wickieup, and east toward the mining town of Bagdad and the Aquarius Mountains.

The road is graded its entire length, but a few rough sections and moderate grades make a high-clearance vehicle preferable.

Yuccas and granite outcrops combine to form a striking landscape

Current Road Information

Bureau of Land Management
Kingman Field Office
2755 Mission Blvd.
Kingman, AZ 86401
(928) 718-3700

Map References

BLM   Bagdad, Alamo Lake
USGS 1:24,000   Greenwood Peak, Signal
          Mtn., Arrastra Mtn., Kaiser Spring
          1:100,000 Bagdad, Alamo Lake
Arizona Atlas & Gazetteer, p. 41
Arizona Road & Recreation Atlas, pp. 79, 72

Route Directions

▼ 0.0   From West #17: Signal Road, 8.1

miles west of US 93, zero trip meter
and turn southeast on a graded dirt
road. Turn is marked by a road sign for
Seventeen Mile Road. Immediately,
there is a graded road on left.

7.7 ▲   Trail ends at the intersection with
West #17: Signal Road. Turn left to
continue to Signal; turn right to exit to
US 93.

        GPS: N34°30.89′ W113°35.57′

▼ 0.2   SO Two tracks on left.
7.5 ▲ SO Two tracks on right.

▼ 0.5   SO Small track on right goes to the site of
Greenwood City. The unmarked turn
is at the base of the hill. Also track on
left.

A view of the trail with an ocotillo in the foreground

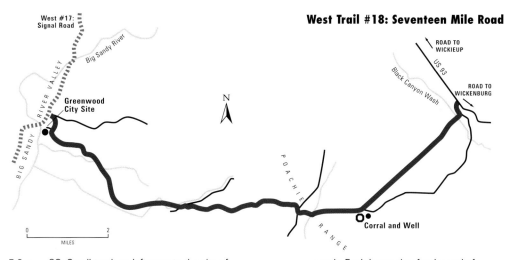

7.2 ▲ SO Small track on left goes to the site of Greenwood City. The unmarked turn is at the base of the hill. Also track on right.
Intersection is at:
GPS: N34º30.49' W113º35.57'
Greenwood City is at:
GPS: N34º30.45' W113º35.71'

▼ 0.7 BR Two tracks on left.
7.0 ▲ BL Two tracks on right.
GPS: N34º30.32' W113º35.47'

▼ 1.8 SO Track on left.
5.9 ▲ SO Track on right.

▼ 2.1 SO Cross through wash.
5.6 ▲ SO Cross through wash.

▼ 3.0 SO Cross through wash.
4.7 ▲ SO Cross through wash.

▼ 4.2 SO Cross through wash. Arrastra Mountains Wilderness on right.
3.5 ▲ SO Cross through wash. Arrastra Mountains Wilderness on left.

▼ 4.6 SO Cross through wash.
3.1 ▲ SO Cross through wash.

▼ 5.6 SO Cattle guard.
2.1 ▲ SO Cattle guard.

▼ 7.7 SO Track on left and right down and up

wash. Each has a sign for the end of Mohave County Road Maintenance. Zero trip meter.
0.0 ▲ Continue to the southwest.
GPS: N34º28.59' W113º29.18'

▼ 0.0 Continue to the northeast.
1.5 ▲ SO Track on left and right up and down wash. Each has a sign for the end of Mohave County Road Maintenance. Zero trip meter.

▼ 0.4 SO Track on right on left-hand bend.
1.1 ▲ SO Track on left on right-hand bend.
GPS: N34º28.45' W113º28.80'

▼ 1.1 SO Cross through wash.
0.4 ▲ SO Cross through wash.

▼ 1.3 SO Cross through wash.
0.2 ▲ SO Cross through wash.

▼ 1.5 SO Corral on right and well on right. Zero trip meter.
0.0 ▲ Continue to the west.
GPS: N34º28.43' W113º27.62'

▼ 0.0 Continue to the east.
3.9 ▲ SO Corral on left and well on left. Zero trip meter.

▼ 0.1 SO Track on right.
3.8 ▲ SO Track on left.

▼ 2.6   SO Cross through wash.
1.3 ▲   SO Cross through wash.
         GPS: N34º29.76' W113º25.53'

▼ 2.7   SO Track on left.
1.2 ▲   SO Track on right.

▼ 3.2   SO Cross through wash.
0.7 ▲   SO Cross through wash.

▼ 3.4   SO Cross through wide Black Canyon
             Wash.
0.5 ▲   SO Exit wash crossing.

▼ 3.5   SO Exit wash crossing.
0.4 ▲   SO Cross through wide Black Canyon
             Wash.

▼ 3.6   BL Track on right.
0.3 ▲   BR Track on left.

▼ 3.9   Cattle guard; then trail ends at inter-
             section with US 93. Turn right for
             Wickenburg; turn left for Wickieup.
0.0 ▲   Trail commences on US 93, 0.8 miles
             northwest of mile marker 144. Zero trip
             meter and turn west onto the graded
             dirt road at the sign for Seventeen Mile
             Road.
         GPS: N34º30.71' W113º24.97'

WEST REGION TRAIL #19

Flag Mine Trail

STARTING POINT Hualapai Mountain Road at
  Hualapai Mountain Park
FINISHING POINT West #15: Alamo Lake Road
TOTAL MILEAGE 34 miles
UNPAVED MILEAGE 32.1 miles
DRIVING TIME 5 hours
ELEVATION RANGE 2,000–7,000 feet
USUALLY OPEN April to November
BEST TIME TO TRAVEL April to November
DIFFICULTY RATING 5
SCENIC RATING 9
REMOTENESS RATING +0

Special Attractions

■ Extensive section of shelf road.
■ Picnicking, hiking, and camping at
  Hualapai Mountain Park.
■ Old mining buildings of the Boriana
  Mine.
■ Long, moderately challenging trail.

History

Hualapai Mountain Park, the pretty and
popular refuge at the start of this trail, was
developed during the 1930s by the Civilian
Conservation Corps, which constructed the
small stone cabins, picnic areas, and hiking
trails. The word Hualapai (pronounced wal-
a-pie) means "pine tree folk" and comes from
the name of the Indian tribe that once in-
habited this area.

  The Flag Mine, or American Flag Mine, as
it is sometimes called, was discovered in 1871
by a group of Cornishmen, who established a
small settlement with a post office. Although
the mines in the area were small, they were
worked steadily until the late 1880s. (There is
another settlement in Arizona called American Flag; that one is located along *Arizona
Trails South Region*, Trail #27: Oracle Control
Road on the north side of the Santa Catalina
Mountains.)

  The Boriana Mine was a hard-rock mine
that was operational for some time during
the early 1900s.

Description

This trail commences at the Hualapai Mountain Park, a peaceful sky island far above the
arid plains surrounding Kingman. The park
offers excellent camping and picnicking facilities, with many areas to choose from. In addition there are 16 stone and timber cabins
available for rent year-round. Miles of hiking
trails invite exploration. In winter there is often snow on the top of the mountain, and although there is access to the park, the Flag
Mine Trail is closed.

  The Flag Mine Trail leads out from the
park along a graded dirt road that passes
many private cabins as it heads away from
Hualapai Peak. The standard quickly drops
to a well-used trail that almost immediately

The closed portal of the Boriana Mine

The shelf road above Boriana Mine

starts to follow a wide shelf road. The longest stretch of the trail travels along a shelf road that is wide enough for a single vehicle and has adequate passing places. The grade is very easy and the surface for the most part is fairly smooth and granitic.

The trail passes by the Flag Mine, 3.5 miles from the start. A large adit can be seen in the hillside. The trail then intersects Antelope Wash Road, which passes the Wild Cow Springs Recreation Site. This pleasant campground at 6,200 feet has shady sites set in a wide gully. A fee is charged for camping and picnicking. It is open from May 1 to November 1.

The trail continues along the shelf road just below the crest of a ridge. There are expansive views to the east over Big Sandy River Valley to the Aquarius Mountains, and farther along over the pretty Moss Basin. To the west there are views over Wabayuma Peak and the wilderness area and surrounding canyons.

As the trail leaves Moss Basin, there are some rough spots; the roughest occurs where the trail starts to switchback down the south side of Moss Basin and farther south where there are some steep, loose-surfaced sections.

As the trail starts to descend the southern side of the range, the extensive remains of the Boriana Mine can be seen in Boriana Canyon. You can gaze down into the canyon and see the single-width shelf road descending to the mine far below.

The trail follows Mackenzie Creek through the jumbled rocks and prolific vegetation of Boriana Canyon before becoming a graded dirt road at private property. It is an easy run to join West #15: Alamo Lake Road, a few miles east of Yucca and I-40.

Camping along the trail is limited because of the shelf road, but there are a few small, pleasant sites tucked into the vegetation close to the trail. The best camping can be found in the developed campgrounds at Wild Cow Springs and Hualapai Peak.

This trail is marked as road #2123 on the BLM map of the region.

Current Road Information
Bureau of Land Management
Kingman Field Office
2755 Mission Blvd.
Kingman, AZ 86401
(928) 718-3700

THE PAI INDIANS

The Pai Indians have a long history in northwestern Arizona. After excavating and studying pieces of pottery, scholars believe that they were living just east of the Colorado River as early as A.D. 700. They survived by hunting, gathering, and gardening along the banks of the Colorado River. During the 1300s, they spread eastward onto the Colorado Plateau. Around 1750, there was a great schism in the Pai civilization. Lore attributes the separation to a mudball fight between children. As parents ran to settle things between the children, hostilities arose among the adults as well. A group of Indians, the Yavapai, split off from the main Pai tribe and headed south. Settlers later dubbed the Pai Indians the Walapai (or Hualapai) to differentiate them from their southern enemies. In the years that followed, many heated and very bloody conflicts occurred between the two tribes.

For many decades, encounters between Pai Indians and white settlers were quite peaceful. Then a Prescott teamster murdered a Walapai Indian, Wauba Yuma, and the Walapai War (1868-69) exploded. Pitched battles and skirmishes between the Indians and U.S. Army Colonel William Price were common. Before long, the tribal chiefs were forced to surrender and the Walapais were relocated to the Colorado River Indian Reservation, where they stayed until 1875. Many of their leaders were imprisoned on Alcatraz and Angel Islands in California. The majority of the tribe was forcibly relocated to the Colorado River bottom. Because they were mountain people, many of them sickened and died. They sent word to General George Crook that they would rather die fighting in their mountain territory then die slowly along the river bottom.

However, throughout the conflict, a small band of Walapai along the Colorado River remained aloof. Americans referred to this group as the Havasupai to distinguish them from their warring brethren.

Farther south, the Yavapai were finding trouble of their own. American gold miners began to enter their territory in search of wealth. The miners were promptly attacked, which caused retribution from the U.S. government. Beginning in 1872, the Yavapai fought a nine-year battle for their territory. The northern Walapai aided U.S. forces in destroying their mutual enemy. Eventually, the Yavapai were defeated and moved to the San Carlos Indian Reservation. In 1903, President Theodore Roosevelt created a large Yavapai reservation near the Verde and Salt Rivers. A reservation was formed for the Walapai on the Colorado Plateau, while the Havasupai were relocated to a small reservation at the bottom of Cataract Canyon. In 1975, their land was extended considerably in order to include traditional hunting grounds.

Culturally, the three Pai tribes are quite similar. Where possible, they survived in the dry climate by using irrigation or natural springs to provide water for their crops. They also prized the fruits of yucca plants and enjoyed the mescal hearts of the plentiful agave cacti. They wore and traded buckskin, and also hunted rabbits and wildcats. Generally their houses were pole-framed structures covered in brush, similar to Apache wickiups. Today they make a living in tourism, mining, and breeding livestock.

Map References

BLM   Valentine, Bagdad, Needles
USGS 1:24,000   Hualapai Peak, Dean
      Peak, Wabayuma Peak, Creamery
      Canyon, Yucca SE

1:100,000 Valentine, Bagdad, Needles
Arizona Atlas & Gazetteer, pp. 30, 31
Arizona Road & Recreation Atlas, p. 63
Recreational Map of Arizona (incomplete)

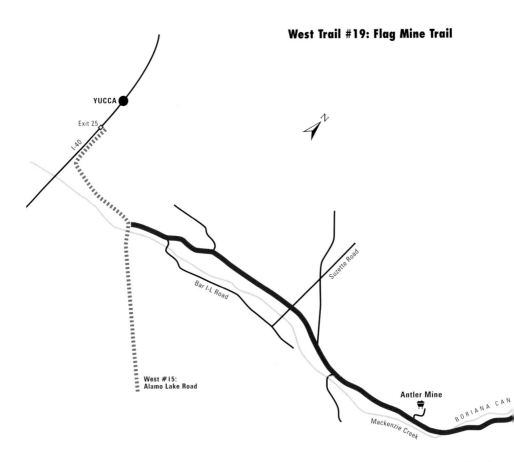

Route Directions

▼ 0.0　　From Kingman, take Hualapai Mountain Road 9.7 miles to the boundary of the Mohave County Hualapai Mountain Park. Zero trip meter and continue on the paved road into the park.

1.9 ▲　　Trail ends at the boundary of the Mohave County Hualapai Mountain Park. Continue along the paved road to Kingman.
GPS: N35°06.54′ W113°53.97′

▼ 0.1　　SO　Road on right to Camp Stephens.

1.8 ▲　　SO　Road on left to Camp Stephens.

▼ 0.7　　SO　Road on right to Deer Canyon Picnic Area.

1.2 ▲　　SO　Road on left to Deer Canyon Picnic Area.

▼ 0.9　　SO　Ranger station and camper registration on right—fee charged for camping.

1.0 ▲　　SO　Ranger station and camper registration on left—fee charged for camping.
GPS: N35°06.08′ W113°53.09′

▼ 1.1　　BL　Road on right is park entrance to picnicking and camping areas.

0.8 ▲　　BR　Road on left is park entrance to picnicking and camping areas.
GPS: N35°05.97′ W113°53.02′

▼ 1.2　　SO　Track on right goes to recreation area.

0.7 ▲　　SO　Track on left goes to recreation area.

▼ 1.3　　SO　Track on right goes to recreation area.

0.6 ▲　　SO　Track on left goes to recreation area.

▼ 1.5　　SO　Track on left.

0.4 ▲　　SO　Track on right.

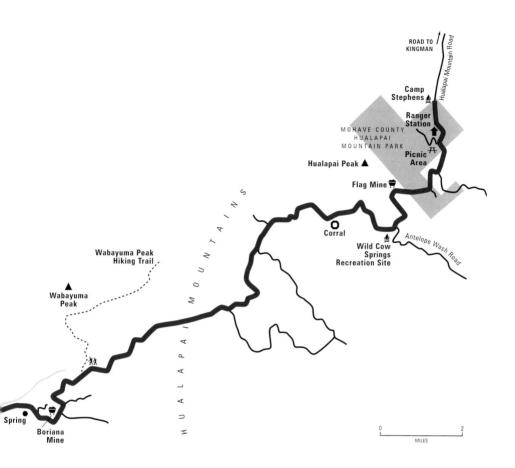

▼ 1.6	SO	Leaving county park into private property.
0.3 ▲	SO	Entering Mohave County Hualapai Mountain Park.

▼ 1.7	SO	Crumb Road on right; then Ponderosa Drive on left.
0.2 ▲	SO	Ponderosa Drive on right; then Crumb Road on left.

▼ 1.8	SO	Road on right.
0.1 ▲	SO	Road on left.

▼ 1.9	TR	Turn right onto Flag Mine Road at BLM sign for Wild Cow Springs Recreation Site. Zero trip meter.
0.0 ▲		Continue to the northwest.
		GPS: N35°05.56′ W113°52.46′

▼ 0.0		Continue to the south. Road is now graded gravel.
3.1 ▲	TL	Turn left onto paved Hualapai Mountain

Road opposite the Pine Lake Fire Department. Zero trip meter.

▼ 0.2	SO	Road is now graded dirt. Remain on Flag Mine Road; there are many driveways on the right and left for next 0.5 miles.
2.9 ▲	SO	Road is now paved.

▼ 0.3	SO	Track on right is Ridge Road (deadend).
2.8 ▲	SO	Track on left is Ridge Road (dead end).
		GPS: N35°05.44′ W113°52.57′

▼ 0.4	SO	Track on left is Halmar Road.
2.7 ▲	SO	Track on right is Halmar Road.

▼ 0.7	BR	Two tracks on left to viewpoint; bear right on wide shelf road.
2.4 ▲	BL	Two tracks on right to viewpoint; bear left, remaining on Flag Mine Road. There are many driveways on the right

and left for next 0.5 miles.
GPS: N35°05.19' W113°52.35'

▼ 1.6   BL   Track on right is short, steep dead end.
Adit of the Flag Mine on right.

1.5 ▲   BR   Track on left is short, steep dead end.
Adit of the Flag Mine on left.
GPS: N35°04.62' W113°52.88'

▼ 1.8   SO   Track on left.

1.3 ▲   SO   Track on right.

▼ 2.0   SO   Turnouts on right and left.

1.1 ▲   SO   Turnouts on right and left.

▼ 2.8   SO   Track on left.

0.3 ▲   SO   Track on right.

▼ 3.1   BR   Track on left is Antelope Wash Road to
Wild Cow Springs Recreation Site. BLM
sign at intersection. Zero trip meter.

0.0 ▲   Continue west toward Kingman.
GPS: N35°04.14' W113°52.13'

▼ 0.0   Continue southeast toward Yucca.

5.3 ▲   SO   Track on right is Antelope Wash Road to
Wild Cow Springs Recreation Site. BLM
sign at intersection. Zero trip meter.

▼ 0.7   SO   Cross through wash.

4.6 ▲   SO   Cross through wash.

▼ 0.8   SO   Faint track on left; then cross over wash.

4.5 ▲   SO   Cross over wash; then faint track on
right.

▼ 2.0   SO   Track on left to camping area.

3.3 ▲   SO   Track on right to camping area.
GPS: N35°03.57' W113°53.37'

▼ 2.3   SO   Faint track on left; then corral on left.

3.0 ▲   SO   Corral on right; then faint track on right.
GPS: N35°03.31' W113°53.40'

▼ 2.4   SO   Faint track on right.

2.9 ▲   SO   Faint track on left.

▼ 2.5   BR   Track on left. Shelf road starts.

2.8 ▲   BL   Track on right. End of shelf road.
GPS: N35°03.17' W113°53.52'

▼ 2.7   SO   Track on right.

2.6 ▲   SO   Track on left.

▼ 3.3   SO   Track on right; then cattle guard.

2.0 ▲   SO   Cattle guard; then track on left.
GPS: N35°03.12' W113°54.13'

▼ 4.6   SO   Small track on right.

0.7 ▲   SO   Small track on left.
GPS: N35°02.27' W113°54.49'

▼ 5.3   SO   Well-used track on left. Zero trip meter.

0.0 ▲   Continue to the north.
GPS: N35°01.74' W113°54.23'

▼ 0.0   Continue to the south.

7.5 ▲   SO   Well-used track on right. Zero trip
meter.

▼ 2.4   SO   Track on left.

5.1 ▲   SO   Track on right.
GPS: N35°00.43' W113°53.62'

▼ 2.9   SO   Start of switchbacks.

4.6 ▲   SO   End of switchbacks.

▼ 3.2   BL   Track on right.

4.3 ▲   BR   Track on left.

▼ 3.5   SO   End of switchbacks.

4.0 ▲   SO   Start of switchbacks.
GPS: N34°59.94' W113°53.98'

▼ 5.1   SO   Cattle guard.

2.4 ▲   SO   Cattle guard.

▼ 7.0   SO   Track on left.

0.5 ▲   SO   Track on right.
GPS: N34°57.61' W113°54.81'

▼ 7.1   SO   Cattle guard.

0.4 ▲   SO   Cattle guard.

▼ 7.5   SO   Wabayuma Peak hiking trailhead on
right at information board. Small parking area on left. Hiking trail enters
wilderness area. Zero trip meter.

0.0 ▲   Continue to the north.
GPS: N34°57.20' W113°54.90'

Boriana Mine, near the southern end of the trail

▼ 0.0   Continue to the south.
2.8 ▲ SO Wabayuma Peak hiking trailhead on left at information board. Small parking area on right. Zero trip meter.

▼ 1.4 BR Track on left through fence line.
1.4 ▲ BL Track on right through fence line.
        GPS: N34°56.64′ W113°54.78′

▼ 1.7 BR Two tracks on left through fence line. Trail starts to descend to Boriana Canyon.
1.1 ▲ BL Two tracks on right through fence line.
        GPS: N34°56.42′ W113°54.62′

▼ 2.7 SO Track on right goes to Boriana Mine. End of shelf road.
0.1 ▲ SO Track on left goes to Boriana Mine. Shelf road begins and climbs out of Boriana Canyon.

▼ 2.8 SO Track on right through gate is the main entrance into Boriana Mine. Zero trip meter.
0.0 ▲   Continue to the northeast.
        GPS: N34°56.09′ W113°54.99′

▼ 0.0   Continue to the southwest.
9.2 ▲ SO Track on left through gate is the main entrance into Boriana Mine. Zero trip meter.

▼ 0.2 SO Track on right through gate is old washed-out entrance to Boriana Mine.
9.0 ▲ SO Track on left through gate is old washed-out entrance to Boriana Mine.

▼ 0.3 SO Track on left goes to spring, just off the trail.
8.9 ▲ SO Track on right goes to spring, just off the trail.
        GPS: N34°55.98′ W113°55.29′

▼ 0.5 SO Cross over wash.
8.7 ▲ SO Cross over wash.

▼ 1.5 SO Cross through Mackenzie Creek on concrete ford.
7.7 ▲ SO Cross through Mackenzie Creek on concrete ford.
        GPS: N34°55.30′ W113°55.96′

▼ 1.8 SO Cross through wash.
7.4 ▲ SO Cross through wash.

▼ 2.3   SO   Track on left.
6.9 ▲   SO   Track on right.
           GPS: N34°54.62′ W113°56.28′

▼ 2.4   SO   Track on right goes to corral.
6.8 ▲   SO   Track on left goes to corral.

▼ 2.6   SO   Cross through wash.
6.6 ▲   SO   Cross through wash.

▼ 3.3   SO   Track on right.
5.9 ▲   SO   Track on left.
           GPS: N34°53.89′ W113°56.76′

▼ 4.1   SO   BLM sign the other way to Wild Cow Springs Recreation Site.
5.1 ▲   SO   BLM sign for Wild Cow Springs Recreation Site straight on.

▼ 4.2   SO   Cross over Mackenzie Creek.
5.0 ▲   SO   Cross over Mackenzie Creek.
           GPS: N34°53.22′ W113°57.19′

▼ 4.8   SO   Track on left.
4.4 ▲   BL   Track on right.

▼ 5.2   SO   Cross through wash. Antler Mine on right.
4.0 ▲   SO   Cross through wash. Antler Mine on left.

▼ 5.3   SO   Two tracks on right to the Antler Mine.
3.9 ▲   SO   Two tracks on left to the Antler Mine.
           GPS: N34°52.68′ W113°58.17′

▼ 5.9   SO   Track on left opposite house. Trail is now graded dirt road.
3.3 ▲   SO   Track on right opposite house. Trail is now a formed trail.

▼ 6.2   SO   Cattle guard.
3.0 ▲   SO   Cattle guard.

▼ 6.6   SO   Graded road on left.
2.6 ▲   SO   Graded road on right.

▼ 7.2   SO   Cattle guard.
2.0 ▲   SO   Cattle guard.

▼ 7.4   SO   Track on left.
1.8 ▲   SO   Track on right.

▼ 8.2   SO   Track on right.
1.0 ▲   SO   Track on left.

▼ 9.2   SO   Graded road on right is Suzette Road; also track on left. Zero trip meter at sign for Suzette Road.
0.0 ▲   Continue to the northeast.
           GPS: N34°52.31′ W114°02.24′

▼ 0.0   Continue toward Yucca.
4.2 ▲   SO   Graded road on left is Suzette Road; also track on right. Zero trip meter at sign for Suzette Road.

▼ 0.6   SO   Track on right.
3.6 ▲   SO   Track on left.

▼ 0.9   SO   Track on right.
3.3 ▲   SO   Track on left.

▼ 1.9   SO   Graded road on right.
2.3 ▲   SO   Graded road on left.

▼ 2.1   SO   Track on right.
2.1 ▲   SO   Track on left.

▼ 3.0   SO   Track on right.
1.2 ▲   SO   Track on left.

▼ 3.4   SO   Track back on left is Bar I-L Road. Also small track on left.
0.8 ▲   BL   Small track on right. Also track on right is Bar I-L Road.
           GPS: N34°51.27′ W114°05.89′

▼ 4.1   SO   Track on right.
0.1 ▲   SO   Track on left.

▼ 4.2   Trail ends at the junction with paved West #15: Alamo Lake Road. Turn right for Yucca; turn left for Lake Alamo National Wildlife Refuge.
0.0 ▲   Trail commences at the junction of Boriana Mine Road and paved West #15: Alamo Lake Road, 3 miles east of Yucca. Zero trip meter and turn northeast on the wide, graded dirt Boriana Mine Road.
           GPS: N34°50.99′ W114°06.60′

Mohave Mountains Trail

STARTING POINT I-40 at exit 13
FINISHING POINT Mohave Mountains
TOTAL MILEAGE 12.6 miles
UNPAVED MILEAGE 12.6 miles
DRIVING TIME 2 hours (one-way)
ELEVATION RANGE 1,200–3,400 feet
USUALLY OPEN Year-round
BEST TIME TO TRAVEL Fall to spring
DIFFICULTY RATING 3
SCENIC RATING 7
REMOTENESS RATING +1

Special Attractions

■ Stone ruin at Scotts Well.
■ Wide variety of Mohave Desert scenery.

Description

The large, blocky Mohave Mountains are intersected by narrow washes that cut into them. This trail travels up one main wash and two smaller spurs to the slopes of the mountains. There are no trails that climb over the mountains because of the steep face on the northern side.

Mohave Mountains Trail leaves from I-40 at exit 13 and proceeds south, initially along a roughly graded, dirt road. After 4.6 miles the trail passes an active mining property. After this the trail drops in standard to a lumpy, ungraded trail that runs along a slight ridge, affording views ahead of the Mohave Mountains. On the return trip, the gently sloping ridge gives views back to the Black Mountains.

The trail then enters a gravelly wash with many side trails that lead right and left. Remain in the main wash until 10.9 miles from the start of the trail. Here the wash forks; the left-hand, smaller canyon leads along a twisty trail that runs partly in the wash and partly along a formed trail to finish at private property where there is a small stone cabin ruin and a tank at Scotts Well. This pretty, narrow canyon has some scattered Joshua trees. Some sections in the wash can be a bit brushy with some close-growing tamarisk, but a small fire has reduced the worst of it. The second spur continues up the main canyon for another 1.8

Joshua trees growing in the wash beside the trail

West Trail #20: Mohave Mountains Trail

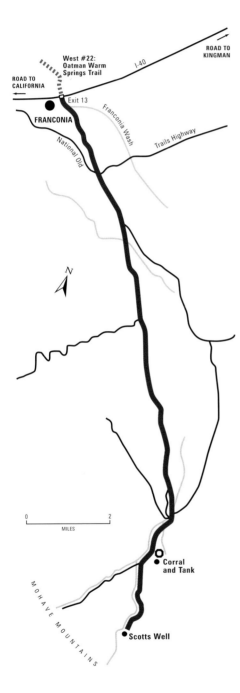

miles. It is possible to continue a short distance past that point, but the trail is used mainly by ATVs and is very narrow and scratchy for a vehicle.

The Mohave Mountains represent somewhat of a crossover between the Mohave and Sonoran Desert vegetations. The canyons on the south side have a population of Joshua trees (the representative plant of the Mohave Desert communities), while the northern slope has vegetation characteristic of the Sonoran Desert, including saguaro cacti. A keen eye will spot a couple of saguaros growing on the northern side of the mountain up the slopes of the main wash. Wildlife includes Gambel's quail, coyote, and bighorn sheep.

Current Road Information

Bureau of Land Management
Lake Havasu Field Office
1785 Kiowa Avenue
Lake Havasu City, AZ 86403
(928) 505-1200

Map References

BLM   Needles
USGS 1:24,000   Franconia, Buck Mtns.,
           Crossman Peak
           1:100,000 Needles
Arizona Atlas & Gazetteer, p. 30
Arizona Road & Recreation Atlas, pp. 62, 63

Route Directions

▼ 0.0   From I-40 at exit 13, zero trip meter at the top of the exit ramp and turn south on the unsigned, graded dirt road. West #22: Oatman Warm Springs Trail leads off to the north from this point.
           GPS: N34°44.02' W114°15.42'

▼ 0.1   SO Pipeline on left and right; remain on main trail.
▼ 0.6   SO Track on right along power lines.
▼ 1.9   SO National Old Trails Highway crosses on the right and left.
           GPS: N34°42.73' W114°14.19'

▼ 3.1   BR Track on left.
           GPS: N34°41.85' W114°13.33'

▼ 3.4	SO	Cross through wash.
▼ 4.6	TL	Turn left directly in front of fenced property of AL\FAR Mining. Sign directs through traffic to the left. Zero trip meter.
		GPS: N34°40.62' W114°12.60'

▼ 0.0		Continue on lesser standard trail. Immediately, there is a track on right and track on left. Continue to the south-southeast.
▼ 0.1	SO	Pass through fence line.
		GPS: N34°40.51' W114°12.58'

▼ 0.5	SO	Track on right.
▼ 0.9	SO	Cross through wash.
▼ 2.6	SO	Pass through wire gate.
		GPS: N34°38.53' W114°11.56'

▼ 2.7	SO	Quarry on left.
▼ 4.0	SO	Faint track on right.
▼ 4.3	SO	Faint track on right.

▼ 4.4	SO	Track on right; then trail runs alongside the large, sandy wash. Well-used track on left at the edge of wash. Zero trip meter.
		GPS: N34°37.01' W114°10.96'

▼ 0.0		Continue southeast alongside wash.
▼ 0.1	SO	Track on left. Trail now runs in wash course.
▼ 0.4	SO	Track on left.
		GPS: N34°36.68' W114°10.84'

▼ 0.5	SO	Track on left in wash; then crossroads in wash. Small track on right and well-used tracks straight on and to the left. Continue straight ahead in wash.
		GPS: N34°36.58' W114°10.80'

▼ 0.7	BR	Fork in wash; track on left.
▼ 1.6	SO	Corral and tank on the left.
		GPS: N34°35.68' W114°11.20'

Stone ruins at Scotts Well

▼ 1.9	BL	Fork in wash; track on right is spur trail that goes 1.8 miles up the wash. **GPS: N34°35.52′ W114°11.36′**
▼ 2.4	SO	Exit wash through small stone walling.
▼ 2.5	SO	Re-enter wash. **GPS: N34°34.95′ W114°11.21′**
▼ 2.8	SO	Exit wash. **GPS: N34°34.75′ W114°11.15′**
▼ 3.0	SO	Re-enter wash.
▼ 3.4	SO	Exit wash. **GPS: N34°34.27′ W114°11.29′**
▼ 3.6		Trail ends at a gate and stone ruin on private property. Old mine ruin and tank. **GPS: N34°34.15′ W114°11.34′**

WEST REGION TRAIL #21

Falls Springs Wash Trail

STARTING POINT Arizona 95, north of Lake Havasu City
FINISHING POINT Falls Springs Wash
TOTAL MILEAGE 10.1 miles
UNPAVED MILEAGE 5 miles
DRIVING TIME 45 minutes (one-way)
ELEVATION RANGE 300–3,100 feet
USUALLY OPEN Year-round
BEST TIME TO TRAVEL Fall to spring
DIFFICULTY RATING 4
SCENIC RATING 6
REMOTENESS RATING +0

Special Attractions

■ Northernmost point of the saguaro cactus distribution.
■ Well-used trail traveling up a wash.
■ Bison Falls.

Description

This trail leaves from the eastern side of Lake Havasu City's limits along a well-used, dirt road marked by an information board. It is an easy ride as it travels along the ridge be-

fore dropping to enter Falls Springs Wash. The wash is smooth as it climbs steadily up to the south side of the Mohave Mountains. The vegetation is the ubiquitous creosote bush, ocotillo, and some fairly large, scattered saguaro—this is the northernmost point of their distribution.

The trail then turns right into a narrow and twisty side canyon. The left turn at this point dead-ends 2 miles farther at a locked gate marking the start of the trail up to the radio towers.

Continue along the main trail for 0.9 miles to the bottom of the small, rocky Bison Falls. A constructed stone dam halfway up the falls testifies to the efforts of early miners to secure a water supply in this harsh landscape.

Two trails climb around the falls, one on either side. They rejoin almost immediately. Both are very rocky and narrow. Neither one is much harder than the other; the left-hand one is steeper and looser, but the right-hand one is extremely narrow just before it rejoins the other and has a rocky section at the bottom.

At the top of Bison Falls there is a short, narrow, brushy section. However, it soon opens out again and the trail continues in the wash. A well-used track to the left goes 0.6 miles along a narrow ridge top and shelf road to some old diggings. Nothing remains except the shaft and tailings. The main trail continues in the wash until it forks at the very end of the trail. The left-hand fork goes a short distance to the few remains of an old mining camp; all that is left are the tumbled stone walls of a cabin at the top of the small pour-off and some tin-can dumps. The right-hand fork at the end of the trail soon turns into a loose, rubbly 4WD trail that climbs steeply and may result in vehicle damage.

Current Road Information

Bureau of Land Management
Lake Havasu Field Office
2610 Sweetwater Ave.
Lake Havasu City, AZ 86406
(928) 505-1200

Looking across a mine shaft to the trail

West Trail #21: Falls Springs Wash Trail

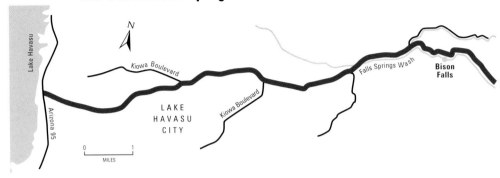

Map References

BLM   Needles
USGS   1:24,000   Lake Havasu City South,
       Lake Havasu City North, Crossman Peak
       1:100,000 Needles
Arizona Atlas & Gazetteer, pp. 30, 40

Route Directions

▼ 0.0   From Arizona 95, north of Lake Havasu
           City, turn east on Industrial Boulevard
           at the stoplight and zero trip meter.
           Industrial Boulevard is 1 mile south of

Wal-Mart on Arizona 95. Continue
east—Industrial Boulevard turns into
Havasupai Boulevard.
GPS: N34°29.61 W114°21.50'

▼ 3.1   TR   Continue along Kiowa Boulevard.
▼ 5.1   TL   Turn onto Bison Boulevard. Follow
                paved road to the end where it turns
                into a dirt single-lane trail. Zero trip
                meter at the information board.
                GPS: N34°31.27' W114°16.32'

▼ 0.0   Trail heads out from the information

Falls Springs Wash approaching Mohave Mountains

board at the end of Bison Boulevard.

▼ 0.4 SO Track on left.
▼ 1.0 SO Track on left.
       GPS: N34º31.78′ W114º15.40′

▼ 1.2 BL Bear left at concrete foundation in large open area, heading down toward wash.
▼ 1.4 BR Ignore small tracks on left and right; remain on main trail. Bear right up wash under power lines.
       GPS: N34º31.95′ W114º15.24′

▼ 2.1 SO Track on right and small track on left.
       GPS: N34º32.27′ W114º14.53′

▼ 2.2 SO Small track on right.
▼ 2.6 BR Wash forks; well-used track on left goes 2 miles to a locked gate. Zero trip meter.
       GPS: N34º32.57′ W114º14.13′

▼ 0.0   Continue to the northeast.
▼ 0.9 TR Trail forks in front of Bison Falls with old concrete dam in the wash. Both ways join up fairly quickly. Both are narrow and rocky—the right fork is slightly easier, but it is narrower.
       GPS: N34º32.66′ W114º13.32′

▼ 1.0 SO Tracks rejoin at top of pour-off.
▼ 1.7 SO Track on left climbs 0.6 miles along the 0ridge, then along a narrow shelf road to some diggings. There is a view back to Lake Havasu.
       GPS: N34º32.63′ W114º12.67′

▼ 2.3 TL Fork in wash.
       GPS: N34º32.32′ W114º12.15′

▼ 2.4   Trail ends at small pour-off in the wash. Immediately above the pour-off on the left, there is a small stone ruin—part of an old mining camp. No diggings, just the ruin and tin-can dumps. Hiking trail continues to the mine, visible above the head of the valley.
       GPS: N34º32.34′ W114º12.49′

Oatman Warm Springs Trail

STARTING POINT Route 66, 0.7 miles south of Golden Shores
FINISHING POINT I-40 at exit 13
TOTAL MILEAGE 29.9 miles
UNPAVED MILEAGE 29.9 miles
DRIVING TIME 2.5 hours
ELEVATION RANGE 600–2,000 feet
USUALLY OPEN Year-round
BEST TIME TO TRAVEL Fall to spring
DIFFICULTY RATING 3 (spur could be classed as a 4)
SCENIC RATING 8
REMOTENESS RATING +1

Special Attractions
■ Oatman Warm Springs.
■ Trail running along the edge of the Warm Springs Wilderness.
■ Far-reaching views of the Black and Mohave Mountains.
■ Wildflower-viewing in spring.

Description
This trail combines a long, interesting drive, a short walk, and wide-ranging views. It leaves from the community of Golden Shores along a wide, graded (though often washboardy) road. The turnoff for the trail proper is 6.4 miles along this road. The turn is well-used but very narrow, and with no marker it is easy to miss. If you come to a windmill, a stone tower, and a dwelling on the graded road, you have gone 1 mile too far.

The trail runs along a ridge for much of the first leg, giving 360-degree views ahead over the Black Mountains and back over the Mohave Mountains. Although the trail is easy for a 4WD vehicle, it is very lumpy and you will be forced to go slowly. Take your time. Fast speeds risk tire damage and make for a very uncomfortable ride for the vehicle's occupants. Vegetation is sparse along the rocky ridge top—a mix of creosote bush, large ocotillo, paloverde, and barrel cactus. The trail is at its best in spring when the ocotillos are waving their red flaglike blooms and the yellow flowers of the paloverde are out. You are likely to see wildlife along this trail. Gambel's quail are abundant, coyotes roam the slopes, and there are wild burros that have strayed down the mountains from the mines around Oatman.

The section of trail that leads off as a spur to Oatman Warm Springs is slightly tougher than the rest of the trail because it has a couple of loose, steep hills; but anyone who has come this far is unlikely to have trouble. This short spur ends at a small turnaround on the boundary of the Warm Springs Wilderness. From here, hike past the gate along the old trail for approximately 1 mile to Oatman Warm Springs. A cold spring is reached first at approximately 0.3 miles. Coordinates for the warm springs are GPS: N34°53.80' W114°18.48'. The springs are small and not suitable for bathing because no pool has been built, but the hike is pleasant and goes through some wonderful wilderness scenery.

From the springs, retrace your steps to the main trail and continue around the loop to Franconia. The second leg winds through the edge of the Black Mountains through some rugged mountain scenery. On the whole, it is a smoother road than the outward leg.

A spur trail enters the wilderness area along a vehicle access corridor, 2.5 miles from the top of the loop. This spur goes 1.3 miles before ending on a small platform raised above the valley at some old diggings. There is little to see, although the view is pleasant. Access to the trail is narrow and brushy.

The main trail crosses many washes and then joins a graded road that leads to a talc mine, which is just visible to the left, high on the mountain. The mine is private property. From the mine, the trail runs across the flats to join I-40 after crossing over the railroad tracks.

Current Road Information

Bureau of Land Management
Kingman Field Office
2755 Mission Blvd.
Kingman, AZ 86401
(928) 718-3700

An off-camber section of the trail

Viewpoint at the talc mine looking back down on the distant trail

West Trail #22: Oatman Warm Springs Trail

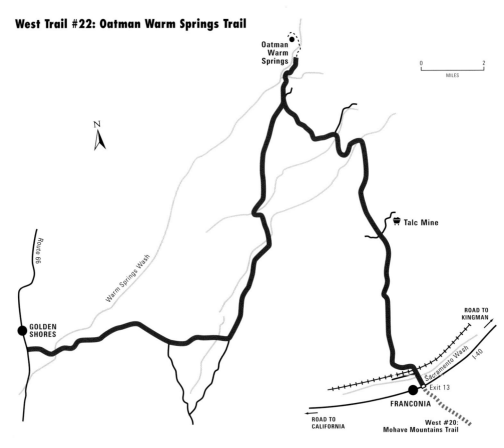

Map References

BLM   Needles
USGS   1:24,000   Warm Springs SW,
   Warm Springs, Warm Springs SE,
   Franconia
   1:100,000 Needles
Arizona Atlas & Gazetteer, p. 30
Arizona Road & Recreation Atlas, p. 62

Route Directions

▼ 0.0 From Route 66, 0.7 miles south of the
    community of Golden Shores, turn east
    on wide, graded dirt road and zero trip
    meter. Turn is unmarked, but the road
    runs just north of the radio facility,
    which is a short, white, square building.
6.4 ▲ Trail finishes on Route 66, 0.7 miles
    south of the community of Golden
    Shores. Turn left for Topock and I-40;
    turn right for Oatman.
    GPS: N34°46.12' W114°28.61'

▼ 0.9 TL Turn left in front of fenced enclosure.
     Track on right; then cross through
     Warm Springs Wash.
5.5 ▲ TR Cross through Warm Springs Wash;
     then turn right in front of fenced enclo-
     sure. Track straight on.

▼ 2.2 SO Track on left.
4.2 ▲ SO Track on right.

▼ 4.9 SO Cross through wash.
1.5 ▲ SO Cross through wash.

▼ 5.1 SO Track on right.
1.3 ▲ SO Track on left.

▼ 5.5 SO Track on right.
0.9 ▲ SO Track on left.

▼ 6.2 SO Cross through wash; then private
     entrance on right.

0.2 ▲	SO	Private entrance on left; then cross through wash.

| 6.4 ▼ | TL | Turn onto smaller, well-used but unmarked single-lane trail and zero trip meter. Track on right opposite the turn. |
| 0.0 ▲ | | Continue on graded road to the west. **GPS: N34°45.81' W114°21.71'** |

| 0.0 ▼ | | Continue on smaller trail and immediately tracks on right and left. |
| 8.0 ▲ | TR | Tracks on left and right; then turn onto larger graded road. |

| 0.9 ▼ | BL | Track on right is private property; bear left and immediately cross through wash. Tracks on left and right up and down wash. |
| 7.1 ▲ | SO | Cross through wash; tracks on left and right up and down wash. Then track on left is private property. **GPS: N34°46.63' W114°21.26'** |

| 1.6 ▼ | SO | Survey marker on right. |
| 6.4 ▲ | SO | Survey marker on left. |

| 3.5 ▼ | SO | Cross through wash. Warm Springs Wilderness boundary on left. |
| 4.5 ▲ | SO | Cross through wash. Warm Springs Wilderness boundary finishes on right. |

| 4.3 ▼ | SO | Cross through wash. |
| 3.7 ▲ | SO | Cross through wash. |

| 4.4 ▼ | SO | Cross through wash. |
| 3.6 ▲ | SO | Cross through wash. |

| 5.4 ▼ | BL | Two faint tracks on right. |
| 2.6 ▲ | BR | Two faint tracks on left. **GPS: N34°49.90' W114°20.05'** |

| 8.0 ▼ | SO | Track on right is return part of loop. Zero trip meter. Continue straight on to start the spur to Oatman Warm Springs. |
| 0.0 ▲ | TR | Return to the start of the spur and turn right (as you are now looking) to continue around the loop on well-used, single-track dirt road. Zero trip meter. **GPS: N34°52.09' W114°19.12'** |

Spur to Oatman Warm Springs

0.0 ▼		Start of spur to Oatman Warm Springs.
0.1 ▼	SO	Track on right.
0.3 ▼	SO	Trail descends to join the large Warm Springs Wash.
0.5 ▼	SO	End of descent. Enter large wash channel.
0.8 ▼	SO	Cross through wash.
1.1 ▼	SO	Cross through wash.
1.5 ▼	UT	Spur ends at turnaround and gate blocking vehicle travel into the wilderness area. From here, hike the short distance to the springs. **GPS: N34°53.10' W114°18.59'**

Continuation of Main Trail

| 0.0 ▼ | TL | Return to the start of the spur and turn left (as you are now looking) to continue around the loop on well-used, single-track dirt road. Zero trip meter. |
| 2.5 ▲ | TR | Track on left is return part of loop; turn right and start the spur to Oatman Warm Springs. Zero trip meter. **GPS: N34°52.09' W114°19.12'** |

| 0.1 ▼ | SO | Cross through wash. |
| 2.4 ▲ | SO | Cross through wash. |

| 0.4 ▼ | SO | Track on right on saddle. |
| 2.1 ▲ | SO | Track on left on saddle. **GPS: N34°51.78' W114°19.03'** |

| 0.5 ▼ | SO | Cross through wash. |
| 2.0 ▲ | SO | Cross through wash. |

| 1.1 ▼ | SO | Cross through wash. |
| 1.4 ▲ | SO | Cross through wash. |

| 1.3 ▼ | SO | Cross through wash. |
| 1.2 ▲ | SO | Cross through wash. |

| 1.5 ▼ | SO | Cross through wash. |
| 1.0 ▲ | SO | Cross through wash. |

| 2.5 ▼ | BR | Track on left enters a wilderness corridor and travels 1.3 miles to some diggings. Zero trip meter. |
| 0.0 ▲ | | Continue toward Oatman Warm Springs. |

GPS: N34°51.04' W114°17.46'

▼ 0.0   Continue to the southeast.
4.7 ▲ BL Track on right enters wilderness corridor and travels 1.3 miles to some diggings. Zero trip meter.

▼ 0.1 SO Cross through wash.
4.6 ▲ SO Cross through wash.

▼ 0.6 SO Cross through wash.
4.1 ▲ SO Cross through wash.

▼ 1.3 SO Cross through wash.
3.4 ▲ SO Cross through wash.

▼ 2.4 SO Cross through wash.
2.3 ▲ SO Cross through wash.

▼ 2.8 SO Cross through wash. Track on right down wash.
1.9 ▲ SO Cross through wash. Track on left down wash.
GPS: N34°49.63' W114°16.60'

▼ 3.2 SO Cross through wash.
1.5 ▲ SO Cross through wash.

▼ 3.4 SO Cross through wash.
1.3 ▲ SO Cross through wash.

▼ 4.1 SO Enter wash.
0.6 ▲ SO Exit wash.

▼ 4.3 SO Exit wash.
0.4 ▲ SO Enter wash.

▼ 4.5 SO Cross through wash.
0.2 ▲ SO Cross through wash.

▼ 4.7 SO Track on right; then cross through wash with tracks on right and left up and down wash; immediately followed by major track on left that goes to private property. A talc mine is visible up the mountain to the left. Zero trip meter.
0.0 ▲   Continue toward wash, bearing right at narrow track on left in the wash.
GPS: N34°48.17' W114°16.25'

▼ 0.0   Continue to the southeast. Trail standard improves slightly.
2.1 ▲ BL Wider track on right goes to private property. Bear left on narrower track toward wash and zero trip meter.

▼ 0.4 SO Cross through wash. Trail now follows along the wide sandy wash, crossing it often in the next 1.4 miles.
1.7 ▲ SO Cross through wash.

▼ 1.8 SO Cross through wash. Trail swings away from wash.
0.3 ▲ SO Cross through wash. Trail now follows along the wide sandy wash, crossing it often in the next 1.4 miles.
GPS: N34°46.63' W114°16.39'

▼ 2.1 TR T-intersection with well-used graded trail. Turn right and zero trip meter.
0.0 ▲   Continue toward Oatman Warm Springs.
GPS: N34°46.49' W114°16.26'

▼ 0.0   Continue toward Franconia.
3.2 ▲ TL Turn left on roughly graded trail and zero trip meter.

▼ 0.7 SO End of Warm Springs Wilderness on left.
2.5 ▲ SO Warm Springs Wilderness starts on right.

▼ 1.1 SO Faint track on right after small hillock. Views of Mohave Mountains ahead.
2.1 ▲ SO Faint track on left. Keep right of the hill on main trail.

▼ 1.7 SO Tracks on left and right along transmission line.
1.5 ▲ SO Tracks on left and right along transmission line.

▼ 2.0 SO Start to cross wide wash. Many tracks on right and left for the next 0.6 miles; remain on main trail.
1.2 ▲ SO Exit wash.

▼ 2.6 SO Track on right; exiting wash channel.
0.6 ▲ SO Trail enters wash channel. Many tracks on right and left for the next 0.6 miles; remain on main trail.

▼ 2.7	BR	Track on right; then track on left.
0.5 ▲	BL	Bear left after the railroad crossing. Remain on main trail; many tracks on right and left.

▼ 2.8	TR	Stop sign at railroad crossing; turn right after crossing. Track on left.
0.4 ▲	TL	Turn left and cross over railroad crossing. Stop sign at crossing. Track straight ahead.
		GPS: N34°44.48' W114°15.51'

▼ 2.9	TL	Turn left, heading toward freeway; cross wide, sandy Sacramento Wash.
0.3 ▲	TR	Turn right away from freeway; cross wide, sandy Sacramento Wash.

▼ 3.2		Track on right; then trail ends at the junction with I-40, just east of Franconia.
0.0 ▲		Trail starts at exit 13 on I-40, just east of Franconia. Exit freeway, zero trip meter, and proceed north on wide, graded dirt road toward the railroad crossing. West #20: Mohave Mountains Trail leads off to the south at this point. Immediately there is a turn to the left. Exit is signed—Franconia Road.
		GPS: N34°44.14' W114°15.49'

WEST REGION TRAIL #23

Moss Mine Trail

STARTING POINT Silver Creek Road, 4.5 miles from Route 66 and Oatman
FINISHING POINT Moss Mine
TOTAL MILEAGE 2 miles
UNPAVED MILEAGE 2 miles
DRIVING TIME 20 minutes (one-way)
ELEVATION RANGE 2,000–2,200 feet
USUALLY OPEN Year-round
BEST TIME TO TRAVEL Fall to spring
DIFFICULTY RATING 3
SCENIC RATING 8
REMOTENESS RATING +0

Special Attractions

- Extensive remains of Moss Mine.
- Access to a network of other 4WD trails.
- Can be combined with West #24: Moss-back Wash Trail and West #25: Thumb Butte Trail to make a full-day tour.

History

John Moss, who was responsible for opening up the Moss Mine and hence this area of Arizona for mining, was a colorful character. He was born in 1823 in Utica, Iowa. By the time he was in his early twenties he was already prospecting for gold in Eldorado Canyon, Nevada. When Eldorado Canyon became too crowded for him, he crossed the river and began prospecting in Mohave County.

Most mentions of John Moss refer to him as Captain Moss. The title seems to have been honorary, as there is no record of military service in his career. He was always friendly to the local Indians, learning to speak their language and winning their trust and friendship in return. This friendship with the Mojave Indians accounts for the version of his discovery of Moss Mine that paints him in the most favorable light. Supposedly, in 1863 the Mojave leader, Chief Iretaba, grateful to Moss for his friendship, showed him some outcroppings of rock likely to be productive. Moss noticed the glint of gold and was quick to establish his claim.

The alternative version of the discovery of the mine tells of a prospector who came to Moss to ask his opinion of some ore he had found. Moss proclaimed it valueless, but wheedled the location of the ore out of the man. He then quickly staked the claim, driving off the original discoverer when he returned.

The Moss Mine was truly amazing. John Moss extracted more than $200,000 worth of gold from a hole 10-feet square by 10-feet deep. He then sold the claim to Dahren Black, who was backed by a consortium from the East. Later, the Gold Giant Mining and Milling Company from Los Angeles became the operator but soon discovered that the only gold was in the original small hole. When that played out, the company sank many

Moss Mine gantry

holes trying to locate the lode, but they never found it for the simple reason that there wasn't one! John Moss's original hole is to the right of the headframe. The surrounding holes were the attempts to find more riches.

Another of John Moss's discoveries was the Mossback Mine, just over the hill from the Moss Mine. Moss also tried to establish the first town site in Mohave County. As a result of his find other mines sprang up along Silver Creek. The settlement became known as Fort Silver, although it had nothing to do with the military directly. It may have been known as "Fort" because the soldiers from Fort Mohave prospected here while on furlough. They constructed a rock cabin, which they used as a base while they explored the hills.

John Moss is perhaps best remembered for something other than mining. He was well respected among the Mojave and was concerned about the bloodshed between Indians and white settlers. He thought that if the Indians realized the sheer number of white people, they would see the futility of their attacks and would stop.

His friendship with Chief Iretaba enabled him to persuade the chief to accompany him to Washington to meet President Abraham Lincoln. The chief was gone far longer than the planned three months, and he did indeed meet the president. As part of Moss's campaign to convince Iretaba that the white population was more numerous than he ever imagined, every time their train passed through a town at night, Moss would wake his friend to show him the lights and would try to convince him that they were traveling through one large city rather than isolated settlements.

After leaving Mohave County, Moss moved to Colorado, where he had a checkered career involving a diamond-mining scam. In spite of all the wealth he had accumulated over the years, he ultimately died in poverty.

Description

This short spur trail leads along a rutty trail to the remains of the Moss Mine. The major attraction is the mine, which has some interesting ruins of stone buildings, many adits and shafts, and a steel headframe. The ruins make excellent subject matter for photographers.

There are many side trails leading from Moss Mine and along some of the washes. A keen explorer will be able to find one of several different routes through to West #24: Mossback Wash Trail. However, these unmapped trails can be confusing to follow and it is easy to get lost. Make sure you are carrying at least a topographic map and compass if you are planning to attempt any of these routes.

Current Road Information

Bureau of Land Management
Kingman Field Office
2755 Mission Blvd.
Kingman, AZ 86401
(928) 718-3700

Map References

BLM   Davis Dam
USGS 1:24,000   Oatman
      1:100,000 Davis Dam
Arizona Atlas & Gazetteer, p. 30

Route Directions

▼ 0.0   Proceed along Silver Creek Road for 4.5 miles from Route 66 and Oatman. Then turn north onto an unmarked trail that leaves along a wash. Zero trip meter. Immediately bear right,

staying on the better-used major track. Lesser-used track on left.
GPS: N35°04.70′ W114°26.94′

▼ 0.1   BR   Enter main Silver Creek Wash. Vehicles travel left down wash as well. Trail immediately forks; bear right following main trail.
GPS: N35°04.79′ W114°26.93′

▼ 0.2   SO   Two tracks on left and two tracks on right down and up wash. Remain on main trail toward the far side of the wash.

▼ 0.3   BL   Track on right up wash is West #24: Mossback Wash Trail. Also track on left out of wash. Continue straight on up small side wash to the north.
GPS: N35°04.92′ W114°26.72′

▼ 0.5   SO   Crest ridge at head of wash.
▼ 0.8   SO   Two tracks on left.
▼ 0.9   SO   Cross through wash.
▼ 1.1   SO   Track on left.
▼ 1.2   SO   Cross through wash; tracks on right and left up wash.
GPS: N35°05.63′ W114°26.62′

▼ 1.3   SO   Track on left up wash. Stone remains

Old stone building ruins at Moss Mine

West Trail #23: Moss Mine Trail

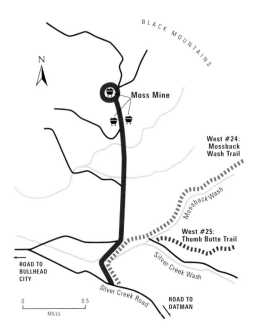

of the Moss Mine on both sides of the trail. Adit down in wash on left. Many small tracks on right and left around mine. Remain on main trail.
GPS: N35°05.81' W114°26.67'

▼ 1.5   BL   Track on right is end of small loop at the end of the trail. Zero trip meter.
GPS: N35°05.94' W114°26.71'

▼ 0.0   Start of loop at end of trail.

▼ 0.2   BR   Steel headframe on right and many adits in the hillside. Bear right before the headframe and swing up ridge. Climb up ridge for a view back over Moss Mine.
GPS: N35°05.97' W114°26.82'

▼ 0.4   TR   T-intersection. Track on left and faint track straight on.
GPS: N35°06.02' W114°26.65'

▼ 0.5   End of trail at the end of the small loop.
GPS: N35°05.94' W114°26.71'

Stone ruin near Moss Mine with a mine gantry visible further up the wash

Mossback Wash Trail

STARTING POINT West #25: Thumb Butte
Trail, 8.5 miles from the northern end
FINISHING POINT Silver Creek Road, 4.5 miles
from Oatman and Route 66
TOTAL MILEAGE 5.6 miles
UNPAVED MILEAGE 5.6 miles
DRIVING TIME 1 hour
ELEVATION RANGE 2,000–2,500 feet
USUALLY OPEN Year-round
BEST TIME TO TRAVEL Fall to spring
DIFFICULTY RATING 4
SCENIC RATING 8
REMOTENESS RATING +1

Special Attractions

■ Viewing wild burros and bighorn sheep.
■ Spectacular scenery in the Black
Mountains.
■ Mossback Mine and German Soldiers'
Caves.

Description

This narrow, winding single track meanders
through some spectacular Black Mountains
scenery before dropping into Mossback
Wash. It leaves from West #25: Thumb
Butte Trail along a wash, before climbing out
and winding its way over ridges, dropping
often to cross through narrow gully washes.

After 2.6 miles, the trail passes Mossback
Mine, another of John Moss's claims. The
mine has large tailings heaps and adits. Nearby are caves reputed to have been the hideout
of some German prisoners of war from World
War II who escaped from the camp in Kingman.

The trail comes very close to meeting West
#25: Thumb Butte Trail at the mine, just as the
main trail drops into Mossback Wash. From
here to the end, the trail, which runs along
Mossback Wash, is easy, gravelly, and smooth.
Sections are fairly narrow, but even the widest
vehicle will have no trouble fitting through.

The trail ends at the junction with Silver
Creek Wash and shares the exit to the main

dirt Silver Creek Road with West #23: Moss
Mine Trail. From Silver Creek Road, it is 4.5
miles to Route 66 and Oatman.

Current Road Information

Bureau of Land Management
Kingman Field Office
2755 Mission Blvd.
Kingman, AZ 86401
(928) 718-3700

Map References

BLM   Davis Dam
USGS 1:24,000   Oatman
          1:100,000 Davis Dam
Arizona Atlas & Gazetteer, p. 30

Route Directions

▼ 0.0   Trail starts on West #25: Thumb Butte
         Trail, 8.5 miles from the northern junc-
         tion with Arizona 68; at an unmarked
         junction in the wash. Turn west in the
         wash and zero trip meter.
4.0 ▲   Trail ends at the junction with West
         #25: Thumb Butte Trail. Turn left in the
         wash to exit to Arizona 68; turn right
         to return to Silver Creek Road via the
         Thumb Butte Trail.
         GPS: N35°07.33′ W114°25.13′

▼ 0.5 BL Bear left out of wash and swing up hill.
           Track continues in wash and is a diffi-
           cult route out via Pass Canyon.
3.5 ▲ BR Descend hill and bear right up wash.
           Track on left down wash is a difficult
           route out via Pass Canyon.
           GPS: N35°07.14′ W114°25.63′

▼ 0.7 TR Cross through wash; then track on left.
3.3 ▲ TL Turn sharp left; track continues straight
           on; then cross through wash.
           GPS: N35°07.05′ W114°25.54′

▼ 0.9 SO Descend ridge and head up the wash.
3.1 ▲ SO Exit wash and climb up ridge to the
           right.

▼ 1.3 BR Exit wash to the right and climb ridge.
2.7 ▲ BL Descend small ridge and bear left,

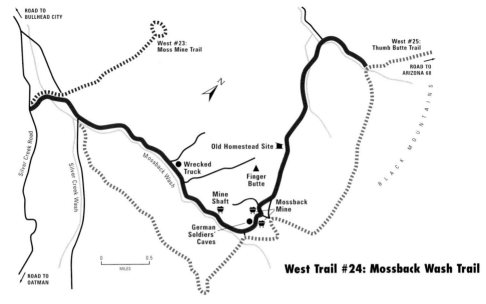

West Trail #24: Mossback Wash Trail

entering wash.
GPS: N35º06.73' W114º25.15'

▼ 1.6　SO　Cross through wash. Tracks up and
　　　　　　down wash.
2.4 ▲　SO　Cross through wash. Tracks up and
　　　　　　down wash.

▼ 1.7　SO　Pass through forest thicket, by the site
　　　　　　of old homestead and past a spring.
2.3 ▲　SO　Pass through forest thicket, by the site
　　　　　　of old homestead and past a spring.
　　　　　　GPS: N35º06.40' W114º25.03'

▼ 1.9　SO　Cross through wash.
2.1 ▲　SO　Cross through wash.

▼ 2.3　SO　Track on right.
1.7 ▲　BR　Track on left.
　　　　　　GPS: N35º06.06' W114º24.60'

▼ 2.4　SO　Track on left.
1.6 ▲　SO　Track on right.

▼ 2.5　BL　Two tracks on right.
1.5 ▲　BR　Two tracks on left.

▼ 2.6　TR　Track on left; then turn right at T-inter-
　　　　　　section and enter wash. Track on left
　　　　　　leads a short distance to join West

#25: Thumb Butte Trail. Second track
on left up wash. Mossback Mine is on
the right.

1.4 ▲　TL　Track on right; then second track on
　　　　　　right, which joins West #25: Thumb
　　　　　　Butte Trail. Turn left and exit wash;
　　　　　　then track on right.
　　　　　　GPS: N35º05.82' W114º24.50'

▼ 2.7　SO　Track on left and the German Soldiers
　　　　　　Caves on right; then track on left.
1.3 ▲　SO　Track on right; then another track on
　　　　　　right and the German Soldiers Caves on
　　　　　　left. The Mossback Mine is on the left.

▼ 2.8　BL　Track on right; then track on left.
1.2 ▲　BR　Track on right; then track on left. Bear
　　　　　　right up wash.

▼ 2.9　SO　Track on left up wash.
1.1 ▲　BL　Track on right up wash.
　　　　　　GPS: N35º05.59' W114º24.47'

▼ 3.2　SO　Mine shaft on right up bank.
0.8 ▲　SO　Mine shaft on left up bank.

▼ 3.8　SO　Track on right.
0.2 ▲　SO　Track on left.

An old water tank beside the trail

One of the caves of Mossback Mine where German soldiers hid

BIGHORN SHEEP

Bighorn sheep are grayish brown with yellowish white rump patches and short brown tails. Some have whitish fur around their muzzles, eyes, bellies, and calves. They have muscular bodies and thick necks. Ewes weigh around 150 pounds, and rams range from 150 to 250 pounds. Both the male and female have horns that grow continually and never molt. The ram's horns are massive and coil up and back around his ears in a C shape up to 40 inches long. The ewe's horns are thin and only slightly curved—no more than a half curl. Bighorn sheep are active by day, dwelling on cliffs, mountain slopes, and rolling foothills. They feed on a wide variety of grasses and shrubs. Rams challenge each

Bighorn sheep

other in butting contests in which they simultaneously charge each other. Their combined speed can be more than 40 miles per hour just before impact, and their foreheads meet with a crack that can be heard a mile away. These contests can last for as long as 20 hours. Horn size determines status among rams, but these ramming contests establish hierarchy among rams with horns of similar size.

Many bighorns died in the twentieth century from hunting, habitat fragmentation, and diseases contracted from domestic livestock. Reintroduction programs and habitat protection have assisted in increasing their populations, but they are still endangered.

▼ 4.0   SO   Two tracks on right marked by an old orange wrecked truck on right of wash. Zero trip meter.

0.0 ▲   Continue toward Mossback Mine.
GPS: N35°05.40′ W114°25.51′

▼ 0.0   Continue along in the wash.

1.6 ▲   SO   Two tracks on left marked by an old orange wrecked truck on left of wash. Zero trip meter.

▼ 0.3   BL   Track on right at fork in wash.

1.3 ▲   SO   Track on left is previous track rejoining.

▼ 0.5   SO   Track on right is previous track rejoining.

1.1 ▲   BR   Track on left at fork in wash.

▼ 1.1   TR   T-intersection with the larger Silver Creek Wash. Track on left goes 0.1 miles to the start of West #25: Thumb Butte Trail. Turn right and join Silver Creek Wash.

0.5 ▲   BL   Track on right runs up Silver Creek

Wash and goes 0.1 miles to the start of West #25: Thumb Butte Trail. Bear left into the smaller Mossback Wash.
GPS: N35°04.95′ W114°26.49′

▼ 1.3   TL   Track on right is West #23: Moss Mine Trail. Also track straight on, leading out of wash. Remain in Silver Creek Wash and turn left.

0.3 ▲   TR   Remain in Silver Creek Wash and turn right. Track straight ahead is West #23: Moss Mine Trail; also track on left out of wash.
GPS: N35°04.92′ W114°26.72′

▼ 1.4   SO   Two tracks on left and two tracks on right up and down main wash. Continue straight ahead to north side of wash.

0.2 ▲   SO   Two tracks on left and two tracks on right down and up wash. Remain on main trail toward far side of wash.

▼ 1.5   BL   Bear left up smaller side wash. Bear

extreme right into main Silver Creek Wash, up the south side.

0.1 ▲   BR   Enter main Silver Creek Wash. Vehicles travel left down wash as well. Trail immediately forks; bear right following main trail.
GPS: N35°04.79' W114°26.94'

▼ 1.6   Track on right; then trail ends at the junction with major graded dirt Silver Creek Road. Turn left for Route 66 and Oatman; turn right for Bullhead City.

0.0 ▲   Trail starts on Silver Creek Road, 4.5 miles northwest of Route 66 and Oatman. Turn north onto an unmarked trail that leaves along a wash. Zero trip meter. Immediately bear right, staying on the better-used major track. Lesser-used track on left.
GPS: N35°04.70' W114°26.94'

Thumb Butte Trail

STARTING POINT Arizona 68, 19.5 miles west of junction with US 93

FINISHING POINT Silver Creek Wash, 0.1 miles east of West #24: Mossback Wash Trail

TOTAL MILEAGE 14.5 miles

UNPAVED MILEAGE 14.5 miles

DRIVING TIME 3 hours

ELEVATION RANGE 2,000–2,700 feet

USUALLY OPEN Year-round

BEST TIME TO TRAVEL Fall to spring

DIFFICULTY RATING 5

SCENIC RATING 8

REMOTENESS RATING +1

Special Attractions

■ Spectacular scenery in the Black Mountains.

■ Old mine remains.

■ Thumb Butte.

■ Wild burros.

Description

This extremely pretty route takes the backcountry traveler along the western side of the Black Mountains, through rugged terrain, gravelly washes, and remnants of the mining era. The trail leaves Arizona 68 to the west of Union Pass on an unmarked but well-used gravel road, 19.5 miles west of Kingman. A series of turns leads to increasingly smaller and less-traveled roads, passing around the distinctive rock spire of Thumb Butte.

The road shown on most maps of the region as leading south from Arizona 68 is closed to public access by a mining claim. An alternate route around exists: Follow the coal slurry pipeline as it travels up a loose desert wash to the junction with the original road. Take care you don't miss the turn—a sharp right out of the wash just past the wash wall. Vehicle tracks that continue in the wash are traveling east to rejoin Arizona 68.

Once on the formed vehicle trail, you will find the road rough and rocky. The trail crosses many washes as it winds its way south, often traveling in a wash bed that can be narrow in places. Vegetation seen along the trail includes creosote bush, Mohave yucca, cholla, and a few barrel cacti. The rugged Black Mountains make a spectacular backdrop to the stony trail. This is the Mohave Desert at its best.

The junction with West #24: Mossback Wash Trail is reached 8.5 miles from the start. This shorter trail loops around and comes close to rejoining the Thumb Butte Trail. The main trail continues to the south, skirting the boundary of the Mount Nutt Wilderness Area. Camping is limited because of the rugged terrain and rocky soils, but it is possible to find a few isolated spots.

The trail comes close to joining West #24: Mossback Wash Trail a second time at the Mossback Mine. The final part of the trail is slightly more difficult and travel is very slow, so anyone not wanting to tackle this harder section down Grapevine Wash could go out on the Mossback Wash Trail

The rockiest and most difficult section of the trail

Bullhead Jeep Club members explore the trail

for a slightly faster, easier exit. From this second convergence with the Mossback Wash Trail, the Thumb Butte Trail is the lesser used and a bit rougher. There are a couple of loose, rubbly descents, in particular the one to Grapevine Wash. The exit leading from the junction of Grapevine Canyon travels in the wash. The formed trail at this point leads to some interesting scenery and a short vehicle access corridor into the wilderness area; however, it is not the through route as it appears on the maps because of gated private property. Instead, the trail travels west down Grapevine Wash. Some drivers may not like this section—it can be quite brushy in places, and squeezing through a couple of tight spots in the wash will require some careful wheel placement over large boulders. The trail widens out as it goes downstream, and the end is wide and gravelly.

The trail ends where Grapevine Wash joins Silver Creek Wash, which is 0.1 miles from the junction with West #24: Mossback Wash Trail. From here, it is another 0.4 miles along the wash to the graded dirt Silver Creek Road that leads to Oatman. If you travel the trail in reverse, it can be tricky finding the right entrance to Grapevine Canyon. Follow the reverse directions at the start of the Mossback Wash Trail and instead of turning up Mossback Canyon, continue for 0.1 miles in the main Silver Creek Wash. Grapevine Canyon is the next side canyon leading to the east. It is smaller than the start of Mossback Wash, but usually there are vehicle tracks leading up the wash. A GPS is extremely useful for finding the route along this trail.

Current Road Information
Bureau of Land Management
Kingman Field Office
2755 Mission Blvd.
Kingman, AZ 86401
(928) 718-3700

Map References
BLM   Davis Dam
USGS 1:24,000   Union Pass, Oatman
       1:100,000 Davis Dam
Arizona Atlas & Gazetteer, p. 30
Arizona Road & Recreation Atlas, p. 62
(incomplete)

Route Directions

▼ 0.0   From Arizona 68, 19.5 miles west of the junction with US 93, turn south onto gravel road at the unmarked junction and zero trip meter. The trail swings away from the highway up a rise.

0.9 ▲ Trail ends at the junction with Arizona 68. Turn left for Bullhead City; turn right for Kingman.

GPS: N35°11.13′ W114°27.26′

▼ 0.1 TL Smaller track on right at the top of a rise.

0.8 ▲ TR Smaller track on left. Turn right and descend rise to the highway.

▼ 0.2 SO Track on left; then track on right. Thumb Butte is directly ahead.

0.7 ▲ SO Track on left; then track on right.

▼ 0.4 SO Cross through wash.

0.5 ▲ SO Cross through wash.

▼ 0.6 SO Track on left.

0.3 ▲ SO Track on right.

▼ 0.7 SO Track on left.

0.2 ▲ SO Track on right.

▼ 0.8 SO Track on left at small mine hole; then track on right. Cross through wash.

0.1 ▲ SO Cross through wash. Track on left; then track on right at small mine hole.

▼ 0.9 TR Turn onto unmarked, graded road. Zero trip meter. Views to the right to Bullhead City.

0.0 ▲ Continue toward Arizona 68. Thumb Butte is to the right.

GPS: N35°10.76′ W114°26.71′

▼ 0.0 SO Continue on slightly smaller graded road.

7.6 ▲ TL Turn onto unmarked graded road. Zero trip meter. Views to the left to Bullhead City.

▼ 0.1 BR Track on left.

7.5 ▲ BL Track on right.

▼ 0.2 SO Track on right.

7.4 ▲ SO Track on left.

▼ 0.4 SO Enter wash; then track on left.

7.2 ▲ SO Track on right; then exit wash.

The trail follows the west side of the Black Mountains

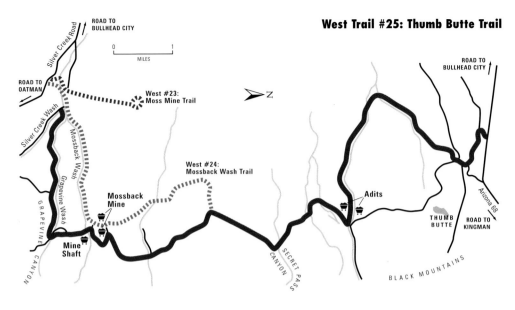

▼ 0.8   SO   Track on left; then exit wash.
6.8 ▲   SO   Enter wash; then track on right.

▼ 0.9   SO   Track on right; then cross through wide wash. Track on left up wash.
6.7 ▲   SO   Track on right up wash; then track on left.

▼ 1.0   SO   Exit wash crossing.
6.6 ▲   SO   Cross through wide wash.

▼ 1.2   BL   Track on right. Bear left down wash.
6.4 ▲   BR   Track on left.
        GPS: N35°09.89' W114°27.45'

▼ 1.8   TL   Turn out of wash.
5.8 ▲   TR   Turn right and enter wash.
        GPS: N35°09.43' W114°27.61'

▼ 2.2   TL   T-intersection. Track on right. Turn left up the wash. Trail is following along a poorly marked pipeline (high-pressure coal slurry pipeline).
5.4 ▲   BR   Track on left. Bear right and leave the wash and pipeline.

▼ 3.2   BL   Faint track on right. Wrap around the wash diversion around pipeline.
4.4 ▲   BR   Swing right around the wash diversion around pipeline. Faint track on left.
        GPS: N35°09.09' W114°26.19'

▼ 4.0   SO   Small mine adits on right and left.
3.6 ▲   SO   Small mine adits on right and left.
        GPS: N35°09.37' W114°25.52'

▼ 4.2   SO   Track on left.
3.4 ▲   BL   Track on right.
        GPS: N35°09.37' W114°25.33'

▼ 4.3   TR   Exit wash. Track straight on continues up wash.
3.3 ▲   TL   Enter wash. Track on right continues up wash.
        GPS: N35°09.37' W114°25.29'

▼ 4.5   SO   Cattle guard.
3.1 ▲   SO   Cattle guard.

▼ 4.9   SO   Cross through wash.
2.7 ▲   SO   Cross through wash.

▼ 5.0   SO   Cross through wash.
2.6 ▲   SO   Cross through wash.

▼ 5.1   SO   Cross through wash.
2.5 ▲   SO   Cross through wash.

▼ 5.4   SO   Cross through wash; then proceed up small wash.
2.2 ▲   SO   Exit small wash; then cross through wash.

▼ 5.6 SO Exit wash.
2.0 ▲ SO Enter wash.

▼ 5.9 SO Cross through wash.
1.7 ▲ SO Cross through wash.

▼ 6.1 SO Enter wide wash crossing.
1.5 ▲ SO Exit wash crossing.

▼ 6.2 SO Exit wash crossing.
1.4 ▲ SO Enter wide wash crossing.

▼ 7.1 SO Enter wash.
0.5 ▲ SO Exit wash.

▼ 7.4 SO Tailings on right.
0.2 ▲ SO Tailings on left.

▼ 7.6 TL Join second wash and turn left. Zero trip meter. Track on right is West #24: Mossback Wash Trail.
0.0 ▲   Continue to the north in wash.
      GPS: N35º07.33' W114º25.13'

▼ 0.0   Continue to the east in wash.
2.3 ▲ TR Turn into well-used wash and zero trip meter. Track continuing straight on in the wash is West #24: Mossback Wash Trail.

▼ 0.5 SO Exit wash.
1.8 ▲ SO Enter wash.
      GPS: N35º07.12' W114º24.69'

▼ 1.3 SO Cross through wash. Track on right down wash.
1.0 ▲ SO Cross through wash. Track on left down wash.
      GPS: N35º06.58' W114º24.15'

▼ 1.4 SO Enter wash.
0.9 ▲ SO Exit wash.

▼ 1.5 BR Exit wash; old trail into wilderness area on the left is now closed to vehicles.
0.8 ▲ BL Enter wash and bear left. Old trail into wilderness area on the right is now closed to vehicles.
      GPS: N35º06.40' W114º24.02'

▼ 2.3 TL Turn sharp left up ridge. Mossback Mine is ahead. Continuing on at this point joins West #24: Mossback Wash Trail at Mossback Mine. Zero trip meter.
0.0 ▲   Continue to the northeast.
      GPS: N35º05.91' W114º24.40'

▼ 0.0   Continue to the east.
1.4 ▲ TR Descend ridge and turn sharp right. Turning left at this point joins West #24: Mossback Wash Trail at the Mossback Mine. Zero trip meter.

▼ 0.1 SO Track on right.
1.3 ▲ SO Track on left.

▼ 0.5 TL Mine shaft on left at junction. Track on right joins West #24: Mossback Wash Trail just south of Mossback Mine.
0.9 ▲ TR Mine shaft on right at junction. Continuing straight at this point joins West #24: Mossback Wash Trail just south of the Mossback Mine.
      GPS: N35º05.63' W114º24.38'

▼ 0.6 SO Cross through Mossback Wash. Track on right down wash.
0.8 ▲ SO Cross through Mossback Wash. Track on left down wash.

▼ 0.9 BL Track on right.
0.5 ▲ SO Track on left.
      GPS: N35º05.33' W114º24.25'

▼ 1.3 BL Track on right; then enter Grapevine Canyon.
0.1 ▲ BR Exit Grapevine Canyon; then track on left. Climb loose, rocky section.
      GPS: N35º05.09' W114º24.17'

▼ 1.4 TR Turn down main wash in Grapevine Canyon. Do not exit main wash up well-used trail on the far side (it dead-ends 0.6 miles farther in wilderness corridor). Zero trip meter.
0.0 ▲   Continue away from Grapevine Canyon.
      GPS: N35º05.07' W114º24.13'

▼ 0.0		Continue down wash.
2.3 ▲	TL	Turn left out of wash. Track continues up wash; also track on right (it dead-ends 0.6 miles farther in wilderness corridor). Zero trip meter.

▼ 0.8	SO	Faint track on left up wash. Remain on best-used trail and pick the best line through for your vehicle.
1.5 ▲	BL	Faint track on right up wash. Remain on best-used trail and pick the best line through for your vehicle. **GPS: N35°05.01' W114°24.93'**

▼ 1.3	SO	Faint track on right up wash. Remain on best-used trail.
1.0 ▲	BR	Faint track on left up wash. Remain on best-used trail. **GPS: N35°04.96' W114°25.44'**

▼ 1.6	TR	Tailings piles of mine on left; then T-intersection. Track on right continues down wash; track on left.
0.7 ▲	TL	Track on right exits wash to mine. Remain in wash; then pass tailings piles of mine on right. **GPS: N35°04.84' W114°25.72'**

▼ 2.3		Trail ends at the junction with the major Silver Creek Wash. Turn right for West #24: Mossback Wash Trail, Moss Mine, and the graded dirt road to Oatman.
0.0 ▲		Trail starts at the junction of the major Silver Creek Wash and Grapevine Canyon Wash. There are no signs. To get to the start, follow the reverse directions from the start of West #24: Mossback Wash Trail. Thumb Butte Trail starts a farther 0.1 miles to the east down the main Silver Creek Wash. Zero trip meter and proceed east up Grapevine Canyon in the wash, following the vehicle tracks. **GPS: N35°04.91' W114°26.39'**

Portland Mine Road

STARTING POINT US 93, 0.3 miles south of mile marker 45
FINISHING POINT Princess Cove Road
TOTAL MILEAGE 31.8 miles
UNPAVED MILEAGE 31.8 miles
ELEVATION RANGE 800–3,800 feet
DRIVING TIME 5 hours
USUALLY OPEN Year-round
BEST TIME TO TRAVEL Fall to spring
DIFFICULTY RATING 4
SCENIC RATING 9
REMOTENESS RATING +1

Special Attractions

■ Winding trail in the Black Mountains.
■ Access to Lake Mead National Recreation Area.
■ Wild burros and bighorn sheep.
■ Views of Lake Mohave and the Newberry Mountains.

History

The Portland Mine Road was put in by the miners working the Portland Mine. This gold mine is still sporadically worked by investors.

The wild burros that abound in the region are descended from burros miners used as pack animals and for transport. When miners left the region in the 1860s, they turned their burros loose. The animals are descended from African burros, and many show the characteristic cross-shaped dark stripe across the shoulders and down their back; others have dark stripes on their legs. The burros are rounded up yearly, and many are taken to Kingman for adoption. It is necessary to keep their numbers in check as they compete with native bighorn sheep for food.

At the lower end of the trail, the settlement of Katherine Landing and the Katherine Mine both took their name from the sister of Kingman's Stanley C. Bagg. Bagg established the mine in 1920, and it was active until 1942, although after 1929 it had very limited production.

Description

The Portland Mine Road is one of a number of designated vehicle access trails within the Lake Mead Recreation Area. The long trail leaves from US 93, 3 miles south of the Pierce Ferry Road. Initially, it follows the wide, graded dirt Cottonwood Road that leads to several subdivisions. The turn is well marked from US 93.

After 8.1 miles, the trail turns off onto an ungraded, smaller trail. The trail leads down to Lost Cabin Wash; there is a well at the head of the wash. You will have the best chance of finding a shady campsite along this section of the trail as it passes through stands of juniper trees, Mohave yucca, and creosote bush.

Lost Cabin Wash, within the Black Mountains, is loose and gravelly, and the soil acts like sand, with the ability to bog down a vehicle. Your engine will work hard—in hot weather watch out for overheating. The trail continues in the wash, passing the currently unmarked turn for Jeep Cove (currently open to vehicles although this status may change), and then swings up the ridge to the Portland Mine. The road runs around the fenced perimeter of the mine before dropping to run along the equally gravelly Portland Wash.

As you exit the wash, you reach perhaps the best part of the trail as it runs along a ridge with views of Lake Mohave, the Eldorado and Newberry Mountains, and the Black Mountains. This is also the roughest part of the trail; it is loose, rutty, and washed out in places, especially on the many steep descents that cross through dry washes. In places these descents can be narrow, but currently, with a careful driver, even the widest vehicles can travel the road. However, conditions can change after every rainstorm. The road is not actively maintained; most of

Deep loose sand where the trail follows along in Lost Cabin Wash

the maintenance comes from trail users. If in doubt, walk the trail first. Many times, some minor work on the road will make it passable again and keep the trail open for other users in time to come.

There is very little shade along this trail, especially along the ridge tops in the recreation area. It can be uncomfortably hot in summer months. Winter is an excellent time to visit; temperatures are mild, it is easier to see wildlife, and there are very few visitors.

Vehicle-based camping within the Lake Mead National Recreation Area is allowed in designated primitive spots only.

Current Road Information

Bureau of Land Management
Kingman Field Office
2755 Mission Blvd.
Kingman, AZ 86401
(928) 718-3700

Lake Mead National Recreation Area
601 Nevada Way
Boulder City, NV 89005
(702) 293-8990

Map References

BLM   Davis Dam
USGS   1:24,000   Grasshopper Junction
       NW, Spirit Mtn. NE, Spirit Mtn.
       SE, Grasshopper Junction
       1:100,000 Davis Dam
Trails Illustrated, #204 Lake Mead National
       Recreation Area
Arizona Atlas & Gazetteer, pp. 22, 30
Arizona Road & Recreation Atlas, pp. 62, 54
Other: Lake Mead National Recreation
       Area Map

Route Directions

▼ 0.0   On US 93, 0.3 miles south of mile
         marker 45, zero trip meter and turn
         west across cattle guard onto graded
         dirt road at the sign for Cottonwood
         Road. Immediately track on left.
         Remain on the major graded dirt road,
         ignoring tracks on left and right, which
         lead mainly into subdivided lots.
8.1 ▲   Trail ends on US 93, 3 miles south of
         Pierce Ferry Road. Turn right for
         Kingman; turn left for Hoover Dam.
         GPS: N35°29.40′ W114°19.48′

Lost Cabin Well

A rutted section of the trail

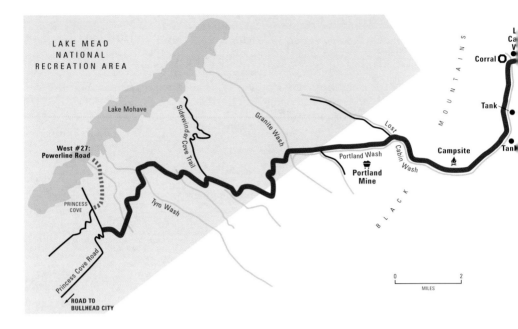

▼ 2.9   BR   Track on left is Cheryl Avenue; remain on the main Cottonwood Road.

5.2 ▲   SO   Track on right is Cheryl Avenue; remain on the main Cottonwood Road.

▼ 8.1   BL   Turn onto unmarked, graded dirt road, which heads southwest, initially staying close to Cottonwood Road. Zero trip meter.

0.0 ▲   Continue on Cottonwood Road toward US 93.

GPS: N35°29.45′ W114°28.39′

Portland Mine tailings along the trail

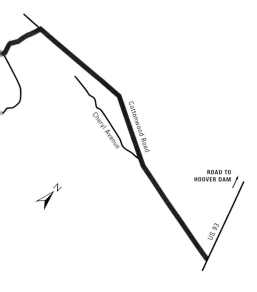

West Trail #26: Portland Mine Road

▼ 0.0   Continue on smaller trail. There are many small, shallow wash crossings for the next 3.2 miles.

3.2 ▲   SO   Turn onto wide graded road and zero trip meter.

▼ 1.4   SO   Track on right and track on left.

1.8 ▲   SO   Track on left and track on right.
       GPS: N35º28.29' W114º28.64'

▼ 3.1   SO   Track on right goes short distance to Lost Cabin Well; track on left.

0.1 ▲   SO   Track on right; track on left goes short distance to Lost Cabin Well.
       GPS: N35º27.06' W114º29.48'

▼ 3.2   TL   T-intersection. Track on right goes short distance to Lost Cabin Well. Zero trip meter.

0.0 ▲   Continue to the northeast away from the wash. There are many small, shallow wash crossings for the next 3.2 miles.
       GPS: N35º26.94' W114º29.51'

▼ 0.0   Continue to the southeast, traveling in Lost Cabin Wash. Corral on right.

6.5 ▲   TR   Corral on left; then track ahead goes short distance to Lost Cabin Well.

Swing right, out of Lost Cabin Wash.

▼ 0.1   SO   Pass through fence line.
6.4 ▲   SO   Pass through fence line.

▼ 1.5   SO   Tank on left.
5.0 ▲   SO   Tank on right.

▼ 2.1   SO   Tank on left.
4.4 ▲   SO   Tank on right.

▼ 4.0   SO   Campsite on right out of wash.
2.5 ▲   SO   Campsite on left out of wash.
       GPS: N35º24.19' W114º27.94'

▼ 4.5   SO   Small track on left.
2.0 ▲   SO   Small track on right.

▼ 6.0   SO   Trail enters narrow gap.
0.5 ▲   SO   Trail leaves narrow gap.
       GPS: N35º23.59' W114º29.76'

▼ 6.4   SO   Track on right continues down Lost Cabin Wash to Jeep Cove. Trail leaves Lost Cabin Wash and climbs up ridge.

0.1 ▲   SO   Track on left follows Lost Cabin Wash to Jeep Cove.

▼ 6.5   TR   Track straight on goes into Portland Mine. Zero trip meter.

0.0 ▲   Continue away from the mine and descend down the ridge to join Lost Cabin Wash.
       GPS: N35º23.25' W114º29.96'

▼ 0.0   Trail follows along the fence line marking the boundary of the Portland Mine on the left.

2.2 ▲   TL   T-intersection. Track on right goes into Portland Mine. Zero trip meter.

▼ 0.8   SO   Trail leaves fence line and enters Portland Wash.

1.4 ▲   SO   Exit Portland Wash and follow along the fence line marking the boundary of the Portland Mine on the left.

▼ 1.2   SO   Drill hole on left.
1.0 ▲   SO   Drill hole on right.

▼ 2.1   SO Track on left up wash.
0.1 ▲   SO Track on right up wash.
        GPS: N35°21.62′ W114°30.93′

▼ 2.2   SO Entering Lake Mead National
            Recreation Area on unimproved road.
            Zero trip meter.
0.0 ▲   Continue out of the Lake Mead
            National Recreation Area.
        GPS: N35°21.56′ W114°31.06′

▼ 0.0   Continue into Lake Mead National
            Recreation Area.
5.6 ▲   SO Leaving Lake Mead National
            Recreation Area. Zero trip meter.

▼ 0.7   BL Swing left out of wash and climb up
            ridge.
4.9 ▲   BR Descend ridge and enter Portland
            Wash.
        GPS: N35°21.07′ W114°31.56′

▼ 0.8   SO Cross through Granite Wash.
4.8 ▲   SO Cross through Granite Wash.

▼ 1.4   SO Descend from ridge-rutted, washed-
            out section.
4.2 ▲   SO Ascend ridge-rutted, washed-out sec-
            tion.

▼ 1.6   SO Cross through wash.
4.0 ▲   SO Cross through wash.

▼ 2.0   SO Cross through wash.
3.6 ▲   SO Cross through wash.

▼ 4.2   SO Cross through wash.
1.4 ▲   SO Cross through wash.

▼ 4.5   SO Enter wash.
1.1 ▲   SO Exit wash.

▼ 5.1   SO Exit wash; then washed-out climb
            from wash.
0.5 ▲   SO Washed-out descent; then enter wash.

▼ 5.6   SO Sidewinder Cove Trail on right
            descends to the lake. Zero trip meter.
0.0 ▲   Continue along ridge.
        GPS: N35°18.74′ W114°32.47′

▼ 0.0   Continue along ridge.
6.2 ▲   SO Sidewinder Cove Trail on left descends
            to the lake. Zero trip meter.

▼ 0.1   SO Small track on left.
6.1 ▲   SO Small track on right.

▼ 0.4   SO Old bulldozer line on right.
5.8 ▲   SO Old bulldozer line on left.
        GPS: N35°18.52′ W114°32.74′

▼ 0.7   SO Rutted descent around head of wash.
5.5 ▲   SO Rutted ascent around head of wash.

▼ 1.2   SO Cross through wash.
5.0 ▲   SO Cross through wash.

▼ 2.4   SO Cross through wash.
3.8 ▲   SO Cross through wash.

▼ 2.8   SO Start to cross wide Tyro Wash.
3.4 ▲   SO Exit Tyro Wash.
        GPS: N35°17.50′ W114°33.99′

▼ 3.0   SO Exit Tyro Wash.
3.2 ▲   SO Start to cross wide Tyro Wash.

▼ 3.8   SO Enter wash.
2.4 ▲   SO Exit wash.

▼ 4.0   SO Exit wash.
2.2 ▲   SO Enter wash.

▼ 4.5   SO Cross through wash.
1.7 ▲   SO Cross through wash.

▼ 4.7   SO Cross over wash.
1.5 ▲   SO Cross over wash.

▼ 4.8   SO Cross over wash.
1.4 ▲   SO Cross over wash.

▼ 5.2   SO Cross over wash.
1.0 ▲   SO Cross over wash.

▼ 5.5   SO Cross over wash.
0.7 ▲   SO Cross over wash.

▼ 5.6   SO Cross through wash.

0.6 ▲	SO	Cross through wash.
▼ 6.1	SO	Cross through wash.
0.1 ▲	SO	Cross through wash.
▼ 6.2		Trail ends at the junction with the major gravel road to Princess Cove. Turn left for Bullhead City; turn right for Princess Cove.
0.0 ▲		Trail starts at the junction with the major gravel road to Princess Cove, opposite mile marker 3. Road is signed to the Portland Mine Road, Recreation Road #5. Zero trip meter. **GPS: N35º15.79' W114º33.18'**

WEST REGION TRAIL #27

Powerline Road

STARTING POINT Princess Cove Road, 0.7 miles past mile marker 3
FINISHING POINT Lake Mohave
TOTAL MILEAGE 2.2 miles
UNPAVED MILEAGE 2.2 miles
DRIVING TIME 45 minutes (one-way)
ELEVATION RANGE 650–900 feet
USUALLY OPEN Year-round
BEST TIME TO TRAVEL Fall to spring
DIFFICULTY RATING 6
SCENIC RATING 8
REMOTENESS RATING +0

Special Attractions

■ Challenging trail for smaller stock vehicles.
■ Access to Lake Mohave.
■ Views of the Newberry Mountains.

Description

This road is not the complete track designated as Recreation Road #2. Although it is only the spur that gives access to the lake, it is the most interesting part of the trail. The trail begins on Princess Cove Road, 3.7 miles from the junction with the paved Katherine Landing–Cabinsite Point Road. It is one of a series of designated vehicle trails within the Lake Mead National Recreation Area; all are marked by yellow arrows and route numbers. The short, challenging trail winds down to a narrow point jutting out into Lake Mohave. You will have to share the view with a pylon, but it is still a magnificent point.

There is no shade along the trail or at the end, so it is extremely hot in summer. Just before the end of the trail, there is vehicle access to the water down a short wash that leads to a pleasant spot for a swim. The trail is narrow in places and subject to ruts and washouts. It is best suited for smaller vehicles; full-size trucks will find the tight turns and gullies difficult as will lower-clearance 4WDs or ones with side steps. Good wheel articulation is an advantage as several holes and ruts have to be negotiated. There are several moderately steep, loose descents to cross washes, and the low-traction surface makes tires with good grip essential.

Current Road Information

Lake Mead National Recreation Area
601 Nevada Way
Boulder City, NV 89005
(702) 293-8990

Map References

BLM   Davis Dam
USGS 1:24,000   Spirit Mtn. SE
          1:100,000 Davis Dam
Trails Illustrated, #204 Lake Mead National
     Recreation Area
Arizona Atlas & Gazetteer, p. 30
Arizona Road & Recreation Atlas, p. 62
Other: Lake Mead National Recreation
     Area Map

Route Directions

▼ 0.0	Trail begins on Princess Cove Road, 3.7 miles from the junction with the paved Katherine Landing–Cabinsite Point Road, 0.7 miles past mile marker 3. Zero trip meter and turn west at the sign for Powerline Road, Lake Mead Recreation Road #2. **GPS: N35º15.95' W114º33.88'**

The descent into the wash is rocky and rutted

The trail ends on a narrow peninsula jutting into Lake Mohave

▼ 0.1 BR Cross through wash. Track on left follows wash to lake.
▼ 0.2 BL Trail forks; track on right.
▼ 0.4 SO Tracks rejoin.
▼ 0.5 SO Cross over wash; the crossing is narrow and washing out.
▼ 0.7 SO Cross through wash.
▼ 0.9 TR Track continues ahead and goes 0.8 miles to a promontory over Lake Mohave. This route avoids the more difficult sections of the main trail.
  GPS: N35°16.35′ W114°34.13′

▼ 1.0 SO Track on left goes to pylon. Main trail has tricky off-camber descent with holes and a loose surface.
▼ 1.1 SO Cross through wash.
▼ 1.4 SO Track on left to pylon.
▼ 1.5 SO Track on left is easier route down to the wash. Main trail descends difficult section with large ruts. If the easier route is taken, swing right in the wash to rejoin the main trail.
  GPS: N35°16.61′ W114°34.63′

▼ 1.7 SO Cross through wash. Vehicles can

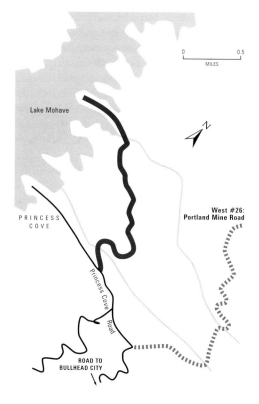

West Trail #27: Powerline Road

travel a short distance to the left
down the wash to the lake.
GPS: N35°16.66′ W114°34.70′

▼ 2.2   Trail ends on the promontory over
Lake Mohave.
GPS: N35°16.62′ W114°35.22′

Packsaddle Mountain Loop Trail

STARTING POINT US 93, 0.9 miles north of
mile marker 52
FINISHING POINT Chloride, 4.4 miles from US 93
TOTAL MILEAGE 16.5 miles
UNPAVED MILEAGE 16.5 miles
DRIVING TIME 2.5 hours
ELEVATION RANGE 3,600–6,300 feet
USUALLY OPEN Year-round
BEST TIME TO TRAVEL Fall to spring
DIFFICULTY RATING 2 to the Cherum Peak trail-
head, 4 from there to Chloride
SCENIC RATING 9
REMOTENESS RATING +0

Special Attractions

■ Chloride town site and many historic
mining remains.
■ Network of 4WD trails around Chloride,
leading to other mining remains.
■ Hiking trail to Cherum Peak.
■ Long, winding shelf road with panoramic
views.

History

From as early as the 1840s, men searched for
minerals in the mountains around Chloride.
However, the first real mention on paper
comes with the formation of the Chloride
Mining District in 1863. Miners traveled
from afar to these remote and rugged re-
gions to seek their fortunes. Even the last
stage of the trip—from Yuma, up the Colorado River to the site of Hardyville, now
submerged under water near Laughlin, and
the long desert trek through Hualapai country—was a feat in its own right.

Gaining its name from the silver chloride
that most were seeking, the town had its
own post office by 1870; but the real rush
came at the turn of the twentieth century.
This rush, which raised Chloride's population from 700 to 2,000, was the biggest Arizona had seen since Tombstone in 1879–
1880. The Butterfield Stagecoach operated
out of Chloride from 1868 to 1919. Near
the turn of the century, the Atchison, Tope-
ka & Santa Fe Railroad Company raced day
and night to build the connecting railroad
from nearby Kingman to Chloride. The railroad was in service until 1935. The Tennessee, Diana, Mollie Gibson, Merrimac,
and Elkhart Mines were shipping not only
silver but also gold, lead, copper, turquoise,
barium, and zinc to the processing plant. As
many as 75 mines were active between 1900
and 1920.

As in many mining communities across
the country, tales of fortunes gained and lost
were common in Chloride. One of interest
concerned Andy Flynn, a railroad brake-
man, cowboy, and prospector for 11 years.
The story was recounted in the *San Francisco Chronicle*. Having worked the nearby
White Hills silver mines and witnessed the
ore removed there, Andy staked his own
claim, the Mollie Gibson. With a borrowed
$50 he worked to find out what exactly he
had claimed. After six weeks he was out of
money and had insufficient food to continue his efforts. Desperate, Flynn walked to
Kingman after attempts to get additional
cash in Chloride failed. With no other options Andy went to work for the railroad
and was financially able to return to his diggings one month later. This time, after some
blasting, he was surprised to find a promis-
ing-looking ore body. Much to his disbelief
the ore was assayed at $600 a ton. Within
days he was offered $20,000 for his claim.
He scoffed at the offer, realizing he had
struck it rich. One month later he sold just
half his claim for $75,000 and continued to
extract ore at the rate of nearly $3,000 a
month.

Chloride was a distribution point for surrounding mines and ranches as far away as Eldorado Canyon. Various stores, the weekly *Arizona Arrow*, and more than a dozen saloons were all testimony to the town's success. The Tennessee Mine went through stages of success; a company invested in a flotation plant (set just below the mine) that was better than the previous one. By 1948 the Tennessee Mine had produced more than $7 million and was the deepest mine in Mohave County. When the mines finally ceased to produce in the late 1940s, Chloride was winding down as a town.

Never reaching the status of ghost town, Chloride has managed to attract enough residents who enjoy a relaxed approach to life and businesses that promote the colorful past in the few remaining buildings.

Visitors also come to Chloride to see the murals of Roy Purcell (see page 166), painted by the artist in the 1960s.

Description

The trail leaves US 93, 15.5 miles north of the junction with Arizona 68. The well-used dirt road initially follows alongside Big Wash, gradually climbing as it makes its way to the Cerbat Mountains. There are a few primitive campsites along this stretch, set within the juniper, Mohave yucca, and cactus. Six miles from the start, the trail starts to climb in earnest, switchbacking its way up the side of the range. This long section of shelf road is usually wide enough for two vehicles to pass easily. The trail is graded, but it can be rough in spots. All along the fairly steep climb, there are views back along Big Wash and then higher up over Detrital Valley to the Black Mountains. Near the Packsaddle Recreation Area, there is a distant view across the Hualapai Valley to the Music Mountains.

The small Packsaddle Recreation Area is reached in 8 miles. It has three small sites—each equipped with a picnic table and fire ring. There is a pit toilet but no water. The walk-in sites can accommodate only small tents, and they are more sheltered than those at Windy Point Recreation Area, 1.3 miles farther along.

From Packsaddle the trail runs along the

Big Wash lies below the shelf road on Packsaddle Mountain

ridge top, through jumbled boulders and windswept vegetation. There are views to Chloride, 2,000 feet below. The Windy Point Recreation Area has some lovely campsites with great views west over Detrital Valley. These seven sites are more exposed than the ones at Packsaddle. Most of them are only large enough for small tents, although there are a couple of larger ones. A fee is charged for camping. The sites have picnic tables and fire rings but no water.

Two miles farther, the hiking trailhead to Cherum Peak is reached, and the BLM's trail maintenance ends. At this point 2WD vehicles should turn around and return to US 93. High-clearance 4WDs can continue to Chloride. The trail descends a series of switchbacks, which run along a single-lane shelf road; the road has a rougher, looser surface and steeper grade than the ascent from Big Wash. There are limited passing places.

The trail passes the turnoffs first to the Samoa Mine and then to the Rainbow Mine, with its wooden chute. It then passes directly by the tailings, adits, tramway, and loading hopper of an unnamed mine.

The road passes other turns to mining remains before passing by the rock paintings done by Roy Purcell. Directly beside the trail, these distinctive murals are impossible to miss. A sign on the rocks says, "The Journey, Images from an inner search for self." The trail standard improves from this point to enable passenger vehicles access to the murals. Tracks on the right and left lead to some of Chloride's famous mines.

The trail ends on the eastern edge of Chloride, at the start of the paved road. Continue into town to explore some of the shops that sell antiques, memorabilia, and rocks and to visit the saloon or cafe. There are many interesting old buildings to photograph.

The end of the trail is marked CR 125 to Chloride, which is 13.5 miles from the junction with Arizona 68.

An off-camber section of the trail

Roy Purcell's murals from the 1960s

Current Road Information

Bureau of Land Management
Kingman Field Office
2755 Mission Blvd.
Kingman, AZ 86401
(928) 718-3700

Map References

BLM   Davis Dam
USGS   1:24,000   Grasshopper Junction,
        Chloride
        1:100,000 Davis Dam
Arizona Atlas & Gazetteer, p. 22
Arizona Road & Recreation Atlas, pp. 54, 55
Recreational Map of Arizona

Route Directions

▼ 0.0   Trail commences on US 93, 15.5 miles
         north of the junction with Arizona 68,
         0.9 miles north of mile marker 52. Zero
         trip meter and turn northeast on grad-
         ed dirt road at the sign for Big Wash
         Road. Immediately cross cattle guard.
8.4 ▲   Trail ends on US 93. Turn right for

Hoover Dam; turn left for Kingman.
        GPS: N35°25.06' W114°16.38'

▼ 0.2   SO Track on left.
8.2 ▲   SO Track on right.

▼ 0.4   SO Track on left.
8.0 ▲   SO Track on right.

▼ 0.9   SO Track on left goes to corral and tank.
7.5 ▲   SO Track on right goes to corral and tank.

▼ 1.4   SO Track on right.
7.0 ▲   SO Track on left.

▼ 2.3   SO Track on right.
6.1 ▲   SO Track on left.

▼ 3.0   SO Track on right.
5.4 ▲   SO Track on left.

▼ 3.2   SO Cattle guard.
5.2 ▲   SO Cattle guard.
         GPS: N35°27.08' W114°13.84'

▼ 3.4   SO Track on right goes to well.

West Trail #28: Packsaddle Mountain Loop Trail

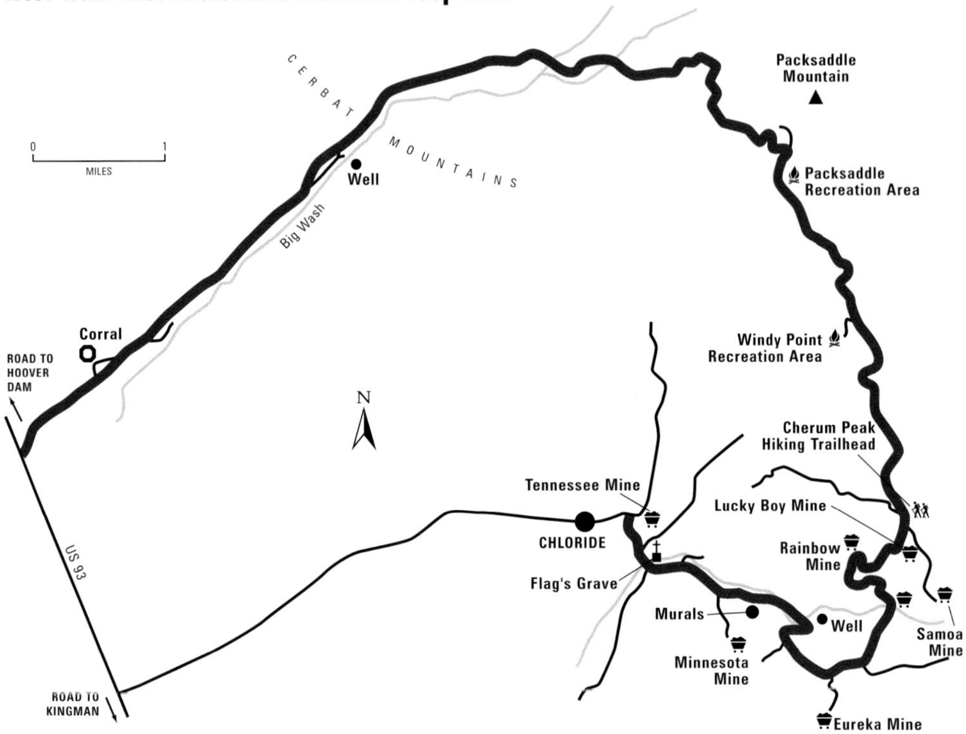

CERBAT MOUNTAINS

Packsaddle Mountain ▲

0 ___ 1
MILES

Well

Big Wash

🔥 Packsaddle Recreation Area

Corral
ROAD TO HOOVER DAM

Windy Point 🔥 Recreation Area

N

Cherum Peak Hiking Trailhead

Tennessee Mine

Lucky Boy Mine

CHLORIDE

Rainbow Mine

US 93

Flag's Grave

Murals

Well

Samoa Mine

ROAD TO KINGMAN

Minnesota Mine

🔥 Eureka Mine

5.0 ▲ SO Track on left goes to well.

▼ 3.5 SO Track on right.
4.9 ▲ SO Track on left.

▼ 4.0 SO Track on right.
4.4 ▲ SO Track on left.

▼ 4.2 SO Track on right.
4.2 ▲ SO Track on left.

▼ 4.9 SO Campsite on right.
3.5 ▲ SO Campsite on left.

▼ 5.0 SO Track on right.
3.4 ▲ SO Track on left.

▼ 5.2 SO Cross over wash; trail starts to climb.
3.2 ▲ SO Cross over wash.

▼ 5.6 SO Cross over wash; then campsite on right.
2.8 ▲ SO Campsite on left; then cross over wash.

▼ 6.2 SO Start of switchbacks and wide shelf road.

2.2 ▲ SO End of switchbacks and shelf road.

▼ 7.3 SO Cattle guard. Views over Detrital Wash to the Black Mountains.
1.1 ▲ SO Cattle guard. Views over Detrital Wash to the Black Mountains.

▼ 8.0 SO Track on left. Views to the left over the Hualapai Valley to the Music Mountains.
0.4 ▲ SO Track on right. Views to the right over the Hualapai Valley to the Music Mountains and views ahead down Big Wash.

▼ 8.4 SO Packsaddle Recreation Site on right and left. Zero trip meter at sign.
0.0 ▲   Continue toward Big Wash. Start of switchbacks and shelf road.
            GPS: N35°27.13′ W114°10.15′

▼ 0.0   Trail starts to descend. Views on right to Chloride.
1.3 ▲ SO Packsaddle Recreation Site on left and right. Zero trip meter at sign.

▼ 1.3   SO   Track on right goes to Windy Point Recreation Site. Zero trip meter.

0.0 ▲   Continue toward Packsaddle Recreation Site.

        GPS: N35°26.23' W114°09.46'

▼ 0.0   Continue to the southeast along the top of the ridge.

1.8 ▲   SO   Track on left goes to Windy Point Recreation Site. Zero trip meter.

▼ 0.9   BL   Track on right goes to radio tower; gate at bottom.

0.9 ▲   SO   Track on left goes to radio tower; gate at bottom.

        GPS: N35°25.62' W114°09.24'

▼ 1.5   SO   Diggings immediately below the track on right, and remains of small cabin down in the valley.

0.3 ▲   SO   Diggings immediately below the track on the left, and remains of small cabin down in the valley.

        GPS: N35°25.13' W114°09.13'

▼ 1.8   SO   Track on right; end of BLM road maintenance. 4WD road ahead; other vehi-

cles turn here. Parking area on right. Zero trip meter.

0.0 ▲   Continue on graded dirt road; parking area on left.

        GPS: N35°24.99' W114°08.99'

▼ 0.0   BR   Continue on smaller trail. Cherum Peak hiking trail on left. Also vehicle trail on left goes to the Samoa Mine. Diggings of the Lucky Boy Mine are immediately below the road on the left. Trail standard drops and is looser and more roughly graded and starts to switch back down a narrow shelf road.

2.4 ▲   SO   End of climb. Diggings of the Lucky Boy Mine are immediately below the road on the right. Vehicle trail on right goes to the Samoa Mine; then Cherum Peak hiking trail on right. Start of BLM maintained road.

▼ 0.8   BL   Track on right goes short distance into Rainbow Mine. Wooden chute remains.

1.6 ▲   BR   Track on left goes short distance into Rainbow Mine. Wooden chute remains.

        GPS: N35°24.71' W114°09.40'

The remains of an old mine tramway along the trail

ROY PURCELL AND HIS MURALS

A tall, wiry, red-haired boy named Roy Purcell was born in 1936. He grew up in Utah and worked as a miner while studying for his masters degree in creative writing and fine arts at Utah State University. During that time, he was inspired to paint a giant mural upon the face of the Cerbat Mountains, near the small town of Chloride, Arizona. Chloride had been a successful mining town around the turn of the twentieth century, but it experienced severe decline when the mines closed in the 1940s. During the summer of 1966, Purcell lived in a cave while he worked on this gigantic 2,000 square-foot exercise of abstract Modernism. The mural, titled "The Journey," brought Purcell to national attention and now draws visitors from around the world to the remote location. He also completed several other somewhat odd, but provocative murals.

Purcell's murals

The attention gained from these murals resulted in Purcell receiving a commission from the Kingman Museum. After the project was completed, Purcell became the director of the Mojave Museum of History and Arts where he started working with the medium for which he has become best known: etching. Next, he worked as director of the Southern Nevada Museum for four years before establishing himself as a free-lance artist.

Purcell has maintained his passion for large-scale projects and his fascination with mankind's major historical and cultural journeys. Through his art he has portrayed the life of Christ, Moses and the Exodus, and the Mormon migration to Utah. His other subjects have included Western themes, desert images, world wildlife, and the legacy of the American Indian. Purcell returned to Chloride in 1976 to touch up the murals, which are currently one of the town's biggest attractions.

▼ 1.2   SO   Gate.
1.2 ▲   SO   Gate.

▼ 1.4   SO   Pass by the remains of mine. Tailings, tramway, and loading chute on left.
1.0 ▲   SO   Pass by the remains of mine. Tailings, tramway, and loading chute on right.
         GPS: N35°24.46′ W114°09.07′

▼ 1.5   SO   Track on left goes into mine. Concrete foundations on right.
0.9 ▲   SO   Track on right goes into mine. Concrete foundations on left.

▼ 2.1   SO   Faint track on left.
0.3 ▲   BL   Faint track on right.

▼ 2.2   SO   Faint track on right.
0.2 ▲   SO   Faint track on left.

▼ 2.4   BR   Track on left goes to Eureka Mine. Zero trip meter.
0.0 ▲   Continue toward the top of the ridge.
         GPS: N35°23.96′ W114°09.60′

▼ 0.0   Continue toward Chloride.
2.6 ▲   BL   Track on right goes to Eureka Mine. Zero trip meter.

▼ 0.4   SO   Track on left.
2.2 ▲   BL   Track on right.

▼ 0.7   SO   Cross through wash. Falls on right.
1.9 ▲   SO   Cross through wash. Falls on left.
         GPS: N35°24.28′ W114°09.78′

▼ 1.0   SO   Faint track on right alongside tailings; then cross through wash.
1.6 ▲   SO   Cross through wash; then faint track on left alongside tailings.

▼ 1.4	SO	Roy Purcell's murals on the rocks on the left. Trail standard improves at this point and is graded—suitable for passenger vehicles.
1.2 ▲	SO	Roy Purcell's murals on the rocks on the right. Trail standard is 4WD only from this point.
		GPS: N35°24.48′ W114°10.25′
▼ 1.5	SO	Small track on right; then small track on left.
1.1 ▲	SO	Small track on right; then small track on left.
▼ 1.6	BR	Track on left goes to the Minnesota Mine.
1.0 ▲	BL	Track on right is to the Minnesota Mine.
▼ 1.9	SO	Track on right.
0.7 ▲	SO	Track on left.
▼ 2.1	SO	Track on left; then cross through wash.
0.5 ▲	SO	Cross through wash; then track on right.
▼ 2.3	SO	Track on right. Flag's Grave at the start: "Good ole dog, 1991–1998."
0.3 ▲	SO	Track on left. Flag's Grave at the start: "Good ole dog, 1991–1998."
		GPS: N35°24.72′ W114°11.15′
▼ 2.5	TL	T-intersection with larger graded road. Track on right goes to the Tennessee Mine. Turn left and cross through wash.
0.1 ▲	TR	Cross through wash; then turn from the larger graded road onto a smaller one. Turn is at the painted boulder with directional arrow to the murals.
		GPS: N35°24.88′ W114°11.23′
▼ 2.6		Trail ends on the edge of Chloride where the paved road begins. Continue through Chloride to US 93.
0.0 ▲		Trail starts at the eastern end of the paved main street in Chloride, 4.4 miles from US 93. Cross cattle guard and zero trip meter. Continue on the graded dirt road to the east past the information sign for the Tennessee Schuylkill Mine.
		GPS: N35°24.92′ W114°11.35′

White Hills Trail

STARTING POINT US 93, 0.4 miles north of mile marker 29
FINISHING POINT Pierce Ferry Road (Mohave CR 25)
TOTAL MILEAGE 22.2 miles
UNPAVED MILEAGE 16.9 miles
DRIVING TIME 1.75 hours
ELEVATION RANGE 2,400–4,900 feet
USUALLY OPEN Year-round
BEST TIME TO TRAVEL Fall to spring
DIFFICULTY RATING 3
SCENIC RATING 7
REMOTENESS RATING +1

Special Attractions

■ Historic sites of White Hills and Cyclopic.
■ Joshua tree forest.
■ Views of Hualapai Valley and the White Hills.

History

Long before White Hills was a flourishing mining camp, local Hualapai Indians would scour the region for the iron oxide, which they used to make paint. In 1887, an Indian known as Hualapai Jeff was searching the White Hills area when he came across a sample of silver chloride. He kept the ore, and when he was next in town, he asked about the value of his find. He was told it was worthless iron, so he discarded it.

In the winter of 1891, a rancher named Frank Robinson asked Hualapai Jeff to help him round up some cattle that had strayed over to White Hills in a snowstorm. The men camped near the spot where Jeff had found the silver. Once again Jeff picked up a good specimen. This time he kept it. Shortly after, Judge Henry Schaffer asked him if he knew of any good mineral deposits and Jeff showed him his find. Recognizing nearly pure silver, the judge offered Jeff $200 (a large sum of money at the time) if he would show him the location of the deposits.

Joshua trees beside the trail warmed by the late afternoon sun

In 1892, Jeff led the judge's party of John Barnett and John Sullivan to the White Hills location, where they staked the claims that would become a number of mines: the Horn Silver, the Occident, the Grand Army, the Chief of the Hills, the Treasurer, the Norma, and the Emma. A separate party led by rancher John Robinson arrived 10 days later and also staked claims.

The news traveled rapidly and within two weeks of the find there was a small town of 200 people, with a store, four saloons, three restaurants, and a large number of tents. The demand for lots was so great that would-be residents had to claim their land by sleeping on it. With no permanent housing, many a miner woke up in the company of rattlesnakes that had crawled under the bedding in the night.

The town, set on the edge of the Detrital Valley, grew rapidly and soon had a population of 1,500. The first post office was opened in 1892 by a man named Taggart, who gave the town its official name of White Hills, after the exposed rock of the region.

Many of the initial claims of the judge's party were not immediately worked, and in 1893, all the claims except the Treasurer and the Emma were sold to a consortium from Colorado. This proved a good move for the town, and by 1895, it boasted running water, electricity, and flush toilets. The town was a law abiding one, with a wide main street lined on both sides with businesses. The biggest problem for the population was the scarcity of water, which sold for a dollar a barrel.

White Hills had a very concentrated number of profitable mines in its relatively small area. The ore quality varied, but the consortium's Grand Army Mine produced ore that assayed at 3,000 ounces of silver and 10 ounces of gold per ton. Other profitable mines were the Horn Silver and the Occident.

On the morning of August 5, 1889, the town was swept away in a flash flood caused by heavy rain. Men working in the Grand Army Extension Mine escaped just in time, as the rising waters filled the mine. The schoolhouse and many houses were swept away, and two feet of soil was deposited on the streets of the town. The local paper, *The*

Mohave County Miner, reported the flood. One sentence of its story said, "We might call their affair too much of a good thing. For water sells at one dollar a barrel at White Hills. They just had a million dollar bath."

The town never really recovered; many residents moved themselves and their houses to nearby Chloride. A few miners remained and extracted a fair living from the mines. There have been various attempts to reopen the mines over the years, although most of them were short-lived.

The small settlement of Cyclopic, located at the far end of the trail, was never as large as White Hills. It was established in the early 1890s by three prospectors, Robert Patterson, Sol Rowe, and a man named Glenn. In 1896 they leased the site to a company from Seattle that continued to work it profitably for many years. Unlike White Hills, where silver was the predominate ore, Cyclopic was known for gold. One of the early miners,

Stanley Bagg, named the town after the Cyclops, a mythological one-eyed giant. A post office was established in 1905, and the town and mine continued until 1917.

Description

The White Hills Road is signposted from US 93 at the small settlement of Boulder Inn. There is a crossover on the divided highway at this point. The initially paved road runs in a plumb line across the Detrital Valley toward the White Hills. The settlement of White Hills was located on the western edge of the White Hills. Today it can be found on either side of the road that runs through the subdivision. Most of the site is privately owned. Please respect the landowners' wishes and stay on the road. There is little left to see in any case—mine diggings, tailings piles, adits, and a few pieces of rusted mine equipment.

The trail runs through the subdivision on a wide gravel road. There are many turns to

An old truck abandoned at a corral near the end of the trail

A washed out section of the trail as it climbs the ridge

the right and left on this first part of the route; most of them lead to private property. Remain on the major graded road until it finishes at a T-intersection marked Cyclopic Boulevard. Turn left and travel through the subdivision to the end, at which point the trail starts in earnest, climbing up a rise on a rough, single-track trail.

Immediately, you will see Joshua trees and be treated to wide-ranging Mohave Desert views as the rough track undulates across the western slope of the White Hills. The trail joins a wash and enters the White Hills before leaving the wash at a corral and starting to climb up the ridge.

There are many trails leading off the main trail; most are small but others can look like the main trail, which can make finding the route somewhat confusing. A GPS unit is an asset in picking the correct route. The road surface deteriorates as the trail climbs up on the ridge heading toward the mining settlement of Cyclopic. It can be severely washed out, which can make travel harder for wide vehicles; but it should be passable. The trail descends to Cyclopic, where an old water tank marks the northernmost boundary of the settlement. Little is left in Cyclopic—extensive diggings, tailings heaps, water tanks, and some concrete foundations.

Once past Cyclopic, the trail gradually improves in standard as it passes alongside Table Mountain Plateau and Archibald Corral. The trail ends at the paved Pierce Ferry Road. From here it is 16.2 miles to US 93.

The trail offers some excellent views across the Hualapai Valley to Garnet Mountain. The Mohave Desert vegetation, dense Joshua tree forest, and historic mining sites add interest to a trip in this seldom-traveled region. The naturally gravelly, loose trail is easily traveled by stock vehicles, although future washouts may render the trail more difficult.

Current Road Information

Bureau of Land Management
Kingman Field Office
2755 Mission Blvd.
Kingman, AZ 86401
(928) 718-3700

Map References

BLM   Boulder City
USGS 1:24,000   White Hills West, White Hills East, Senator Mtn., Gold Basin, Mt. Tipton NW
       1:100,000 Boulder City
Arizona Atlas & Gazetteer, p. 22
Arizona Road & Recreation Atlas, pp. 54, 55 (incomplete)
Recreational Map of Arizona (incomplete)

Route Directions

▼ 0.0   From US 93, 0.4 miles north of mile marker 29, just south of Boulder Inn, turn east on White Hills Road at the sign. Information board and historical marker at the turn. Zero trip meter. Remain on the paved road, ignoring small tracks on left and right.

8.8 ▲   Trail ends at US 93 immediately south of Boulder Inn. Turn right for Hoover Dam; turn left for Kingman.
       GPS: N35°41.99′ W114°28.43′

▼ 5.3   SO Road turns to wide, graded dirt road. The site of White Hills is to the north of the road, with some mines on the south side of the road. Continue straight on the major dirt road, ignoring the tracks on left and right, which lead to houses. Continue straight on until the trail reaches a T-intersection.

3.5 ▲   SO The site of White Hills is to the north of the road, immediately before the point where the road becomes paved. Mining sites are on either side of the road.

▼ 8.8   TL T-intersection of White Hills Road and Cyclopic Blvd. (signs for both roads). Turn left onto Cyclopic Blvd. Small track continues ahead. Zero trip meter.

0.0 ▲   Continue through the subdivision; remain on main trail, ignoring tracks on right and left that lead to houses.
       GPS: N35°44.01′ W114°19.10′

▼ 0.0   Continue north on Cyclopic Blvd.

0.8 ▲   TR Turn onto the major dirt White Hills Road, marked with a street sign. Zero

West Trail #29: White Hills Trail

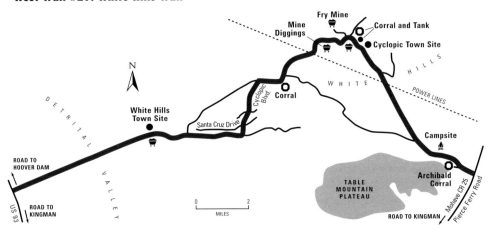

trip meter.

▼ 0.1   SO Rolling Ridge Drive on right.
0.7 ▲   SO Rolling Ridge Drive on left.

▼ 0.3   SO Santa Cruz Drive on left and right.
0.5 ▲   SO Santa Cruz Drive on left and right.

▼ 0.4   SO Cross through wash; followed by
                Escondido Drive on right and left.
0.4 ▲   SO Escondido Drive on right and left; then
                cross through wash.
                GPS: N35°44.36′ W114°19.07′

▼ 0.8   SO Crossroads. Zero trip meter.
0.0 ▲   Continue on wider graded road through
                housing subdivision.
                GPS: N35°44.70′ W114°18.87′

▼ 0.0   Continue on narrower trail and climb up hill.
1.3 ▲   SO Crossroads. Zero trip meter.

▼ 0.1   SO Cross through wash.
1.2 ▲   SO Cross through wash.

▼ 0.2   SO Cross through wash.
1.1 ▲   SO Cross through wash.

▼ 0.3   SO Faint track on right.
1.0 ▲   SO Faint track on left.

▼ 0.6   SO Cross through wash.
0.7 ▲   SO Cross through wash.

▼ 0.8   SO Cross through wash.
0.5 ▲   SO Cross through wash.

▼ 1.0   SO Enter wash channel.
0.3 ▲   SO Exit wash channel.
                GPS: N35°45.62′ W114°18.64′

▼ 1.3   TR Crossroads with slightly wider trail.
                Take the first right. Zero trip meter.
0.0 ▲   Continue on narrower trail.
                GPS: N35°45.75′ W114°18.50′

▼ 0.0   Continue to the northeast.
2.4 ▲   TL Crossroads with narrower trail. Take
                the first left and zero trip meter.

▼ 0.5   SO Track along wash rejoins. Continue in wash.
1.9 ▲   BL Track forks; right-hand track travels in
                the wash.

▼ 0.8   BL Swing left out of wash; corral on right.
1.6 ▲   BR Join the wash; corral on left.

▼ 1.0   SO Cross through wash; then track on right.
1.4 ▲   SO Track on left; then cross through wash.
                GPS: N35°45.93′ W114°17.59′

▼ 1.2   SO Cross through wash.
1.2 ▲   SO Cross through wash.

▼ 1.4   SO Pass through fence line.
1.0 ▲   SO Pass through fence line.

▼ 1.8 SO Cross through wash.
0.6 ▲ SO Cross through wash.

▼ 2.0 SO Track on left.
0.4 ▲ SO Track on right.
GPS: N35°46.55′ W114°17.00′

▼ 2.4 BR Large track on left along power lines. Bear right and follow power lines. Zero trip meter.
0.0 ▲ Continue away from the power lines.
GPS: N35°46.66′ W114°16.55′

▼ 0.0 Continue along power lines.
2.0 ▲ BL Wide track continues on right along power lines. Bear left away from power lines. Zero trip meter.

▼ 0.1 BL Track on right at pylon.
1.9 ▲ BR Track on left at pylon.

▼ 0.2 BL Track on right up wash; bear left and start to climb up ridge.
1.8 ▲ SO Bottom of ridge; track on left up wash.

▼ 0.7 SO Crossroads on saddle. Track on right leads toward old mine diggings.
1.3 ▲ SO Crossroads on saddle. Track on left leads to old mine diggings. Trail now descends from ridge.
GPS: N35°47.02′ W114°16.10′

▼ 1.0 SO Mine diggings on right.
1.0 ▲ SO Mine diggings on left.
GPS: N35°47.03′ W114°15.93′

▼ 1.1 SO Track on right goes to a viewpoint over diggings and a network of small trails around them.
0.9 ▲ SO Track on left goes to a viewpoint over diggings and a network of small trails around them.
GPS: N35°47.05′ W114°15.84′

▼ 1.6 BL Swing away from wash. Track on right goes to more diggings.
0.4 ▲ BR Track on left goes to more diggings. Follow line of wash.
GPS: N35°47.02′ W114°15.24′

▼ 1.7 SO Track on right.
0.3 ▲ SO Track on left.

▼ 1.9 TR T-intersection. Track on left to Fry Mine.
0.1 ▲ TL Track straight on goes to Fry Mine.
GPS: N35°47.21′ W114°15.05′

▼ 2.0 TR Track on left. Old water tank and corral at T-intersection. Zero trip meter.
0.0 ▲ Continue away from Cyclopic.
GPS: N35°47.21′ W114°14.99′

▼ 0.0 Continue toward Cyclopic.
2.1 ▲ TL Old water tank and corral at junction. Zero trip meter.

▼ 0.1 SO Track on right into diggings. Trail is now traveling through the old diggings of Cyclopic. Numerous tracks on right and left into the various diggings.
2.0 ▲ SO Track on left into diggings.

▼ 0.4 SO Concrete foundations on right.
1.7 ▲ SO Concrete foundations on left. Trail is now traveling through the old diggings of Cyclopic. Numerous tracks on right and left into various diggings.

▼ 0.6 SO Cross through wash.
1.5 ▲ SO Cross through wash.

▼ 0.7 SO Cross through wash. Track on right up wash.
1.4 ▲ SO Cross through wash. Track on left up wash.
GPS: N35°46.74′ W114°14.43′

▼ 1.5 SO Track on right.
0.6 ▲ SO Track on left.

▼ 1.7 SO Cross through wash; then track on left.
0.4 ▲ SO Track on right; then cross through wash.
GPS: N35°46.12′ W114°13.65′

▼ 2.1 SO Crossroads under power lines. Zero trip meter.
0.0 ▲ Continue toward Cyclopic.
GPS: N35°45.78′ W114°13.48′

▼ 0.0 Continue toward Pierce Ferry Road. Numerous small wash crossings for next 4.8 miles.

4.8 ▲	SO	Crossroads under power lines. Zero trip meter.
▼ 2.2	SO	Pass through fence line.
2.6 ▲	SO	Pass through fence line.
▼ 2.3	SO	Track on right goes to Butcher Camp. Main trail is now roughly graded.
2.5 ▲	SO	Track on left goes to Butcher Camp. Main trail is now a lesser standard. **GPS: N35°44.04' W114°12.06'**
▼ 2.8	SO	Track on right. Trail now follows along with Table Mountain Plateau on the right.
2.0 ▲	BR	Track on left. Trail leaves Table Mountain Plateau. **GPS: N35°43.64' W114°11.70'**
▼ 3.4	SO	Campsite on left.
1.4 ▲	SO	Campsite on right.
▼ 4.0	SO	Track on left.
0.8 ▲	SO	Track on right.
▼ 4.1	SO	Track on right to Archibald Corral.
0.7 ▲	SO	Track on left to Archibald Corral.
▼ 4.2	SO	Pass through fence line.
0.6 ▲	SO	Pass through fence line. Archibald Corral on left.
▼ 4.3	BL	Track on right to Archibald Corral; then second track on right. Looking ahead at Cerbat Mountains to the south.
0.5 ▲	BR	Track on left; then second track on left to Archibald Corral.
▼ 4.8		Trail ends at the paved Pierce Ferry Road (Mohave CR 25). Turn right for Kingman.
0.0 ▲		Trail starts on the paved Pierce Ferry Road, immediately north of mile marker 17, 16.2 miles from the junction with US 93. Turn northwest on narrow, roughly graded dirt road and zero trip meter. Numerous wash crossings for next 4.8 miles. Table Mountain Plateau is on the left. **GPS: N35°42.99' W114°09.73'**

Eldorado Jeep Trail

STARTING POINT US 93, 0.1 miles south of mile marker 20
FINISHING POINT Colorado River
TOTAL MILEAGE 13 miles
UNPAVED MILEAGE 13 miles
DRIVING TIME 1 hour (one-way)
ELEVATION RANGE 700–3,100 feet
USUALLY OPEN Year-round
BEST TIME TO TRAVEL Fall to spring
DIFFICULTY RATING 3
SCENIC RATING 7
REMOTENESS RATING +1

Special Attractions

■ Old gold, silver, and copper mining remains.
■ Colorado River access and camping in the Lake Mead National Recreation Area.
■ Chance to see bighorn sheep and wild burros.

History

The Eldorado Jeep Trail runs down a canyon that is unnamed on the topographic maps of the region. It likely takes its name from the Eldorado Mountains on the far side of the Colorado River in Nevada. Eldorado Canyon, a well-known gold and silver mining area, exits to the Colorado River immediately south of the end of this trail on the Nevada side.

The trail's exit to the Colorado River may be near the site of the Eldorado Camp, a short-lived army camp that existed as a military outpost for a few months in 1867. The camp, which was located on the west side of the Colorado River, just north of Eldorado Canyon, was founded to protect the miners in Eldorado Canyon from Indian attacks and to assist in the safe passage of steamboats upstream to Utah. However, when the first soldiers arrived to establish the camp on January 1, 1867, they found no steamboats, only three miners, and a few scattered peaceful Paiute. But orders were orders, so the troops constructed the outpost and sat back to wait

THE HOOVER DAM

A testament to human ingenuity, engineering, and endurance stands on the Arizona-Nevada border in Black Canyon—the Hoover Dam. On September 30, 1930, while the depression devastated lives and sank the economy, the construction of Hoover Dam began. Work was hard to come by and many Americans were hungry and jobless. When word spread about the dam, workers came from all over the country seeking employment. Boulder City, Nevada, was created in order to house employees and their families, and it is estimated that the city accommodated more than 4,000 workers during construction of the dam. In order to build the dam, the mighty Colorado had to be diverted from the construction site. Four tunnels, 50 feet in diameter, were drilled through the canyon walls. For added support, the tunnels were then lined with concrete. In 1932, the Colorado's course changed as it spilled through these man-made openings. The holes were closed when the dam was completed, but only after the Colorado River had flowed through the diversion tunnels for two years.

Hoover Dam

The construction of the dam was no easy task. In the summer, workers had to endure temperatures above 100°F; in the winter, frigid temperatures plagued the hardy workers. The job was dangerous. One particularly unnerving job was performed by the high-scalers. These men rappelled down the canyon walls to chip away loose rock. They were agile and unafraid of being dangled by a slim rope over a deep crevice. Daredevils were drawn to this job and soon contests arose about who could swing out the highest, the farthest, and who could perform the best stunts. The high-scalers were not the only ones at risk. Ninety-six people lost their lives during the dam's construction. Rocks or dropped tools falling from above would often end the life of a worker. In the face of this danger, the men began to improvise. They coated cloth hats with coal tar, creating crude but effective hard hats.

As time passed, the dam rose. The dam is, in fact, not a giant block of concrete. Individual columns, trapezoidal in shape, make up the dam. The shape allowed the heat to dissipate as the concrete cooled. Concrete was first poured on June 6, 1933. By the dam's completion there were 3.25 million cubic yards in place. This amount of concrete could pave a highway 16-feet wide from San Francisco to New York City. On May 29, 1935, the last concrete was poured. Turbines were then installed to use the river's waters to generate electricity. Today, 17 turbines are housed in the Hoover power plant. They produce a maximum of 10,348,020,500 kilowatt-hours a year. Most of this power, about 56 percent, goes to southern California. Arizona receives 19 percent and Nevada gets 25 percent.

Lake Mead was formed by Hoover Dam. When full, it contains roughly 31,250,000 acre-feet of water (two years worth of flow from the Colorado River), has a shoreline of more than 550 miles, and covers an area of about 227 square miles. It is the largest man-made lake in the world, twice the size of Rhode Island. More than 6 million people visit the lake yearly. The waters are used for boating, water skiing, swimming, and fishing. The surrounding Lake Mead National Recreation Area contains several enjoyable backcountry trails.

The trail follows the wash through a gap in the Black Mountains

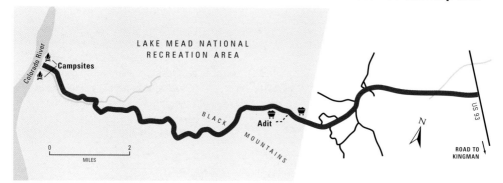

for further instructions. They were eventually recalled seven months later.

Description

This trail leads off from the southbound lane of the main divided US 93, 0.9 miles south of the signed Temple Bar Road. The junction is unmarked, but it is 0.1 miles south of mile marker 20. There is an informal crossing of the divided highway for vehicles traveling north. The trail immediately leads away from the highway. It travels through BLM land for the first stretch as it follows along the wash line, sometimes traveling in the wash. The vegetation is sparse—mainly creosote bush and tall Mohave yuccas.

The trail leads toward the Black Mountains and for the first 3.2 miles is fairly wide and easy. It then turns off onto a smaller, single-lane trail, marked as the Eldorado Jeep Trail. Trails open for vehicle travel within the national recreation area are marked with a route number and yellow arrow. Travel on unmarked trails is not permitted. The trail now gradually descends toward Lake Mohave, twisting through the Black Mountains.

The remains of some old mines can be seen. They have been unused for a long time. Sharp-eyed travelers should watch for bighorn sheep on the cliffs, especially in the early mornings and evenings. Somewhat easier to spot are the small herds of wild burros that roam the area around Lake Mohave.

Vehicle-based camping is restricted to designated primitive sites in the Lake Mead National Recreation Area. The only camping area along this trail is at the very end. As the trail continues to descend through the recreation area, there are views over Lake Mohave to the Eldorado Mountains on the far side. The trail ends at a designated primitive camping area (currently no fee) on the Colorado River. There are no facilities—only two or three small sites set within the tamarisks in the wash. Do not camp here if there is any danger of flash flooding. There are many fish to be caught in Lake Mohave, including large-mouth bass, rainbow trout, bullhead catfish, crappie, and bluegill.

The trail surface is gravelly, loose, and similar to sand in how it affects vehicles, which will tend to bog down in the deep, loose areas of the washes. In the hot summer air, watch engine temperatures when you climb back up the trail. On the return trip, 4WD will be necessary for traction.

Current Road Information

Bureau of Land Management
Kingman Field Office
2755 Mission Blvd.
Kingman, AZ 86401
(928) 718-3700

Lake Mead National Recreation Area
601 Nevada Way
Boulder City, NV 89005
(702) 293-8990

Map References

BLM   Boulder City
USGS 1:24,000   Householder Pass,
      Mojave Mine, Fire Mtn.
      1:100,000 Boulder City
Arizona Atlas & Gazetteer, p. 22
Arizona Road & Recreation Atlas, p. 54
Trails Illustrated, #204 Lake Mead National
      Recreation Area
Other: Lake Mead National Recreation
      Area Map

Route Directions

▼ 0.0   From the junction of US 93, 0.1 miles
         south of mile marker 20, turn south-
         west on unmarked trail. Zero trip
         meter. Immediately cross cattle guard
         and pass under power lines.
         GPS: N35°45.143' W114°30.145'

▼ 0.9 SO Cross through wash.
▼ 1.2 SO Cross through wash.
▼ 1.6 SO Cross through wash.
▼ 2.0 SO Enter wash.
▼ 2.6 SO Track on left.
           GPS: N35°44.82' W114°32.97'

▼ 2.7 BR/SO Trail forks; track on left, immediately
             followed by track on right.
▼ 2.8 SO Cross through wash.
▼ 2.9 SO Track on right.
▼ 3.0 SO Cross through wash. Vehicles travel
           left and right down the wash.
▼ 3.2 BR Track on left to diggings, immediately
           followed by fork. Track on left toward
           TV towers. Bear right at fork at sign
           "Eldorado Jeep Trail." Zero trip meter.
           GPS: N35°44.34' W114°33.26'

▼ 0.0   Continue along the small trail. Road is
         now marked as Lake Mead Recreation
         Area #54.
▼ 0.1 SO Second entrance to track on left.
▼ 0.5 SO Small track on right.
▼ 0.7 SO Small track on left.
           GPS: N35°43.89' W114°33.82'

▼ 0.9 SO Track on right on small saddle. Track
           descends down wash, which quickly

becomes narrower and starts to twist.
▼ 1.3 SO Entering Lake Mead National
           Recreation Area. Zero trip meter.
           GPS: N35°43.80' W114°34.59'

▼ 0.0   Continue into recreation area.
▼ 0.2 SO Old mining remains on right.
           GPS: N35°43.85' W114°34.65'

▼ 0.3 SO Old mine shaft on right.
▼ 0.4 SO Foot trail on left to old diggings; then
           old diggings on right of track.
▼ 0.9 TL Track on right; turn in front of large
           mine adit, following the wash down-
           stream. Track on right is dead end.
▼ 6.3 SO Narrow section of trail in canyon.
▼ 6.6 BL Trail joins another wash; bear left
           down wash, heading downhill.
           GPS: N35°43.34' W114°39.99'

▼ 8.0 SO Colorado River comes into view.
▼ 8.5   Trail ends at designated primitive
           campsites on the Colorado River.
           GPS: N35°43.83' W114°41.62'

Santa Maria Mountains Loop Trail

STARTING POINT Williamson Valley Road (CR
   5), 22 miles north of the intersection
   with Iron Springs Road in Prescott
FINISHING POINT Williamson Valley Road (CR
   5), 14 miles north of the starting point
TOTAL MILEAGE 35.3 miles
UNPAVED MILEAGE 35.3 miles
DRIVING TIME 2.5 hours
ELEVATION RANGE 4,600–6,500 feet
USUALLY OPEN Year-round
BEST TIME TO TRAVEL Dry weather
DIFFICULTY RATING 2
SCENIC RATING 8
REMOTENESS RATING +1

Special Attractions

■ Long trail passing through a variety of forest vegetation.
■ Excellent backcountry camping.
■ Old Walnut Creek Cemetery and Walnut Creek Station.

Description

This long trail follows a wide loop through the Santa Maria Mountains in the Prescott National Forest. The main attraction of this lightly traveled trail is the range of forest scenery through which it passes. Initially, it travels through open ranchland as it heads toward the forest boundary. As the trail starts to climb into the forest, the landscape changes to low hills vegetated with pinyon, juniper, and a variety of low shrubs. As the elevation increases, tall ponderosa pines and oaks dominate. Most of the loop is lightly traveled and you may spend a couple of days, especially around the apex of the loop, without seeing another vehicle.

The trail starts off as a graded road and can be driven in a passenger vehicle as far as Camp Wood and the south end of West #32: Walnut Creek Road. There is excellent camping around this intersection in the large, shady areas underneath the pines. Also at this intersection is Merritt Spring, set back in a clearing. At the back of the clearing is an old fruit orchard, indicating that somebody must have made a home here. There is no camping in the immediate area around the spring.

Once past Camp Wood, the trail drops in standard to become a single-lane trail, rough enough to need high clearance, although 4WD is not necessary under normal conditions. It is rutted and less used after it passes the entrance to the 7 Up Ranch. The trail continues to wind through the forest for a few miles before descending from a saddle to follow alongside the south fork of Walnut Creek. This section of the trail has good views to the north over Juniper Mesa.

The trail joins the larger graded road that runs beneath Juniper Mesa alongside Walnut Creek. The old Walnut Creek Guard Station is passed immediately after the north end of West #32: Walnut Creek Road. The site is now jointly managed by the U.S. Forest Service and an educational institution. It is not open to the public. The station and creek take their names from the native Arizona walnut trees in the area.

Shortly after Walnut Creek Guard Station, there is a narrow, faint trail to the north that leads 0.3 miles to the old Walnut Creek Cemetery. This trail can be a little tricky to find. Keep bearing left at the many forks in the trail and you will find the cemetery, surrounded by a fence. The coordinates of the site are given in the route directions, which will make it easier to locate.

Like other trails in this region, the Santa Maria Mountains Loop Trail should be driven in dry weather only. Light snow is possible during winter months.

Current Road Information

Prescott National Forest
Chino Valley Ranger District
735 North Hwy 89
Chino Valley, AZ 86323
(928) 777-2200

Map References

BLM   Prescott
USFS   Prescott National Forest: Chino
       Valley Ranger District
USGS   1:24,000   Simmons, Seepage Mtn.,
       Camp Wood, Juniper Mtns., Indian
       Peak
       1:100,000 Prescott
Trails Illustrated, #857 Apache Creek,
       Juniper Mesa
Arizona Atlas & Gazetteer, pp. 33, 32
Arizona Road & Recreation Atlas, pp. 65, 64
Recreational Map of Arizona (incomplete)

Route Directions

▼ 0.0   From Prescott, take Iron Springs Road
         out of town; then turn north on
         Williamson Valley Road. Follow the
         paved road for 22 miles and turn west
         on unmarked road, which turns to
         graded dirt after the cattle guard. Zero

Small stone building that covers a flowing spring near Merritt Spring

trip meter at the intersection. There is a sign after the cattle guard, marking the road as FR 21 to Camp Wood.

4.8 ▲   Trail ends at the intersection with the paved Williamson Valley Road. Turn right for Prescott.
GPS: N34º49.94' W112º38.81'

▼ 0.5   SO   Track on left.
4.3 ▲   SO   Track on right.

▼ 1.8   SO   Cross through Hitt Wash on concrete ford.
3.0 ▲   SO   Cross through Hitt Wash on concrete ford.

▼ 2.5   SO   Cattle guard.
2.3 ▲   SO   Cattle guard.

▼ 3.5   SO   Cattle guard.
1.3 ▲   SO   Cattle guard.
GPS: N34º49.21' W112º41.97'

▼ 4.8   SO   Entering Prescott National Forest at sign. Then track on right is FR 9805B. Zero trip meter.
0.0 ▲   Continue to the northeast.
GPS: N34º48.78' W112º43.32'

▼ 0.0   Continue to the southwest.
3.4 ▲   SO   Track on left is FR 9805B. Leaving Prescott National Forest at sign. Zero trip meter.

▼ 0.8   SO   Cattle guard.
2.6 ▲   SO   Cattle guard.

▼ 1.1   SO   Cross over creek on bridge.
2.3 ▲   SO   Cross over creek on bridge.
GPS: N34º48.43' W112º44.39'

▼ 1.6   SO   Track on right.
1.8 ▲   SO   Track on left.

▼ 2.2   SO   Track on right is FR 9807B; then cattle guard.
1.2 ▲   SO   Cattle guard; then track on left is FR 9807B.
GPS: N34º48.86' W112º45.45'

▼ 2.3   SO   Cross over Pine Creek on bridge.
1.1 ▲   SO   Cross over Pine Creek on bridge.

▼ 2.4   SO   Ranch road on left.
1.0 ▲   SO   Ranch road on right.

▼ 3.4   SO   Track on left is FR 666 through gate; then well. Zero trip meter.
0.0 ▲   Continue to the east.
GPS: N34º48.72' W112º46.59'

▼ 0.0   Continue to the west.
6.6 ▲   SO   Well; then track on right is FR 666 through gate. Zero trip meter.

▼ 0.6   SO   Cattle guard; then track on right is FR 9821B.
6.0 ▲   SO   Track on left is FR 9821B; then cattle guard.
GPS: N34º48.75' W112º47.26'

▼ 0.7   SO   Cross over creek on bridge.
5.9 ▲   SO   Cross over creek on bridge.

▼ 1.0   SO   Cross through creek; then track on right is FR 9871B.
5.6 ▲   SO   Track on left is FR 9871B; then cross through creek.
GPS: N34º48.53' W112º47.60'

▼ 1.1   SO   Cross over creek on bridge.
5.5 ▲   SO   Cross over creek on bridge.

▼ 1.5   SO   Cattle guard.
5.1 ▲   SO   Cattle guard.

▼ 1.9   SO   Trail #21 on left for hikers, horses, mountain bikes, dirt bikes, and ATVs—no vehicles. Johnson Mountain is on the right.
4.7 ▲   SO   Trail #21 on right for hikers, horses, mountain bikes, dirt bikes, and ATVs—no vehicles. Johnson Mountain is on the left.
GPS: N34º48.06' W112º48.13'

▼ 3.0   SO   Cross through wash; camping area on left.
3.6 ▲   SO   Cross through wash; camping area on right.

▼ 3.1　SO　Track on left is FR 9874B.
3.5 ▲　SO　Track on right is FR 9874B.
　　　　GPS: N34°47.75' W112°49.36'

▼ 3.6　SO　Track on right is FR 9872B.
3.0 ▲　SO　Track on left is FR 9872B.
　　　　GPS: N34°47.69' W112°49.89'

▼ 3.9　SO　Track on right is FR 6869B.
2.7 ▲　SO　Track on left is FR 6869B.

▼ 5.9　SO　Graded road on left is FR 705 to
　　　　Cottonwood Canyon. Follow the sign
　　　　for Camp Wood.
0.7 ▲　SO　Graded road on right is FR 705 to
　　　　Cottonwood Canyon. Follow the sign
　　　　to Prescott.
　　　　GPS: N34°48.01' W112°51.91'

▼ 6.3　SO　Track on right is FR 9877B.
0.3 ▲　SO　Track on left is FR 9877B.
　　　　GPS: N34°48.05' W112°52.45'

▼ 6.4　SO　Trail #5 on left for hikers, horses,
　　　　mountain bikes, dirt bikes, and ATVs—
　　　　no vehicles. Then cattle guard.
0.2 ▲　SO　Cattle guard. Then Trail #5 on right for
　　　　hikers, horses, mountain bikes, dirt
　　　　bikes, and ATVs—no vehicles.

▼ 6.6　SO　Graded road on right is West #32:
　　　　Walnut Creek Road, FR 95, to Camp
　　　　Wood Station. Zero trip meter.
0.0 ▲　　　Continue to the northeast.
　　　　GPS: N34°48.05' W112°52.72'

▼ 0.0　　　Continue to the southwest, following
　　　　the sign to the 7 Up Ranch. Merritt
　　　　Spring is immediately after the inter-
　　　　section on left. Also on left is Trail #9
　　　　for hikers, horses, mountain bikes, dirt
　　　　bikes, and ATVs—no vehicles.
2.5 ▲　SO　Merritt Spring on right. Also on right is
　　　　Trail #9 for hikers, horses, mountain
　　　　bikes, dirt bikes, and ATVs—no vehi-
　　　　cles. Then graded road on left is West
　　　　#32: Walnut Creek Road, FR 95, to
　　　　Camp Wood Station. Zero trip meter.

▼ 0.4　SO　Track on right to a stone building
　　　　covering a flowing spring.
2.1 ▲　SO　Track on left to a stone building cover-
　　　　ing a flowing spring.
　　　　GPS: N34°48.01' W112°53.16'

▼ 1.7　SO　Track on right.
0.8 ▲　SO　Track on left.

▼ 2.1　SO　Trail #9836 on left for hikers, horses,
　　　　mountain bikes, dirt bikes, and ATVs—
　　　　no vehicles.
0.4 ▲　SO　Trail #9836 on right for hikers, horses,
　　　　mountain bikes, dirt bikes, and ATVs—
　　　　no vehicles.
　　　　GPS: N34°47.83' W112°54.77'

▼ 2.5　TR　Turn right onto graded dirt road, FR 9,
　　　　to 7 Up Ranch. FR 21 continues ahead.
　　　　Zero trip meter.
0.0 ▲　　　Continue to the northeast on FR 21.
　　　　GPS: N34°47.80' W112°55.12'

▼ 0.0　　　Continue to the west on FR 9.
3.1 ▲　TL　T-intersection with FR 21. Turn left
　　　　onto graded dirt road following the
　　　　sign for Prescott. Road is now FR 21.
　　　　Zero trip meter.

▼ 0.2　SO　Cross through wash.
2.9 ▲　SO　Cross through wash.

▼ 0.4　SO　Cross through wash.
2.6 ▲　SO　Cross through wash.

▼ 0.5　SO　Cross through wash.
2.5 ▲　SO　Cross through wash.

▼ 0.8　SO　Cross through wash.
2.3 ▲　SO　Cross through wash.

▼ 1.0　SO　Cross through wash.
2.1 ▲　SO　Cross through wash.

▼ 1.6　SO　Track on left.
1.5 ▲　SO　Track on right.

▼ 1.7　SO　Cross through wash.
1.4 ▲　SO　Cross through wash.

This grave in the old cemetery is just off the trail near the Walnut Creek Guard Station

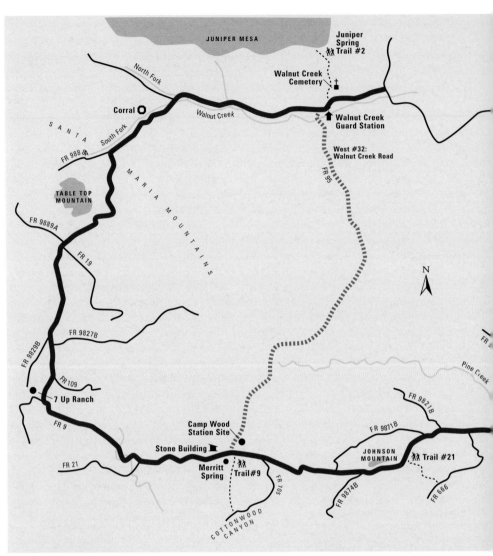

▼ 1.9   SO   Cattle guard.
1.2 ▲   SO   Cattle guard.

▼ 2.0   SO   Track on left.
1.1 ▲   SO   Track on right.

▼ 2.4   SO   Cross through wash; then track on left.
0.7 ▲   SO   Track on right; then cross through wash.

▼ 3.1   TR   Turn right in front of 7 Up Ranch gates and zero trip meter.
0.0 ▲   Continue to the east on FR 9.
          GPS: N34º48.98' W112º57.75'

▼ 0.0   Continue to the north on FR 9.

4.1 ▲   TL   Turn left, remaining on FR 9. The 7 Up Ranch gates are on the right. Zero trip meter.

▼ 0.3   SO   Track on left is FR 9828B.
3.8 ▲   SO   Track on right is FR 9828B.
          GPS: N34º49.24' W112º57.73'

▼ 0.5   SO   Track on right is FR 109.
3.6 ▲   SO   Track on left is FR 109.
          GPS: N34º49.35' W112º57.68'

▼ 1.3   SO   Track on right.
2.8 ▲   SO   Track on left.

#31: Santa Maria Mountains Loop Trail

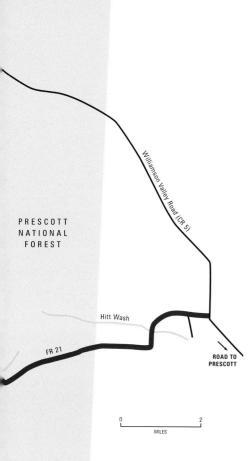

PRESCOTT
NATIONAL
FOREST

Williamson Valley Road (CR 5)

Hitt Wash

FR 21

ROAD TO
PRESCOTT

0   2
MILES

▼ 1.3 ▲   SO   Cross through wash.

▼ 3.5   SO   Cross through wash.
0.6 ▲   SO   Cross through wash.

▼ 3.7   SO   Track on left; then cross through wash.
0.4 ▲   SO   Cross through wash; then track on right.

▼ 4.0   SO   Track on right is FR 19.
0.1 ▲   SO   Track on left is FR 19.

▼ 4.1   SO   Track on left is FR 9889A. There is a
             vehicle travel information sign at the
             intersection. Zero trip meter.
0.0 ▲   Continue to the southwest.
             GPS: N34°52.37′ W112°57.40′

▼ 0.0   Continue to the northeast.
5.4 ▲   SO   Track on right is FR 9889A. There is a
             vehicle travel information sign at the
             intersection. Zero trip meter.

▼ 0.8   SO   Cattle guard.
4.6 ▲   SO   Cattle guard.

▼ 1.2   SO   Saddle. Table Top Mountain on left.
4.2 ▲   SO   Saddle. Table Top Mountain on right.

▼ 1.7   SO   Track on right.
3.7 ▲   SO   Track on left.

▼ 2.4   SO   Cross through wash.
3.0 ▲   SO   Cross through wash.
             GPS: N34°53.67′ W112°56.18′

▼ 2.6   SO   Cross through wash.
2.8 ▲   SO   Cross through wash.

▼ 3.2   BR   Track on left is FR 9888A.
2.2 ▲   BL   Track on right is FR 9888A.
             GPS: N34°54.36′ W112°56.28′

▼ 3.5   SO   Track on left through gate.
1.9 ▲   SO   Track on right through gate.

▼ 3.6   SO   Track on right.
1.8 ▲   SO   Track on left.

▼ 3.7   SO   Cross through wash.
1.7 ▲   SO   Cross through wash.

▼ 1.5   SO   Track on right is FR 9827B.
2.6 ▲   SO   Track on left is FR 9827B.
             GPS: N34°50.20′ W112°57.57′

▼ 1.8   SO   Track on left is FR 9829B.
2.3 ▲   SO   Track on right is FR 9829B.
             GPS: N34°50.43′ W112°57.60′

▼ 2.1   SO   Cross through wash.
2.0 ▲   SO   Cross through wash.

▼ 2.5   SO   Cattle guard.
1.6 ▲   SO   Cattle guard.

▼ 2.8   SO   Cross through wash.

▼ 4.8   SO   Corral on left.
0.6 ▲   SO   Corral on right.

▼ 5.0   SO   Cross through South Fork Walnut Creek.
0.4 ▲   SO   Cross through South Fork Walnut Creek.

▼ 5.1   SO   Cattle guard.
0.3 ▲   SO   Cattle guard.

▼ 5.4   TR   T-intersection; turn right onto wider graded dirt road following the sign to Walnut Creek Station. Zero trip meter. Juniper Mesa is directly ahead.
0.0 ▲   Continue to the southwest.
           GPS: N34°55.55' W112°54.51'

▼ 0.0   Continue to the east.
3.6 ▲   TL   Turn left onto narrower, roughly graded road, FR 9, following the sign to 7 Up Ranch. Track ahead goes to a locked gate in 3 miles.

▼ 0.2   SO   Cross through wash; then cattle guard.

3.4 ▲   SO   Cattle guard; then cross through wash.

▼ 0.3   SO   Track on left.
3.3 ▲   SO   Track on right.

▼ 0.4   SO   Cross through wash.
3.2 ▲   SO   Cross through wash.

▼ 1.3   SO   Cross over creek on bridge.
2.3 ▲   SO   Cross over creek on bridge.

▼ 1.6   SO   Cross through wash.
2.0 ▲   SO   Cross through wash.

▼ 1.8   SO   Ranch entrance on right.
1.8 ▲   SO   Ranch entrance on left.

▼ 2.2   SO   Track on right.
1.4 ▲   SO   Track on left.

▼ 2.5   SO   Ranch entrance on right.
1.1 ▲   SO   Ranch entrance on left.

▼ 2.8   SO   Ranch entrance on right.

Walnut trees surround the old Walnut Creek Guard Station

0.8 ▲	SO	Ranch entrance on left.

▼ 3.3	SO	Exiting the Box L Ranch; then track on left.
0.3 ▲	SO	Track on right; then entering the Box L Ranch; remain on county road. **GPS: N34°55.40′ W112°51.02′**

▼ 3.6	BL	Track on right is West #32: Walnut Creek Road, FR 95. Zero trip meter.
0.0 ▲		Continue to the west, following the sign toward Oro Ranch. **GPS: N34°55.36′ W112°50.68′**

▼ 0.0		Continue to the northeast, road is now marked Yavapai CR 125 following the sign to Prescott.
1.8 ▲	BR	Track on left is West #32: Walnut Creek Road, FR 95. Zero trip meter.

▼ 0.1	SO	Walnut Creek Guard Station on right.
1.7 ▲	SO	Walnut Creek Guard Station on left. **GPS: N34°55.41′ W112°50.61′**

▼ 0.3	SO	Juniper Spring Trail #2 for hikers and horses on left; then cattle guard.
1.5 ▲	SO	Cattle guard; then Juniper Spring Trail #2 for hikers and horses on right. **GPS: N34°55.58′ W112°50.47′**

▼ 0.6	SO	Cross through wash; then small, faint track on left goes 0.5 miles to the old Walnut Creek Cemetery—coordinates for cemetery are GPS: N34°55.79′ W112°50.43′. The spur is 3-rated; keep left at the intersections.
1.2 ▲	SO	Small, faint track on right goes 0.5 miles to the old Walnut Creek Cemetery—coordinates for cemetery are GPS: N34°55.79′ W112°50.43′. The spur is 3-rated; keep left at the intersections. Cross through wash.

▼ 1.8		Trail ends at the intersection with the graded dirt road, CR 5. Turn right for Prescott.
0.0 ▲		Trail commences on CR 5, 36 miles north of Prescott and 14 miles north of the south end of the trail. Zero trip meter and turn southwest on graded dirt road marked Yavapai CR 125.

Junction is 0.2 miles north of the single-lane steel bridge over Walnut Creek. Immediately after the turn, the road is signposted to Walnut Creek Station.
GPS: N34°55.91′ W112°48.98′

Walnut Creek Road

STARTING POINT West #31: Santa Maria Mountains Loop Trail, 1.8 miles from the north end of the loop
FINISHING POINT West #31: Santa Maria Mountains Loop Trail, 14.8 miles from the south end of the loop
TOTAL MILEAGE 10.4 miles
UNPAVED MILEAGE 10.4 miles
DRIVING TIME 1 hour
ELEVATION RANGE 5,200–5,800 feet
USUALLY OPEN Year-round
BEST TIME TO TRAVEL Dry weather
DIFFICULTY RATING 2
SCENIC RATING 8
REMOTENESS RATING +1

Special Attractions

■ Site of the old Camp Wood National Forest Station.
■ Winding trail through the Santa Maria Mountains.
■ Can be combined with part of West #31: Santa Maria Mountains Loop Trail to form a loop trail.

Description

This roughly graded road makes a pleasant alternative to driving the full West #31: Santa Maria Mountains Loop Trail. It connects the two national forest guard stations of Walnut Creek and Camp Wood. Traveling from the north end, the road is initially smoothly graded as it crosses private land, climbing up onto the flank of the Santa Maria Mountains. Looking to the north, there are views of the steep edge of Juniper Mesa rising abruptly from Walnut Creek Valley. Walnut Creek is named for the native Arizona walnut trees that grow in abundance along its course.

As it enters the forest, the trail becomes a single-track road and is not as smooth; a high-clearance vehicle is needed for some of the wash crossings and a few rocky sections, mainly toward the south end. The trail climbs steadily upward, leaving the pinyon and juniper vegetation to enter an area of ponderosa pines. There are many pleasant campsites among the pines, mainly toward the south end of the trail.

The trail passes by the site of Camp Wood National Forest Station, which was actively used by rangers into the 1990s. Only the foundations of the building remain in the clearing because the station was dismantled by the forest service. Opposite the Camp Wood site, a road leads up toward the Hyde Fire Lookout.

The trail ends where it rejoins West #31: Santa Maria Mountains Loop Trail at Merritt Spring, 14.8 miles from the south end. Like other trails in this region, Walnut Creek Road should be driven in dry weather only. Light snow is possible during winter months.

Current Road Information
Prescott National Forest
Chino Valley Ranger District
735 North Hwy. 89
Chino Valley, AZ 86323
(928) 777-2200

Map References
BLM   Prescott
USFS   Prescott National Forest: Chino
      Valley Ranger District
USGS   1:24,000   Indian Peak, Seepage
      Mtn., Camp Wood
      1:100,000 Prescott
Trails Illustrated, #857 Apache Creek,
      Juniper Mesa
Arizona Atlas & Gazetteer, p. 32
Arizona Road & Recreation Atlas, p. 64
Recreational Map of Arizona

Route Directions

▼ 0.0		From West #31: Santa Maria Mountains Loop Trail (CR 125), 1.8 miles from the north end, zero trip meter and turn southwest on the narrow, roughly graded dirt road, FR 95. Road is signed to Camp Wood; then cross through wash.
5.4 ▲		Cross through wash; then trail ends at the intersection with West #31: Santa Maria Mountains Loop Trail (CR 125). Turn right to exit to Prescott; turn left to continue around the loop.
		GPS: N34°55.36′ W112°50.68′
▼ 0.2	SO	Cross through Walnut Creek.
5.2 ▲	SO	Cross through Walnut Creek.
▼ 0.3	SO	Cross through Apache Creek.
5.1 ▲	SO	Cross through Apache Creek.
▼ 0.6	SO	Cattle guard.
4.8 ▲	SO	Cattle guard.
▼ 0.9	SO	Track on right.
4.5 ▲	SO	Track on left.
▼ 1.2	SO	Track on right is FR 95A; then cross through Graver Wash.
4.2 ▲	SO	Cross through Graver Wash; then track on left is FR 95A.
		GPS: N34°54.48′ W112°50.55′
▼ 1.3	SO	Track on right; then cattle guard; then track on left.
4.1 ▲	SO	Track on right; then cattle guard; then track on left.
▼ 2.3	SO	Cattle guard.
3.1 ▲	SO	Cattle guard.
▼ 3.7	SO	Cross through creek.
1.7 ▲	SO	Cross through creek.
		GPS: N34°52.55′ W112°49.43′
▼ 3.9	SO	Track on left.
1.5 ▲	SO	Track on right.
▼ 4.0	SO	Cross through Hitt Wash.

One of the many creek crossings on this trail

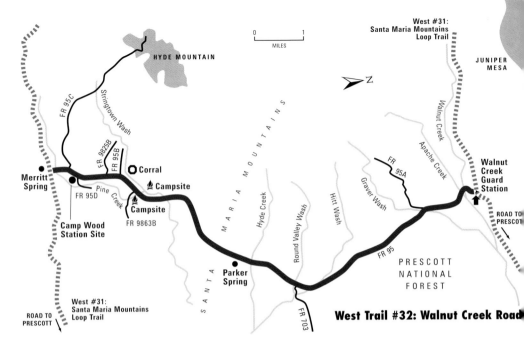

West Trail #32: Walnut Creek Road

1.4 ▲ SO Cross through Hitt Wash.

▼ 4.3 SO Track on left is FR 703.
1.1 ▲ SO Track on right is FR 703.
        GPS: N34°52.01' W112°49.42'

▼ 4.4 SO Cross through Round Valley Wash.
1.0 ▲ SO Cross through Round Valley Wash.

▼ 5.2 SO Track on right.
0.2 ▲ SO Track on left.

▼ 5.4 SO Cross through Hyde Creek. Zero trip
        meter at the crossing.
0.0 ▲   Continue to the north.
        GPS: N34°51.25' W112°50.05'

▼ 0.0   Continue to the south.
3.5 ▲ SO Cross through Hyde Creek. Zero trip
        meter at the crossing.

▼ 0.4 SO Parker Spring on left.
3.1 ▲ SO Parker Spring on right.
        GPS: N34°50.98' W112°50.25'

▼ 0.5 SO Cross through wash.
3.0 ▲ SO Cross through wash.

▼ 1.2 SO Cross through wash.
2.3 ▲ SO Cross through wash.

▼ 1.3 SO Track on right is FR 9821B to mine tailings.
2.2 ▲ SO Track on left is FR 9821B to mine tailings.
        GPS: N34°50.43' W112°50.98'

▼ 1.6 SO Track on right.
1.9 ▲ SO Track on left.

▼ 1.9 SO Cross through wash.
1.6 ▲ SO Cross through wash.

▼ 2.0 SO Cattle guard.
1.5 ▲ SO Cattle guard.

▼ 2.3 SO Cattle guard.
1.2 ▲ SO Cattle guard.

▼ 2.5 SO Cross through Pine Creek; then track
        on left.
1.0 ▲ SO Track on right; then cross through Pine
        Creek.
        GPS: N34°49.93' W112°51.81'

▼ 2.6 SO Track on left.

0.9 ▲	SO	Track on right.

▼ 2.7	SO	Cross through wash.
0.8 ▲	SO	Cross through wash.

▼ 3.0	SO	Cross through Pine Creek; campsites on either side of the trail.
0.5 ▲	SO	Cross through Pine Creek; campsites on either side of the trail.
		GPS: N34°49.54' W112°51.97'

▼ 3.1	SO	Track on left is FR 9863B.
0.4 ▲	SO	Track on right is FR 9863B.

▼ 3.5	SO	Stringtown Wash on right; corral on right; then track on right is FR 95B. Zero trip meter.
0.0 ▲		Continue to the northeast.
		GPS: N34°49.29' W112°52.35'

▼ 0.0	SO	Continue to the southwest.
1.5 ▲	SO	Track on left is FR 95B; then corral on left; Stringtown Wash on left. Zero trip meter.

▼ 0.3	SO	Track on left.
1.2 ▲	SO	Track on right.

▼ 0.4	SO	Track on right is FR 9825B; then cattle guard.
1.1 ▲	SO	Cattle guard; then track on left is FR 9825B.
		GPS: N34°48.96' W112°52.45'

▼ 0.5	SO	Cross through creek; then track on left is FR 9865B.
1.0 ▲	SO	Track on right is FR 9865B; then cross through creek.

▼ 0.9	SO	Cross through creek.
0.6 ▲	SO	Cross through creek.

▼ 1.0	SO	Track on left is FR 95D.
0.5 ▲	SO	Track on right is FR 95D.
		GPS: N34°48.40' W112°52.57'

▼ 1.2	SO	Site of Camp Wood Station on left; then track on right is FR 95C to the Hyde Mountain Lookout Trail.
0.3 ▲	SO	Track on left is FR 95C to the Hyde Mountain Lookout Trail; then site of Camp Wood Station on right.
		GPS: N34°48.30' W112°52.69'

▼ 1.5		Trail ends at the intersection with West #31: Santa Maria Mountains Loop Trail. Turn left for Prescott; turn right to continue around the loop.
0.0 ▲		Trail commences along West #31: Santa Maria Mountains Loop Trail, 14.8 miles from the southern end of the trail. Zero trip meter and turn north on roughly graded dirt road, FR 95, sign-posted to Walnut Creek Station.
		GPS: N34°48.05' W112°52.72'

Tonto Wash Trail

STARTING POINT Iron Springs Road, 10 miles north of Prescott
FINISHING POINT Williamson Valley Road, 15.2 miles north of Prescott
TOTAL MILEAGE 16.2 miles
UNPAVED MILEAGE 15.5 miles
DRIVING TIME 1.5 hours
ELEVATION RANGE 4,600–5,000 feet
USUALLY OPEN Year-round
BEST TIME TO TRAVEL Dry weather only
DIFFICULTY RATING 2
SCENIC RATING 7
REMOTENESS RATING +0

Special Attractions
■ Pleasant, easy trail that crosses through ranchland and Prescott National Forest.
■ Views of Granite Mountain.

Description
This easy trail follows the broad valleys of Tonto Wash and Long Canyon, passing close to Tonto Mountain. The majority of the trail lies within Prescott National Forest; the rest passes through the open ranchland of Arizona's cattle country.

Most of Tonto Wash Trail is an easy graded road. Only a couple of rough rutted sections make high-clearance preferable. There are excellent views of the gray peak of Granite Mountain to the northeast and the Santa

Maria Mountains to the north. Camping is a bit restricted because of private property, but there are many side forest roads leading off from the main trail where it is possible to find a secluded site.

Current Road Information
Prescott National Forest
Bradshaw Ranger District
344 South Cortez St.
Prescott, AZ 86303
(928) 443-8000

Maps References
BLM   Prescott
USFS   Prescott National Forest: Bradshaw
       Ranger District
USGS   1:24,000   Skull Valley, Mt. Josh,
       Simmons, Sullivan Buttes
       1:100,000 Prescott
Trails Illustrated, #857 Apache Creek,
       Juniper Mesa (incomplete)

Trails Illustrated, #858 Bradshaw Mountains
       (incomplete)
Arizona Atlas & Gazetteer, pp. 33, 32
Arizona Road & Recreation Atlas, p. 65

Route Directions

▼ 0.0		Leave Prescott to the northwest along Iron Springs Road. Enter the Prescott National Forest and proceed for 10 miles to Tonto Road. Turn northwest down the graded dirt Tonto Road and zero trip meter.
2.7 ▲		Trail ends at the intersection with Iron Springs Road. Turn left for Prescott; turn right for Skull Valley.
		GPS: N34°33.87' W112°39.95'

▼ 0.1	SO	Cattle guard.
2.6 ▲	SO	Cattle guard.

▼ 0.2	SO	Track on left.
2.5 ▲	SO	Track on right.

A monsoonal storm gathers over Granite Mountain

▼ 0.5 SO Cross through wash.
2.2 ▲ SO Cross through wash.

▼ 0.6 SO Cattle guard; then pass under railroad
           track; then track on left and track on
           right.
2.1 ▲ SO Track on left and track on right; then
           pass under railroad track; then cattle
           guard.
           GPS: N34º34.22' W112º40.49'

▼ 1.4 SO Cross through wash.
1.3 ▲ SO Cross through wash.

▼ 2.2 SO Entering Prescott National Forest over
           cattle guard.
0.5 ▲ SO Leaving Prescott National Forest over
           cattle guard.
           GPS: N34º35.56' W112º40.16'

▼ 2.7 SO Graded road on left is FR 65, sign-post-
           ed for Tonto Spring and Tank Creek
           Mesa. Zero trip meter.
0.0 ▲   Continue to the south.
           GPS: N34º36.06' W112º40.17'

▼ 0.0   Continue to the north.
4.4 ▲ SO Graded road on right is FR 65, sigpost-
           ed for Tonto Spring and Tank Creek
           Mesa. Zero trip meter.

▼ 0.1 SO Track on right.
4.3 ▲ SO Track on left.

▼ 0.4 SO Cattle guard.
4.0 ▲ SO Cattle guard.

▼ 0.5 BR Tonto Ranch Road on left.
3.9 ▲ BL Tonto Ranch Road on right.
           GPS: N34º36.48' W112º39.97'

▼ 0.9 SO Graded road on left.
3.5 ▲ SO Graded road on right.

▼ 1.3 SO Track on right.
3.1 ▲ SO Track on left.

▼ 1.4 SO Cattle guard.
3.0 ▲ SO Cattle guard.
           GPS: N34º37.14' W112º39.47'

▼ 1.6 SO Track on left.
2.8 ▲ SO Track on right.

▼ 1.8 SO Graded road on right is Contreas Road
           to Prescott. Continue toward Fair Oaks
           Road.
2.6 ▲ SO Graded road on left is Contreas Road to
           Prescott. Continue following sign to
           Skull Valley.
           GPS: N34º37.45' W112º39.25'

▼ 1.9 BL Track on right to ranch; then cross
           through Tonto Wash.
2.5 ▲ BR Cross through Tonto Wash; then track
           on left to ranch.

▼ 2.3 SO Track on left is FR 9407S.
2.1 ▲ SO Track on right is FR 9407S.
           GPS: N34º37.88' W112º39.05'

▼ 2.7 SO Ranch entrance on right.
1.7 ▲ SO Ranch entrance on left.

▼ 3.5 SO Track on left.
0.9 ▲ SO Track on right.

▼ 3.7 SO Entering ranch property; remain on
           road. Track on right is FR 41. Continue
           straight on, remaining on FR 102.
0.7 ▲ SO Leaving ranch property. Track on left is
           FR 41. Continue straight on, remaining
           on FR 102.
           GPS: N34º39.13' W112º38.99'

▼ 4.4 TR 4-way intersection. Turn right, remain-
           ing on main graded road. Ahead goes
           to private property. Track on left
           through gate is FR 9269A. Zero trip
           meter.
0.0 ▲   Continue to the southeast.
           GPS: N34º39.66' W112º39.31'

▼ 0.0   Continue to the northeast.
4.3 ▲ TL 4-way intersection. Turn left, remaining
           on main graded road. Graded road on
           right goes to private property. Track
           ahead through gate is FR 9269A. Zero
           trip meter.

West Trail #33: Tonto Wash Trail

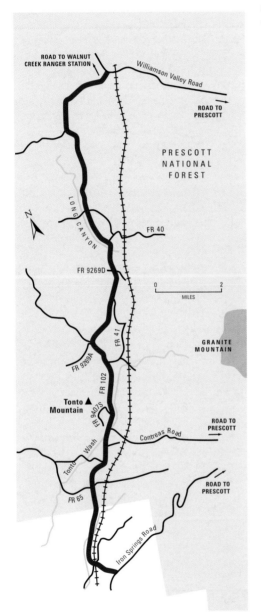

▼ 1.4   SO   Cross through wash; then track on right is FR 41.

2.9 ▲   SO   Track on left is FR 41; then cross through wash.

           GPS: N34°40.69′ W112°38.38′

▼ 2.1   SO   Cross through wash; then track on right. Track on left is FR 9269D.

2.2 ▲   SO   Track on right is FR 9269D. Track on left; then cross through wash.

           GPS: N34°41.26′ W112°38.19′

▼ 2.2   SO   Cattle guard; then track on right.

2.1 ▲   SO   Track on left; then cattle guard.

▼ 2.8   SO   Cross through wash.

1.5 ▲   SO   Cross through wash.

▼ 2.9   SO   Track on right is FR 40.

1.4 ▲   SO   Track on left is FR 40.

           GPS: N34°41.96′ W112°38.17′

▼ 3.3   SO   Track on left.

1.0 ▲   SO   Track on right.

▼ 3.5   SO   Track on left.

0.8 ▲   SO   Track on right.

▼ 4.0   SO   Track on left.

0.3 ▲   SO   Track on right.

▼ 4.3   SO   Track on left; then cattle guard, entering ranch property. Second track on left after cattle guard into ranch. Leaving Prescott National Forest. Zero trip meter.

0.0 ▲   Continue to the south.

           GPS: N34°43.11′ W112°38.74′

▼ 0.0   Continue to the north.

2.4 ▲   SO   Entering Prescott National Forest. Track on right into ranch. Then cattle guard and second track on right. Zero trip meter.

▼ 0.9   SO   Gravel road on right.

1.5 ▲   SO   Gravel road on left.

▼ 1.1   SO   Ranch road on right and left.

1.3 ▲   SO   Ranch road on right and left.

▼ 2.0   SO   Graded dirt road on right.

0.4 ▲   SO   Graded dirt road on left.

▼ 2.4   TR   T-intersection. Turn right onto graded dirt road, following the sign toward Camp Wood and Walnut Creek. Zero trip meter.

0.0 ▲   Continue to the southeast.

GPS: N34°45.04' W112°38.81'

▼ 0.0   Continue to the north.

2.4 ▲   TL   Turn left onto graded dirt road, following the sign to Skull Valley. Zero trip meter.

▼ 0.7   SO   Road turns to paved.

1.7 ▲   SO   Road turns to graded dirt.

▼ 2.4   Trail ends at the intersection with Williamson Valley Road, FR 5. Turn right for Prescott; turn left for Walnut Creek Ranger Station.

0.0 ▲   Trail commences on Williamson Valley Road, FR 5, 15.2 miles from Prescott. Zero trip meter and turn southwest on paved road. The intersection is marked for Fair Oaks Road and is north of the railroad, immediately north of a cattle guard.

GPS: N34°46.40' W112°37.11'

Selected Further Reading

Ahnert, Gerald T. *Retracing the Butterfield Overland Trail Through Arizona: A Guide to the Route of 1857–1861.* N.p.: Westernlore Press, 1973.

Alden, Peter, and Peter Friederici. *National Audubon Society: Field Guide to the Southwestern States.* New York: Alfred A. Knopf, 1999.

Anderson, Dorothy Daniels. *Arizona Legends and Lore.* Phoenix: Golden West Publishers, 1991.

Annerino, John. *Adventuring in Arizona: The Sierra Club Travel Guide to the Grand Canyon State.* San Francisco: Sierra Club Books, 1991.

Arizona: A State Guide. New York: Hastings House, 1940.

Arizona: The Grand Canyon State. 2 Vols. N.p.: Western States Historical Publishers, Inc., 1975.

Bahti, Tom, and Mark Bahti. *Southwestern Indian Tribes.* Las Vegas: KC Publications, 1997.

Barker, Scott. *Arizona off the Beaten Path.* Old Saybrook, Conn.: The Globe Pequot Press, 1996.

Barnes, Will C. *Arizona Place Names.* Tucson, Ariz.: The University of Arizona Press, 1988.

Bischoff, Mike. *Touring Arizona Hot Springs.* Helena, Mont.: Falcon Publishing, Inc., 1999.

Burke, Larry. *Arizona Boonies: The Arizona Even the Zonies Don't Know About.* Phoenix: Niche Publishing, 1998.

Casebier, Dennis G., *Camp Eldorado, Arizona Territory.* N.p.: Arizona Historical Foundation, 1970.

Chronic, Halka. *Roadside Geology of Arizona.* Missoula, Mont.: Mountain Press Publishing Company, 1983.

Cook, James E., Sam Negri, and Marshall Trimble. *Travel Arizona: The Back Roads.* 3rd ed. Edited by Dean Smith and Wesley Holden. Phoenix: Book Division of Arizona Highways Magazine, 1994.

Cowgill, Pete. *Back Roads and Beyond.* 2nd ed. Tucson, Ariz.: Broken Toe Press, 1997.

Cross, Jack L., Elizabeth H. Shaw, and Kathleen Scheifele, eds. *Arizona: Its People and Resources.* Tucson, Ariz.: the University of Arizona Press, 1960.

Crutchfield, James A. *It Happened in Arizona.* Helena, Mont.: Falcon Press Publishing Co., 1994.

Dale, Edward Everett. *The Indians of the Southwest.* London: University of Oklahoma Press, 1949.

Dunning, Charles H. *Rocks to Riches.* N.p.: Southwest Publishing Company, Inc., 1959.

Earle, W. Hubert *Cacti of the Southwest.* Phoenix: Arizona Cactus and Native Flora Society, Inc., 1963.

Elmore, Francis H. *Shrubs and Trees of the Southwest Uplands.* Tucson, Ariz.: Southwest Parks and Monuments Association, 1976.

Etter, Patricia A. *To California on the Southern Route 1849: A History and Annotated Bibliography.* Spokane, Wash.: The Arthur H. Clark Company, 1998.

Farrell, Robert J., and Bob Albano, eds. *Wild West Collections.* 4 vols. Phoenix: Book Division of Arizona Highways Magazine, 1997–99.

Fireman, Bert M. *Arizona: Historic Land.* New York: Alfred A. Knof, 1982.

Florin, Lambert. *Ghost Towns of the West.* New York: Promontory Press, 1993.

Granger, Byrd Howell, *Arizona's Names: X Marks the Place.* N.p.: Falconer Publishing Company, 1983.

Grubbs, Bruce. *Camping Arizona.* Helena, Mont.: Falcon Publishing, Inc., 1999.

Heatwole, Thelma. *Arizona off the Beaten Path!.* Phoenix: Golden West Publishers, 1982.

———. *Ghost Towns and Historical Haunts in Arizona.* Phoenix: Golden West Publishers, 1981.

Hinton, Richard J. *The Handbook to Arizona: Its Resources, History, Towns, Mines, Ruins and Scenery.* Tucson, Ariz.: Arizona Silhouettes,

1954.

Hirschfelder, Arlene. *Native Americans: A History in Pictures.* New York: Dorling Kindersley Publishing, Inc., 2000.

Hoxie, Frederick E., ed. *Encyclopedia of North American Indians.* Boston: Houghton Mifflin Company, 1996.

Jaeger, Edmund C. *Desert Wildlife.* Stanford, Calif.: Stanford University Press, 1950.

Kosik, Fran. *Native Roads.* Tucson, Ariz.: Treasure Chest Books, 1996.

Lamb, Edgar, and Brian Lamb. *Pocket Encyclopedia of Cacti in Colour.* Revised ed. London: Blandford, 1969.

Lingenfelter, Richard E. *Steamboats on the Colorado River, 1852–1916.* Tucson, Ariz.: The University of Arizona Press, 1978.

Lockwood, Frank C. *Pioneer Days in Arizona.* New York: The Macmillan Company, 1932.

———. *Thumbnail Sketches of Famous Arizona Desert Riders 1538–1946.* Tucson, Ariz.: University of Arizona, 1946.

Love, Frank. *Mining Camps and Ghost Towns.* N.p.: Westernlore Press, 1974.

Marks, Paula Mitchell. *And Die in the West.* New York: Simon and Schuster Inc., 1989.

Miller, Donald C. *Ghost Towns of the Southwest.* Boulder, Colo.: Pruett Publishing Company.

Mitchell, James R. *Gem Trails of Arizona.* Baldwin Park, Calif.: Gem Guides Book Co., 1995.

Mitchell, John D. *Lost Mines of the Great Southwest.* Glorieta, N. Mex.: The Rio Grande Press, Inc., 1933.

Morris, Eleanor, and Steve Cohen. *Adventure Guide to Arizona.* Edison, N. Jer.: Hunter Publishing, 1996.

Murbarger, Nell. *Ghost of the Adobe.* Tucson, Ariz.: Treasure Chest Publications, Inc., 1964.

Officer, James E. *Hispanic Arizona, 1536–1856.* Tucson, Ariz.: The University of Arizona Press, 1987.

O'Neal, Bill. *Encyclopedia of Western Gunfighters.* Norman, Okla.: University of Oklahoma Press, 1979.

Paher, Stanley W. *Western Arizona Ghost Towns.* Las Vegas: Nevada Publications, 1990.

Penfield, Thomas. *Dig Here!* San Antonio, Tex.: The Naylor Company, 1962.

Recreation Sites in Southwestern National Forests and Grasslands. N.p.: United States Department of Agriculture, n.d.

Ruland-Thorne, Kate. *Experience Sedona Legends and Legacies.* Sacramento, Calif.: Thorne Enterprises Publications, Inc., 1999.

Schuler, Stanley, ed. *Simon and Schuster's guide to Cacti and Succulents.* New York: Simon and Schuster Inc., 1985.

Searchy, Paula. *Travel Arizona: The Scenic Byways.* Edited by Bob Albano, Evelyn Howell, and Laura A. Lawrie. Phoenix: Book Division of Arizona Highways Magazine, 1997.

Sheridan, Thomas E. *Arizona: A History.* London: The University of Arizona Press, 1995.

Sherman, James E., and Barbara H. Sherman. *Ghost Towns of Arizona.* Norman, Okla.: University of Oklahoma Press, 1969.

Snyder, Ernest E. *Prehistoric Arizona.* Phoenix: Golden West Publishers, 1987.

Stoops, Erik D., and Annette Wright. *Snakes and Other Reptiles of the Southwest.* 5th ed. Phoenix: Golden West Publishers, 1993.

Taylor, Colin F. *The Native Americans: The Indigenous People of North America.* London: Thunder Bay Press, 1991.

Thrapp, Dan L. *Encyclopedia of Frontier Biography.* 3 vols. London: University of Nebraska Press, 1988.

Trimble, Marshall. *Arizona: A Cavalcade of History.* Tucson, Ariz.: Treasure Chest Publications, 1989.

———. *Arizona Adventure!.* Phoenix: Golden West Publishers, 1982.

———. *Roadside History of Arizona.* Missoula, Mont.: Mountain Press Publishing Company, 1986.

Tweit, Susan J. *The Great Southwest Nature Factbook.* Anchorage: Alaska Northwest Books, 1992.

Varney, Philip. *Arizona Ghost Towns and Mining Camps.* Phoenix: Book Division of Arizona Highways Magazine, 1994.

———. *Arizona's Best Ghost Town.* Flagstaff,

Ariz.: Northland Press, 1980.

Wagoner, Jay J. *Arizona's Heritage.* Salt Lake City: Peregrine Smith, Inc., 1977.

———. *Early Arizona: Prehistory to Civil War.* Tucson, Ariz.: The University of Arizona Press, 1975.

Wahmann, Russell. *Auto Road Log.* Cottonwood, Ariz.: Starlight Publishing, 1982.

Waldman, Carl. *Atlas of the North American Indian.* New York: Checkmark Books, 2000.

———. *Encyclopedia of Native American Tribes.* New York: Facts on File, 1988.

Walker, Henry P., and Don Bufkin. *Historical Atlas of Arizona.* 2nd ed. London: University of Oklahoma Press, 1979.

Ward, Geoffrey C. *The West: an Illustrated History.* Boston: Little, Brown and Company, 1996.

Warren, Scott S. *Exploring Arizona's Wild Areas.* Seattle: Mountaineers Books, 1996.

Weight, Harold O. *Lost Mines of Old Arizona.*
Ridgecrest, Calif.: Hubbard Printing, 1959.

Wilderness and Primitive Areas in Southwestern National Forests. N.p.: United States Department of Agriculture, n.d.

Wolle, Muriel Sibell. *The Bonanza Trail: Ghost Towns and Mining Camps of the West.* Chicago: The Swallow Press Incorporated, 1953.

Zauner, Phyllis. *Those Legendary Men of the Wild West.* Sacramento, Calif.: Zanel Publications, 1991.

Selected Web sources

Boyce Thompson Arboretum, Superior, AZ: http://ag.arizona.edu/bta/

Ghost towns and History of the American West, http://www.ghosttowns.com

GORP, http://www.gorp.com

U.S. Bureau of Land Management, Arizona: http://www.blm.gov/az/

U.S. National Forest Service, Southwestern Region (Arizona): http://www.fs.fed.us/r3

Trail Index

About the Authors

Peter Massey grew up in the outback of Australia, where he acquired a life-long love of the backcountry. After retiring from investment banking, he served as a director for a number of companies in the United States, the United Kingdom, and Australia. He moved to Colorado in 1993.

Jeanne Wilson was born and grew up in Maryland. After moving to New York City in 1980, she worked in advertising and public relations before moving to Colorado in 1993.

After traveling extensively in Australia, Europe, Asia, and Africa, the authors covered more than 80,000 miles touring the United States and the Australian outback between 1993 and 1997. This experience became the basis for creating the Backcountry Adventures and Trails guidebook series.

As the research team grew, a newcomer became a dedicated member of the Swagman team.

Angela Titus was born in Missouri and grew up in Virginia, where she attended the University of Virginia. She moved to Alabama and worked for *Southern Living Magazine* traveling, photographing, and writing about the southeastern U.S. She moved to Colorado in 2002.

Since research for the Backcountry Adventures and Trails guidebooks began, Peter, Jeanne, and Angela have traveled more than 75,000 miles throughout the western states.

Photo Credits

Unless otherwise indicated in the following list of acknowledgments (which is organized by page number), all photographs were taken by Bushducks—Maggie Pindar and Donald McGann.

143 Corel; **177** Arizona State Library, Archives & Public Records, Phoenix.

Cover photography: Bushducks—Maggie Pinder and Donald McGann

trail notes

trail notes

trail notes

trail notes

colorado and california trails

backroad & 4-wheel drive trail guides

Colorado Trails–Southwest Region
48 of the region's best scenic backroads and four-wheel drive trails. It covers Silverton, Animas Forks, Ouray, Durango, Telluride, Lake City, and Creede.
ISBN: 978-1-930193-07-9; Price: $29.95

Colorado Trails–Central Region
47 scenic backroads and 4-wheel drive trails near Georgetown, Breckenridge, Leadville, Fairplay, Buena Vista, Aspen, Crested Butte, and Salida.
ISBN 978-1-930193-51-2; Price $29.95

Colorado Trails–Front Range Region
42 scenic backroads and 4-wheel drive trails along the Front Range including trails near Fort Collins, Boulder, Idaho Springs, Denver, Colorado Springs, Cañon City, and Rocky Mountain
National Park.
ISBN 978-1-930193-50-5; Price $29.95

California Trails–Northern Sierra 55 off-road routes located near the towns of Sacramento (east), Red Bluff (east), Truckee, South Lake Tahoe, Sonora, Susanville, Chico, Oroville, Yuba City, Placerville, Stockton (east), Jackson, and Sonora.
ISBN 978-1-930193-23-9; Price $29.95

California Trails–High Sierra 50 trails located near the towns of Fresno (north), Oakhurst, Lone Pine, Bishop, Bridgeport, Coulterville, Mariposa, and Mammoth Lakes.
ISBN 978-1-930193-21-5; Price $29.95

California Trails–North Coast 47 routes located near the towns of Sacramento, Redding (west), Red Bluff, Clear Lake, McCloud, Mount Shasta, Yreka, Crescent City, and Fort Bidwell.
ISBN 978-1-930193-22-2; Price $29.95

California Trails–Central Mountains 52 trails located near the towns of Big Sur, Fresno, San Luis Obispo, Santa Barbara, Bakersfield, Mojave, and Maricopa.
ISBN 978-1-930193-19-2; Price $29.95

California Trails–South Coast 50 trails located near the towns of Los Angeles, San Bernardino, San Diego, Salton Sea, Indio, Borrego Springs, Ocotillo and Palo Verde.
ISBN 978-1-930193-24-6; Price $29.95

California Trails–Desert 51 off-road routes located near the towns of Lone Pine (east), Panamint Springs, Death Valley area, Ridgecrest, Barstow, Baker and Blythe.
ISBN 978-1-930193-20-8; Price $29.95

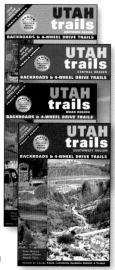